THE
CHURCH
OF
MARY
MAGDALENE

THE
CHURCH
OF
MARY
MAGDALENE

THE SACRED FEMININE
AND THE
TREASURE OF RENNES-LE-CHÂTEAU

JEAN MARKALE
TRANSLATED BY JON GRAHAM

Inner Traditions
Rochester, Vermont

Inner Traditions
One Park Street
Rochester, Vermont 05767
www.InnerTraditions.com

Originally published in French under the title *Rennes-le-Château et l'énigme de l'or maudit* by Éditions Pygmalion/Gérard Watelet, Paris
First U.S. edition published by Inner Traditions in 2004

Library of Congress Cataloging-in-Publication Data

Markale, Jean.
  [Rennes-le-Château. English]
  The church of Mary Magdalene : sacred feminine and the treasure of Rennes-le-Château / Jean Markale ; translated by Jon Graham.
    p. cm.
  Includes index.
  ISBN 0-89281-199-4 (pbk.)
  1. Occultism—France—Rennes-le-Château. 2. Saunière, Bérenger, 1852–1917. 3. Mary Magdalene, Saint—Miscellanea. 4. Treasure-trove—France—Rennes-le-Château. 5. Rennes-le-Château (France)—History—Miscellanea. 6. Eglise Sainte-Marie-Madeleine (Rennes-le-Château, France) I. Title.
  BF1434.F8M3713 2004
  944'.87—dc22
                                                              2004008842

Printed and bound in the United States at Lake Book Manufacturing, Inc.

10 9 8 7 6 5 4 3 2 1

Text design and layout by Mary Anne Hurhula
This book was typeset in Sabon

Roads that climb also descend
—HERACLITUS

Contents

Part 1

THE SITE OF
THE MYSTERY

1

On Roads of Stone and Dust

It is hard for travelers who have been making their way up the upper Aude Valley out of Carcassonne to imagine what is taking place on high—that is to say, on the plateau. The valley is rich in shady groves and ancient picturesque villages such as Limoux and Alet, and the eye is continually drawn to the flowing river whose path is determined by the promontories bordering its winding path. Once travelers have progressed to Couiza, where the Sals River flows into the Aude, they will be tempted to continue southward toward Quillan, the gap leading to those castles constructed "on the flank of the abyss" (to borrow André Breton's expression)—castles that are described as Cathar. For here is a land that bears the imprint of those whom many people have been a bit too quick to call dualists, heretics, and Albigensians. Everything here depends on what travelers truly seek: either the gold of the Holy Grail or the gold of the devil. The quests for both of these—not mutually exclusive—do need to be undertaken over time. From Couiza it is possible to make a detour to the east and, following the Sals Valley, to climb a steep path that leads to the top of the plateau, into the midst of rocks and mineral dust that have accumulated over the centuries. There, "on the flank of the abyss," looms a strange village lost at the end of a cul-de-sac, a hamlet sitting atop the setting sun, and barely distinguishable from the surrounding stone: the village of Rennes-le-Château.

It took me a long time to discover the road to Rennes-le-Château. In truth, for most of my life I had no idea of the existence of this isolated village in the Corbières region or of another hidden in the hollow of a neighboring valley and bearing a similar name: Rennes-les-Bains. The word Rennes brought to my mind only the city located at the confluence of the Ille and Vilaine Rivers, the capital of Brittany. It was customary for me to spend much more time there than in those border zones separating the Aude region from the extremely remote Roussillon, whose French name (so evocative of a blazing sun) conceals the much more authentic but "foreign" name of Catalonia.

Nevertheless, the name Rennes (located in Ille-et-Vilaine) had intrigued me ever since I was a child, for I had heard of the Laplanders, those people who lived in the frozen steppes of the north and hunted reindeer,[1] and I naively wondered about the connection between these animals, described to me as very similar to stags, and this city—or train station, rather—where, night and day, the train that brought me toward Brocéliande stopped, sometimes for a very long while. What is so extraordinary about childhood imagination is the immense and finally terrifying possibility of going as far as we can possibly go in exploration of the fantasy world. Sociocultural censorship has as yet no role to play with children and they breach the ultimate frontiers of reality quite casually and unconsciously. Accordingly, I envisioned extending outside of the Rennes train station a snow-covered plain over which shadowy figures loomed, tracking the animals that fled toward an invisible horizon lost in the night. This was the time of steam locomotives; the puffing of these machines is somewhat reminiscent of the smoking nostrils of an animal at bay, isn't it? I have never been fond of hunters, and my dislike of them is as strong today as it was as a child. In fact, I regard the killing of animals in this way as a criminal act; I have never understood the kind of sordid and sadistic pleasure some derive from shooting at rabbits, partridges, and deer who have never done any ill to anyone and too often have been raised only to serve as moving targets for those who think virility is synonymous with cruelty. But I digress . . . It is normal for human beings to defend themselves against an

---

1. [*Rennes* means "reindeer" in French. —*Translator*]

attack by a ferocious or poisonous animal. It is normal that human beings, in certain penurious times such as the ice ages, would survive at the expense of animals. But what can be said of those slaughters organized for the disturbing pleasure of a few members of the privileged class? It is a matter of perspective, of course. If I were to follow my own words, I would rescue every unfortunate animal whose path I cross.

All of this is to say that initially Rennes reminded me of the animal kingdom, but I eventually accepted the fact that it was the name of a city and that it was once the capital of my ancestors. I did not give the matter any more thought. Had I done so, however, I would not have doubted the possibility of the existence of another village bearing the same name in a region completely foreign to me. I had no connection to the Corbières region. Nobody I spent time with had ever even spoken of it. In fact, it was only later, when I read the labels of certain bottles of trademarked wine, that the name Corbières took on any meaning for me, though I should state for the record that from the time I became impassioned about literature the name brought more readily to mind the Breton poet Tristan Corbière (without the *s*) than a good red wine worthy of some family celebration. At the time when it was my father's pleasure to read to me *Le Curé de Cucugnan,* the famous story attributed to Alphonse Daudet (but actually written by Paul Arène, who was Daudet's black servant), I was far from supposing that the village of Cucugnan was located precisely in the mountainous region of Corbières and not in the completely imaginary Provence created by the author of the immortal *Tartarin.* And yes . . . Cucugnan is not that far from Rennes-le-Château. According to the vision of the steadfast *curé,* it seemed that the residents of Cucugnan allowed themselves to be ensnared in the trap of the devil's gold. Could this also be true of certain inhabitants of Rennes-le-Château?

I must frankly confess that I was completely unaware of Rennes-le-Château for the first fifty years of my life. The magazine and newspaper articles published about it in the '50s and '60s had not left any noticeable trace in my memory. I probably thought at the time that they were merely the ploy of a skilled local businessman who had dreamed up a novel way of bringing tourism to this forsaken Corbières region. I had other subjects for reflection and research that were entirely centered on my personal "poles": in Brittany my cherished Brocéliande Forest and the Barenton Fountain, the Gavrinis Mound, and the Morbihan Gulf that turns so blue when flooded with sunlight; or the New Grange mound in Ireland, the absolute center of all the Celtic mythological tales that motivate me; or the strange circle of Stonehenge on Salisbury Plain in England, where Merlin had used his magic to transport from Ireland this fantastic "Dance of the Giants" that early on I had guessed to be the solar temple of an ancient religion I knew nothing about. Under these conditions, what would have compelled my interest in a village in Corbières, a region I had never frequented? Of course, I had visited Carcassonne and wandered through the old city. I had been affected deeply then, as I still am, by the powerful images that its ramparts—still haunted by the beauty of the centuries of the so-called Dark Ages—inspired in my imagination. But Carcassonne is not Corbières and is even less the Razès. At this time I had never even heard the name Razès spoken.

What is odd about the interest we display for a given subject or a particular place is the circumstance that awakens this interest—a circumstance that often arises from some "act of chance" that is not really luck but more what the surrealists called "objective chance." I have already recounted in other books how it came about that I *lived* in Celtic legends, a situation due as much to my origins and the great amount of time I spent in the Brocéliande Forest as to my meetings with Jean Hani, my literature professor in high school, and the abbot Henri Gillard, the "Rector of Tréhorenteuc," who was my true spiritual mentor. What I have never spoken of previously, however, is my great love for druids and druidism. I will now confess all. In 1948, thanks to my friend the poet Renée Willy, who then "ran" the Librairie Celtique on the rue de Rennes (that name again!) in Paris, a bookstore that closed long ago, I bought a book published three years earlier that turned out to be truly illuminating: Robert Amberlain's *Au pied des Menhirs* (At the Foot of the Menhirs).

This admission may cause snickering among my detractors, who sign petitions that accuse me of both inventing everything I write and, at the same time, "pinching" it from my colleagues. They should get their stories straight before casting aspersions on others . . . but let's continue. I cannot deny that Robert Amberlain's work was a "revelation" to me and encouraged me to undertake more intensive research into Celtic spirituality. This book—which is inspired by a most suspect kind of neo-druidism, is devoid of any serious reference, and is based on vague analogies and romanticized translation of purely apocryphal texts—certainly has no intrinsic value, but it was a key that opened other doors. It is for this reason, despite the book's failings and aberrations, that I am in Robert Amberlain's debt, for he *provoked* me to go further. I later attended the conferences of the druid Erwan Berthou-Kerverziou, now dead, at the Hall of Geography in Paris. I did not understand a word of what he said and realize now that it was better that way: His neo-druidism had more to do with frenzied poetry than scientific research. He was clearly raving. But isn't raving one of the forms that Celtic logic takes? I could say as much about Philéas Lebesgue, who claimed to be "druid of the Gauls." He was merely a "poet and peasant," but he possessed incontestable literary merit.

Likewise, the theme of Rennes-le-Château was imposed upon me by one of those apparently chance meetings that leave an indelible imprint on those who are aware of having enjoyed such an experience. It was in 1981 at a newly opened bookstore in the Montagne Sainte-Geneviève neighborhood in Paris, to which I had been invited thanks to my friend Jean Picollec, the publisher. The ambience was very pleasant. One of the learned assembly who was squeezing in among the books was a young man who made me a present of his latest volume, complete with a charming inscription, and urged me to explore it for anything I might find interesting. The title of this book was *Le Trésor du triangle d'or* (The Treasure of the Golden Triangle), and its author was Jean-Luc Chaumeil. So it is thanks to Jean-Luc Chaumeil that I was ushered straight to the middle of Rennes-le-Château and the mystery of its cursed gold.

I read his book with a bemused curiosity insofar as I have always regarded treasure hunting as merely an inconsequential mind game. Chaumeil spoke of Gisors and the secrets possibly buried beneath the castle of this city on the border of Normandy and the Île-de-France, secrets of the mysterious Templars that Gérard de Sède had helped make known to a wider audience a few years earlier. He also spoke of

Stenay in northern France, the holy city of the Merovingian dynasty; the Saint-Sulpice church in Paris, a monument that I consider to be a triumph of the absolute horror of religious architecture; and finally of Rennes-le-Château, where slept the "secret" of a strange priest, Father Béranger Saunière, in a foggy atmosphere from which emerged the figure of a so-called authentic descendant of the Merovingians, who could make a legitimate claim to the throne of France. All this seemed to me like an excellent piece of historical fiction, and I could attach only relative importance to it without taking any position whatsoever on the hypotheses developed in the work. I simply said to myself, "Why not?" At the time I was more attracted to the Grail and the implications of its legend in Montségur, a short distance from Rennes-le-Château. Therefore, Jean-Luc Chaumeil's book remained "hibernating" on one of my bookshelves.

A seed had been planted in fertile soil, however, even if buried deep. It was impossible to hunt for something at Montségur and remain ignorant of what may have transpired in the area surrounding this prestigious and enigmatic site. From my first climb to Montségur I retained the feeling that this whole region revealed traditions and reminiscences that asked only to be recalled at the level of the conscious mind. Ever since childhood I had been somewhat enthralled by the Merovingian era and had dived with delight into the troubled waters of Augustin Thierry's *Récits des temps mérovingiens*. After all, I told myself, the actual life of my favorite hero, King Arthur, took place around the year 500 B.C.E., the transitional era between the end of the Roman Empire and the beginning of those "barbaric" times ceaselessly embroidered upon by my imagination. Colorful and perfectly odious female figures such as Queen Fredegonde and Queen Brunehaut only added to the problems that occurred to me concerning the transition from one civilization to another. I was already feeling considerable doubt about the reality of the "barbarous" and "savage" invasions of the Christian West. I justly felt, for example, that the Visigoths had left a profound imprint on the Occitan mind-set, and their astounding objects unearthed by archaeologists testified to a culture that was surprisingly refined, although poorly understood and unjustifiably scorned. This period that the Anglo-Saxons have dubbed the Dark Ages held much that fascinated me, for in it I found again the soul of the ancient Britons, those of the Isle of Britain and those who had left there to settle on the Armorican Peninsula. They had a King Arthur, who was only a simple "warrior chief" and not a king, and whose knights were only warriors, sometimes endowed—according to legend—with formidable magical powers that made them more similar to gods incarnate than villains concerned with sacking fortresses. Insofar as I had established that the origin (or at least one of the origins) of the Grail myth was situated exactly within this era, in a West whose Christian veneer had not completely smothered the pagan Celtic and German substratum, I could not refuse consideration of the strange stories, completely unverifiable but terribly seductive, that tell of possibly legitimate Merovingian heirs and of the presence of "secrets" not far from Montségur—secrets that would be dangerous to divulge because they challenge the West's own history as it has been recorded.

History has always appeared to me as a deliberate lie intended to orient people according to the circumstances and ideologies of those in power and then to lead them in a direction chosen by those called the "elites," who are really no more than manipulators of societies. As I have said,[2] I consider history a material expression of myth. This myth is a mental structure inherent to humanity but as such is equivalent to nothing. The sole means of proving the existence of myth is to recognize it in its materialization, in its *incarnation* in men and women who, at the opportune moment, crystallize the unconscious impulse of this humanity that searches for itself. I have not changed my opinion on this but have merely refined it, and have attempted to make it more comprehensible and better adapted to the changes that our universalist and industrial society has forced on primitive values that have been too long considered immutable, dogmatic, and completely sterile. History inspires its heroes when it feels the need. But because free will is the sole wealth of the human being (even if it exists in only one out of a hundred people!), the hero—any hero—influences how history unfolds. The roads that climb are also those that descend.

---

2. Mainly in my preface to *The Celts* (Rochester, Vt: Inner Traditions, 1993) and in my afterword to *La Tradition celtique* (Paris: Payot, 1975).

This digression into the relationship between myth and history is not purposeless: It allows us to measure both the distance that separates a historical event that actually took place and the tale subsequently told about it, however objective, and the goodwill of those who assumed responsibility for driving this story. Because myth is pure potentiality, its only recognized existence is the story (epic, tale, legend) that makes it concrete and accessible to the imaginations of those who hear or read it. But this also holds true for history. Because history itself, de facto, is no longer measurable save through memory (memoirs, writings, various monuments), it appears in the same position as myth. To make it concrete and accessible to all, it must be given a *body,* whether this body is the narrative history of events or scholarly, coded diagrams that introduce the most scientific kinds of notions. This, however, is where history risks being distorted or falsified, for what credit can be given to these testimonies of the past? Even when they are surrounded with the best guarantees of authenticity, there exists the risk of them straying because of errors of appraisal or the deficiencies of sensibility. Pure objectivity is only an illusion; our perception of the past is completely dependent on our present viewpoint, which is loaded with the most varied motivations and the most excessive interpretations. Both myth and history, therefore, suffer the same fate. Soon I had personal confirmation of this regarding all the particulars surrounding the murky affairs of Rennes-le-Château.

At the time when I read Jean-Luc Chaumeil's book, however, I had not yet reached a point of raising such questions. Rennes-le-Château appeared to me more like one of those poles that esoteric (or so-called esoteric) works gladly label as vital centers, where something happens as much by virtue of the geographical situation and the configuration of terrain as by their place in the delicate magnetic, telluric, cosmic, and simply mystical field that covers the surface of the earth. These are privileged spots on the earth that since the dawn of time have been dedicated to celebration by certain cults, to prayer, to so-called miraculous phenomena. Such places are sanctuaries where heaven and earth communicate, sacred sites called *nemeton* by the Celts, and locations on which many Christian churches have been constructed. I thought Rennes-le-Château was one of these privileged places. I did not feel I knew enough yet to attempt to decode it.

One time my wife, Môn, and I, having left Toulouse, where I had just given a conference, had decided to continue our journey toward Catalonia. I saw no good reason to plan a stop in the Razès region, yet our travels would be taking us quite close to the area. We planned to make our way back to Prades by secondary roads and thus had gone back up the Aude Valley. We made a short stop in Limoux, not to enjoy a *blanquette* (a wine I detest), but to refresh ourselves on the terrace of a café under the shade of a row of plane trees. Being more accustomed to the rugged granite landscape of the Atlantic coast, I have always been attracted to what is called the Midi. Somewhat disoriented but nevertheless delighted to find myself in an area totally unfamiliar to me, I began to daydream as we journeyed. We continued southward from there. The town of Alet brought to mind the former name of Saint-Servan, first site of the town and bishopric of Saint-Malo. Couiza flashed by like a single street through a valley. Quillan seemed just another peaceful village slumbering in the May heat. As we turned in the direction of Perpignan, we promised ourselves we would take the first fork that led to the mountain route to Prades.

We therefore passed quite close to the Razès, indifferently noticing several remnants of Cathar castles in the distance. I was in a hurry to reach Prades, located in what was a totally unknown area to me, the interior region of Catalonia called the Cerdana. Actually, the purpose of this trip was much more Môn's than my own. She had spent part of her childhood in Prades, and I had expressed the wish that she show me some of the places she haunted as a young girl. Because of some painful family circumstances, Môn had lost all contact with her paternal family and did not even know at that time where her father was. Several years earlier she had made a long trip through the Pyrenees in hopes of finding him, but until our trip together she had never dared travel through to the end. There was, in fact, a bank of fog in Môn's memory. Would it be dissipated in Prades?

We drove through miles of vineyards before reaching our goal. Once there we visited the cemetery where Môn hoped to find the family plot. It was there we learned that her grandmother was still alive. What a strange day it was, seeing Môn with a grandmother she herself had not seen for twenty-five years. This was to be their last meeting, as it turned out, for the old woman was destined to pass from this earth soon after. Môn also saw her aunt and uncle again and received news about her father. She led me through the streets, searching for the fast freshwater streams that gushed from mountain springs and raced through the town. She brought me to visit the magnificent Abbey of Saint-Michel of Cuxa and recalled the day when, as a child, she had attended a Pablo Casals concert there and shook the hand of this illustrious figure. We left Prades by the mountain road and made a stopover at a strange, empty inn in La Tour de Carol. The windows of our room overlooked the old Spain Road. Everything there was outmoded and shrouded in the remote and long dead past. Accompanying us on that trip was Môn's small dog, who had the odd name of Vespasien.[3] He was old and sick at that time, but I loved him very much, and he shared all our joys and hardships. I have always loved animals, particularly cats, though I must say that Vespasien, a pretty black dachshund, remains in my memory as a very dear friend. From La Tour de Carol (a name that has always moved me), we headed westward toward Brittany. There was not even a question of visiting Rennes-le-Château at that time.

Time passed. I had other subjects of interest, although from time to time my research for a book on Saint Louis brought me into the Occitan regions where the Capet kings had pulled out all the stops to smother a civilization that had aroused the suspicions of the lords of the north. I wondered how the Occitains would have greeted my work about this king who washed the feet of lepers and dispensed justice from beneath an oak tree, thus giving me the title for the book: *Le Chêne de la sagesse* (The Oak of Wisdom).[4] In creating this work, I was compelled to rethink my opinion of the Cathars and what might really have taken place in the Razès during the thirteenth century. Wasn't it in fact rumored that the queen, Blanche de Castille, had buried a treasure or documents somewhere in Razès, most likely in Rennes-les-Bains?

---

3. [Vespasien is the French name for the Roman emperor Vespasian, Titus Flavius Vespasianus (69–79 C.E.). While known primarily for invading Judea in 66 C.E., he also lent his name to the public urinals in France, which are known as Vespasiennes—no doubt due to the fact that in an attempt to restore solvency to the Roman Empire, Vespasian imposed a tax on public bathrooms. —*Translator*]

4. Published in Paris by Éditions Hermé in 1985.

There was food for thought in this strange expanse of earth that I had yet to see for myself.

Then I received what would prove to be an important element in my personal quest: one of the first French editions of a book that enjoyed huge success, *Holy Blood, Holy Grail* by Michael Baigent, Richard Leigh, and Henry Lincoln,[5] a title that seemed guaranteed to earn my appreciation. I devoured this book, however, without supporting all the hypotheses—quite audacious hypotheses—of its authors, who in truth were more akin to sensationalist journalists than writers and historians. Yet whatever the true value of this book may be, for me it had the merit of raising potentially embarrassing questions that had obviously never before been raised or answered, and thus presented extremely original directions for future research.

That said, *Holy Blood, Holy Grail* is an "irritating" work, and my initial reaction was to completely reject all the ideas it prompted. Once I had finished reading it, I viewed it as a deliberate provocation, a deliberate attempt to destabilize traditional Western values. I have often been accused of being an agnostic, which I am not, and a "gravedigger of Western spirituality," which seems an absolute contradiction to my approach, for I am greatly concerned about observations that challenge the profound reality of the Gospels as well as fundamental pre-Christian texts, whether Greek, Germanic, or Celtic. While I often surrendered to full hilarity in reading *Holy Blood, Holy Grail*,[6] I nonetheless retained the impression that its subject matter was of essential importance and that it might prove necessary to revise our old judgments about the historical and legendary data of a Europe that had barely emerged from the so-called Roman Peace[7] to scale the slopes of a new culture. This culture was the result of a harmonious synthesis of all the sources that had watered

---

5. *Holy Blood, Holy Grail* (New York: Delacorte Press, 1982).

6. This was especially true with regard to the so-called genealogies, which have been shamelessly falsified, truncated, revised, and corrected.

7. The *Pax Romana,* which history books depict as a reality that endured for several centuries, is one of the most remarkable swindles committed by historians. Never was an era more troubled and more fertile in revolt, usurpation, civil wars, and other such delights, especially in the territory of Gaul, where a large number of usurpers tried to acquire and hang on to a power that escaped them.

it. At least I had found confirmation of something I had long believed: The Holy Grail, the *sangréal,* in old French, could just as easily designate "royal blood" *(sang royal)* or royal lineage as it could a cup, chalice, or platter that—if we subscribe to the version of the story popularized first by the Clunisians, then by the Cistercians—contained the blood of Christ. But supporting the theory of legitimate descendants of the "hairy kings," meaning the Merovingians, and their debatable origin (Jesus and Mary Magdalene), was out of the question for me, even from a heuristic perspective, though the possibility was worth raising. This was during the time before Scorsese's film *The Last Temptation of Christ* had unleashed such outrage and controversy, yet the book by Kazantzákis on which the film was based had been around for some time without unleashing such debate. Let us not forget that the church of Rennes-le-Château is dedicated to Mary Magdalene and that she is oddly and abundantly depicted in the interior of this sanctuary. This reflects the will of Father Saunière, also the builder of the Magdala Tower in which he wished to house his library. Strange, no? The reading of *Holy Blood, Holy Grail* forced me to ask myself many obviously unanswerable questions. It also compelled me to reread *Le Trésor du triangle d'or* by Jean-Luc Chaumeil, who in this instance turned out to be my "introducing brother" to a strange "closed white assembly," where I was the sole noninitiate.

Here again, however, I found nothing satisfactory. Despite his data, which he claims are authentic but are unverifiable because no reference is ever supplied, Jean-Luc Chaumeil and the authors of *Holy Blood, Holy Grail*—who take themselves a little too much for Anglo-Saxon wizards and heirs of ghosts from Scotland's haunted castles—have fallen into a trap that I think is the most pernicious and characteristic of our age devoted to false prophets and cheap gurus: the famous Priory of Sion. This ghostly priory, allegedly resulting from a scission in the Templar order (beneath the elm of Gisors, thank you for that, Gérard de Sède!) and including among its grand masters people as famous as Claude Debussy and Jean Cocteau, seems to be pure invention. It is a story sewn from whole cloth by failed would-be writers, country squires boasting their Merovingian ancestry, and some crackpots of stage and screen grouped around the brilliant Francis Blanche, who must be laughing in his tomb at the unexpected success of his provocations. This tale has been picked up, revised, and corrected by fans of mysteries of every kind and by treasure seekers who have made the glory of a certain Robert Charroux in a time when the hazel wand is being replaced by the metal detector (colloquially called a "frying pan").

This means, of course, that I did not take any of it seriously, although I had begun spending time at Montségur researching the Cathars, especially the problematic relationship they may have had with the Grail. Still, I was not ready to start exploring Rennes-le-Château, and I know it would have taken a lot to change my mind during this time, when friendly hoaxers were taking advantage of moonless nights to dig holes almost everywhere, even going so far as to set off explosives in a cemetery in search of the fabled treasure of the legendary Béranger Saunière. I felt it was a wise move on my part to stay out of this frenzied lunacy and ignore the mysterious Razès region.

I have learned during my somewhat agitated and adventurous life that I should never undertake anything before having been given the "green light" by those certain obscure powers that guide our actions on earth. I have also realized that our encounters with certain figures are never a matter of chance, and that they necessarily correspond to a stage of the quest we pursue all our lives, especially when we claim, as I have, to be acting independently of any dogma, preconceived ideology, or political and philosophical obligation. I acknowledge no sect and no obedience or affiliation; nor do I set myself up as some sort of guru of any system of thought. I have no students[8] much less disciples, and certainly no "slaves."[9] I am not commissioned by anybody. I say what I think, though I am always ready to admit when I have been wrong. I have encountered only people who have indicated the paths I should follow. I am thinking of André Breton and my former fellow student Jean Cathelin. I am thinking of that mysterious Yann-Ber Kerbiriou who appears from time to time in my life, giving me some totally unexpected information but no address where I can find him again. I am thinking of the women whose oaths have crossed mine over the course

---

8. When I was a professor I did have quite a few students, of course, but that is a different matter.

9. Some have as many as twenty.

of my life and who, like the famous "maidens" who left their imprint on the errantry of Lancelot of the Lake, have each brought me a ray of sunlight that enabled me to go farther in the darkened caverns of the earth and perceive there the presence of monstrous dragons ready to swoop down upon me. I am also thinking of certain books that fell into my hands just at the moment I needed them: *Le Trésor du triangle d'or* and *Holy Blood, Holy Grail,* for instance. But more important has been Michel Lamy's book *Jules Verne, initié et initiateur,* because of its profundity and oblique approach.[10] You may well ask what Jules Verne has to do with the mystery at Rennes-le-Château. It was definitely thanks to Michel Lamy that I grasped what was essential in the fog surrounding Father Saunière and his problematic "cursed gold." It was from that starting point that I figured out just how to enter that particular dark cavern.

It was from Montségur that I was finally launched into this adventure. I always need a connecting door, be it only temporary, or a spring to which I must return from time to time to slake my thirst when the sun is scorching the earth and my blood is thickening and moving sluggishly through my veins. Occitania is in no way my native land, although the two women who have mattered most in my life are both Occitan. It was through them that I was able to wander on the stony paths of the south, even though I sometimes felt inebriated by a light that seemed unreal to me. It was thanks to Môn that I was able to enter Montségur, the very heart of the Cathar mystery. Since that time, Montségur has become not only one of the fundamental poles of my personal quest, but also a place of asylum, an oasis where I feel at home in the fullness of spirit and in close contact with a nature I gladly label Wagnerian, although Wagner most likely never set foot in this sanctuary at the ends of the earth. I like the village of Montségur and know that I have friends there. I love walking on the village streets beneath the amazing shadow of the *pog* and its battlements that always threaten to pierce the sky with their philosopher's-stone teeth. I enjoy spending hours in the bookstore of my friends Raymonde and Nicolas Reznikov.

---

10. Published by Éditions Payot in Paris in 1984. This work seems to have been almost universally ignored by the allegedly alert critics. It is likely that it proved to be "disturbing."

I love the shadowy, completely old-fashioned, strange yet familiar atmosphere of the Costes Hotel. Madame Costes presides there with serenity and generosity like a priestess of ancient times. Then there is
Fernand Costes, who is the true guardian of the temple, by which I
mean the castle. He knows its every corner and stone no matter how
small; he knows every glimmer of light that shines from its darkness. I
have never felt so good, so at ease, so cleansed of my anxieties as in the
village of Montségur. Because I have written a fair number of pages on
subjects related to other specific sites—for example, in my book on
Carnac and the mystery of Atlantis[11]—so it is not surprising that I took
Montségur as my launching point to the other side of the Aude River in
pursuit of the ghosts of Rennes-le-Château.

So that is how one day in September 1985 Môn and I made our
way from the Atlantic slope of the Pyrenees (where Montségur is
located) to the Mediterranean side, crossing the Aude at Quillan and
going back up toward the north to Couiza, that small town we had
passed through a year earlier and seen nothing of which but a single
street running through the floor of a valley. This time, though, we took
the back road that follows the Sals River and then the zigzagging roads
into the mountains, whose peaks, as might be guessed, were arid and
sun-scorched even in those waning days of summer. I am partial to narrow, winding roads. They remind me of my childhood crawls, the time
I discovered the world on all fours, the time when we learn the most
without comprehending it. When we emerged upon the plateau, it was
into a world of complete wonder.

What is unsettling about the Corbières region is the complete contrast between the valleys, which are closed in upon themselves with an
abundance of greenery and fresh running water, and the plateaus,
where there is never any escape from the wind and sun and whose hori-
zons, riddled with stone debris, defy time. Beneath these massifs there
sometimes emerge even darker buttes whose flanks are curiously
crowned by trees that have somehow survived the dog days of summer.
There on one of these buttes, after many turns in the road, we spied a
village whose houses huddled up against one another beneath the

---

11. *Carnac et l'enigme de l'Atlantide,* Jean Markale (Éditions Pygmalion, Paris: 1986).

imposing mass of a castle and the more discreet steeple of a church from which, extending westward, a bizarre construction in the shape of a tower seemed to defy the abyss below. This was Rennes-le-Château, a village, like so many others, built from stone and Roman tile roofs and made up of empty streets that seemed to suggest that no one had ever dared to live there.

I first parked my car in the shade and then, after going through the village, turned my steps toward the tower that so intrigued me. In truth, I was wondering just what I was doing there. In my confusion I was worried that I would go unrecognized and questions would arise about my presence in this place that is so far from my usual haunts. I knew that the inhabitants of Rennes-le-Château had had more than their fill of treasure seekers and other snoopers whose motivations were highly suspect. Would I be considered one of these snoopers come to disturb the tranquillity of a village sleeping beneath the sun? I had no such maleficent intention. It was no concern of mine whether treasure was still buried in the gardens or in the cemetery. I was not concerned with the townspeople and their daily lives. I simply wished *to see;* I wished to be imbued with the atmosphere of this place that had been described to me as both a cursed location and a high sanctuary of the past. I wanted the freedom to form my own opinion.

Our first reaction, then, both Môn's and mine, was one of wonder. The site was simply magnificent and arranged to my personal tastes: oriented toward the setting sun so that a vast landscape of peaks and valleys, some bathed in shadow, was revealed. We shared the impression of finding ourselves in an ideal location where we could live the good life, in a village perched between earth and heaven and sweetly caressed by mountain breezes charged with aromas and tinted with the richest colors of the sun. We directed our steps toward the strange neo-Gothic structure that I had been told was the Magdala Tower, and we leaned over its wall and were lost for a long time in mute contemplation. I knew that Father Saunière had built this tower to house his library. Here was a man after my own heart! I would be delighted to have my own library at such a site, overlooking this kind of serene yet grandiose landscape. It seemed that I would have felt inspired in this tower, amid all my books, and it would have been quite easy to work there, to think deeply on things and meditate there. No doubt Father Saunière had been inspired even to conceive of such a project. By virtue of this, everything disturbing that I had been told about this village priest became pure invention. Any man who could build this kind of observatory for meditating could be only a truth seeker, and a seeker of the truth could never sell his soul to the devil.

We then made our way along the path toward the church, but not before being dumbfounded by the sight of the Villa Bethania, an incredible construction worthy of a place among the most horrible housing developments in the suburbs of Paris before the war! In a region where the traditional stone architecture is remarkable and noteworthy, why build a structure that does not even have the merit of being in the "noodle" style of the architect Guimard and the old Paris Métro stations?[12] Curious . . . The Magdala Tower has an entirely different allure, even if the neo-Gothic mania of the early 1900s is too apparent in its design. I told myself that maybe Father Saunière was not as rich as his biographers have claimed, an observation that did not take long to be confirmed, given the monstrosities he sought to add as adornments to his parish church.

Because it was morning and the church was closed, we had to schedule our visit there for the afternoon. I certainly understood why the residents of Rennes-le-Château took precautions so that tourists are not left alone in their church. Otherwise the church would have been emptied and totally altered long ago by the work of careless snoopers. These precautions, along with the sign at the entrance to the village that tells visitors explicitly that excavations are forbidden within the borders of the township, do not prevent a few "scratchers" from operating on moonless nights, but they protect the essential in the village and, most important, the tranquillity of the people of Rennes. I couldn't complain, then, that the church was closed. For the time being it was still possible for me to study the cross on the so-called Visigoth pillar and observe that the pillar was placed upside down. I could also meditate on the inscription above the door of the church: *Terribilis est locus iste* (This place is terri-

---

12. [The curvilinear, organic forms of the 1890s-era architecture designed by Guimard is now formally referred to as the "noodle style," though originally the term was pejorative. —*Translator*]

ble). This inscription intrigued me for two reasons: The use of the Latin word *iste,* which has a clearly pejorative sense (and is sometimes the equivalent of the second person possessive) plunged me deep in thought. In addition, after reading the words above the door, I could not help but recall that on the request of Father Henri Gillard I myself had written a fairly bizarre inscription above the door of the parish church of Tréhorenteuc (in Morbihan). It can still be seen today—"The door is on the inside"—and while of course it does not share the same idea, I found myself in familiar territory and sensed these two churches were analogous, however vaguely, despite the great distance separating them.

Because it was noon and time for lunch, we found ourselves a table on a charming and well-shaded restaurant patio. The weather was splendid and we felt perfectly in tune with the countryside, though our attention to our meal was distracted by the presence of an impertinent child we took for a little girl because her name was Morgane. Of course, I took this as just one more coincidence, for Morgan le Fay is the great mythical shadow soaring over the Brocéliande Forest and is specifically depicted on the Stations of the Cross in the Tréhorenteuc church. I later learned that this Morgane was in fact a handsome boy, which in no way invalidates the speculations I had formed concerning the relationship between Rennes-le-Château and the Brocéliande Forest. Nor must we lower ourselves to meaningless quarrels over the sex of angels. In any event, this Morgane-Morgan had the face of an angel and the unruliness of a little devil. I hope he forgives me for being as impertinent as he was on that September day in 1985.

Once the time had come, we went back to visit the church, accompanied by a certain number of tourists who were visibly interested in every detail of the structure and seemed buried in great perplexity. It seemed the question of the hour was, "What could all this be hiding?" All of the visitors shared a similar hope of stumbling upon the one detail that had escaped all the rest who had visited the church. I was left with a strange impression: The poor church dedicated to Mary Magdalene was no longer a place of worship or prayer but an alchemical treatise in pictures—coded pictures, of course, to which each person must strive to find the key. I was insistently reminded of the phrase from the Tréhorenteuc church: "The door is on the inside."

I must confess that on this first visit I tried only to be aware. The Rennes-le-Château "affair," as it had been presented to me, with its "aura" of mystery, required some thought before I opened my mouth—and even before I tried to imagine which testimonies concerning treasures, secrets, and a challenge to the basis of the entire Western world just might be valid. I advised myself then: "Don't panic!" I am often accused of raving, though the accusation is unfounded. I am the coldest rationalist to be found in a domain where the irrational serves as the absolute engine for any and all intellectual and spiritual approaches. I have also been labeled an agnostic, though in fact I am a person who has a great belief in the value of religious texts—of all religions—because all address the unattainable Truth. This Truth, I believe, would be more appropriately labeled as deep reality—the reality that the Surrealists attempted to flush out from behind the false appearances and distraction that Blaise Pascal denounced so well. On this September day in 1985, however, I felt myself to be a kind of extraterrestrial in full flabbergasted contemplation of a world beyond comprehension. It is often said that the designs of God are incomprehensible. But I was asking myself if there was *really* any of God's design in this church.

Obviously, the words above the door warn the visitor beforehand that "this place is terrible," but to what place is the inscription referring? From the moment we enter the church we could easily conclude that it is the church itself and that we are being welcomed by a kind of horrible devil. I know full well that this devil, Asmodeus to those in the know, is not in the most glorious position: He is sagging under the weight of the holy water stoup he is obliged to hold. Here we find the devil not in the holy water stoup,[13] but beneath it. It is a detail of little account, yet is disconcerting nonetheless. I felt strangely ill at ease on entering the sanctuary, a sensation that has filled me in only Rennes-le-Château and the Saint-Sulpice church in Paris. This is surely not by chance.

I tried to analyze the origin of this feeling of unease, something Môn experienced as well. Was it because of the inscription over the door? Was it the presence of the grotesque Asmodeus, whose humiliating posture could not hide the fact that he was guardian of the temple?

---

13. [This refers to the French version of the expression "sticks out like a sore thumb": "sticks out like a devil in a stoup of holy water." —*Translator*]

And what of the temple itself? I confess to feeling that the church was created more for marginal celebrations along the lines of "black masses." Throughout the structure there exists a bias toward reversal: Not only is the "Visigoth" pillar upside down outside, but inside the Stations of the Cross are also arranged in a direction that is opposite that found in most churches. What are we supposed to make of the two plaster statues reflecting the purest nineteenth-century Sulpician style, one depicting Joseph and the other Mary, each holding a child and facing the other on either side of the nave? Were there two infant Jesuses? The theme could be Cathar but there is nothing Cathar in the church. And what of the strange painting beneath the altar, placed there, it appears, thanks to Father Saunière? It depicts Mary Magdalene, the patron saint of the parish, inside a cave, contemplating a death's head. Finally, what is the meaning behind the presence of two Saint Anthonys, both the hermit and the saint of Padua? No conclusion can be drawn, a priori, from these "curiosities," but we must admit that they provoke and even nourish a certain unease.

In this regard I cannot refrain from raising anew the problem of aesthetics as related to religion—any religion. We know that from the most ancient times, artistic manifestations were religious before becoming purely aesthetic. It is known that theater, for instance, is based on the sometimes ambiguous rituals borrowed from ceremonies of predominant religions, and that all forms of visual art—both representational and abstract—on the walls of caves or the supporting columns of megalithic monuments assume a kind of transcendence of the human toward the divine. In those civilizations that had not yet created a distinction between the sacred and the profane and that combined both intellectual and manual labor with the act of worshipping the higher powers that give life to the world, beauty in all its forms presided over the shaping of all types of worship, temple construction, and the ornamentation of sanctuaries. Now, the aesthetic of Rennes-le-Château does not correspond in the slightest to this fundamental search of humanity for its Creator. How could so many horrors, so much religious bric-a-brac, accumulate in what remains a religious sanctuary? Are we to believe that the person whose inspiration was responsible for decorating this church, Father Saunière, was a complete ignoramus from the artistic point of view, or that he deliberately ignored the aesthetic aspect in deference to a purely intellectual message? (The specifically spiritual aspect of his message is not at all visible at first glance.)

It should be mentioned in defense of Father Saunière that he lived in a time when there was no longer any understanding whatsoever of the need to harmonize beauty and glorification. This was at the end of the nineteenth century and the beginning of the twentieth, an era that witnessed the construction of the basilicas of Fourvière in Lyon, Sacré-Coeur in Paris, and Sainte-Anne-d'Auray in Brittany, which are, in the unanimous opinion of art lovers, monuments to ugliness in addition to being manifestations of an aggressive and triumphal Catholicism against the rise of secularism. Grillot de Givry, in his remarkable and still relevant work *Lourdes, ville initiatique,* was even then striving to unmask the deception that consists of building just anything "provided it brings in a crowd," and, I might add, a profit. The Lourdes basilica was already a horror in 1900. I can imagine the howls that the worthy—and genuinely faithful—Grillot de Givry would emit at the sight of Lourdes's underground parking lot, which has been pompously dubbed the Basilica of Saint Pius X, and the atrocity of a Stations of the Cross perfectly designed to cause nightmares in the most fervent devotees of the Virgin Mary! Things should be said as they are: Beauty and religion are connected. Ancient times and the Middle Ages have proved the truth of this assertion in a series of monuments that are as glorious in their worship of the deity as they are for humanity.

I was initially tempted to regard the ornamentation of the Church of Saint Magdalene as an example of "miserabilism" before the fact,[14] but I was reminded again of my Brocéliande Forest and that church in Tréhorenteuc that was decorated through the efforts of its rector, Father Henri Gillard, and to which—through my presence as much as my discussions—I had contributed. The two churches by no means share iden-

---

14. [*Miserabilism* is a word coined by André Breton to describe those cultural and political tendencies in a given time that tend to depreciate life rather than exalt it. In the era in which he was writing, he targeted specific movements, such as existentialism, which he described as the offspring of Hitlerite fascism and Stalinism, as the main threat to "sacred language" and the vital connection of the concrete to the abstract, the ideal to the real. —*Translator*]

tical features other than the reverse arrangement of the Stations of the Cross. The ornamentation in Rennes-le-Château, which has been carefully examined by tourists down to its tiniest detail, offers nothing original. It is a Sulpician creation of which other examples can be found in several sanctuaries, including the one in Rocamadour. But ornamentation in Tréhorenteuc is original, painted on location under the direction of Father Gillard, with elements influenced by regional style, including a scene that caused a scandal when it was created in 1948: a depiction of Jesus falling at the feet of the fairy Morgana as a symbolic depiction of lust. Yet, wouldn't there be a close connection between the Morgana of Celtic tradition, "the hottest and lustiest woman of all Brittany," and Mary Magdalene, the so-called repentant sinner, the woman intentionally depicted as one of the sacred prostitutes from antiquity who has been forgiven, sanctified, and incorporated into a triumphant Christianity? Regardless, the ornamentation of the Tréhorenteuc church, while of little note aesthetically speaking, is nonetheless original, as I can personally testify. As I have said, the ornamentation of the church Saint Magdalene of Rennes-le-Chateau is the purest Sulpician style from the decadent era. Could my feelings of unease at my first sight of this sanctuary, with its imitation Masonic checkerboard and the church's inversions and tawdry Baroque atmosphere, have been prompted by the site's *ugliness* rather than by more intangible reasons?

But memory, or rather the function of memorizing, comprises a series of trigger mechanisms that are at work within a delicate instrument. I was reminded then of some of Father Gillard's stories that until that time had brushed only a fairly weak level of my awareness. He had told me of his *"drôle de guerre,"* the one that took place during 1939–1940, the less than glorious end of the war following the debacle of the confrontation of German troops by the French army. During this time he had been wearing the French uniform, for it was right for all good citizens of an age to bear arms. Following a series of troop movements he found himself in Rodez, where he was decommissioned, but before being able to return to Brittany, where his church ministry was calling, he was forced to wait. Because he was a man who could never stand being inactive, he took advantage of this time before repatriation to travel through the surrounding area and explore a region unknown to him before then. He was not far from the Aveyron in Ariège and the Aude. He visited Montségur, where the theme of the Holy Grail connected to that Cathar fortress influenced him to take an interest in the Arthurian romances and this major Western myth. And he learned of a village, he told me, in the Aude region where a priest of modest means had completely restored his ruined parish church, wishing thereby to transform the village into a pilgrimage site that would satisfy both his religious needs and the interests of the town's inhabitants. In short, what Father Gillard discovered down there was the vocation of religious and cultural tourism that he would put into practice in the following years in Tréhorenteuc, the vital center of the legendary Brocéliande. What I did not realize at the time was that this place down there was Rennes-le-Château, which amounts to another example that nothing ever happens by chance. I who had taken part, at least to a certain extent, in the renovation of that forgotten corner of Morbihan and who had, in some way, assisted Father Gillard in the fulfillment of his vow, now found myself that September in 1985, six years after Father Gillard's death, in one of the places that inspired his action. A coincidence? I do not think so.

I then realized a few things: Of course, there was no question of attempting to incorporate Father Saunière into Father Gillard. They were not of the same time nor of the same stamp, and their profound motivations seem to have been fundamentally different. The sole connection between them exists on a superficial level, in their desire to transform modest parish churches into sites of "religious and cultural tourism" and in the indelible imprints they left on their respective edifices. Of course, abbe Gillard was entombed inside the Tréhorenteuc church, a practice that was customary in ancient times, and the abbé Saunière was buried outside the sanctuary but beneath the chevet, in a strange cemetery next to another tomb, that of his servant Marie Dénarnaud, who was also an odd individual.

We made sure to visit the cemetery that September, and gained access to it through a door that brought a smile to my face, for it was an imitation—and a clumsy one at that—of the triumphal portals that have been the glory and reputation of the parish grounds in Finistère. We pulled ourselves together in front of Father Saunière's tomb with the confused sense that this man had unleashed something that went far beyond him. Hadn't I been told that his tomb had been desecrated? What was someone looking for here? A treasure or a secret? I had been told that Father Saunière himself, in circumstances that remain mysterious, had performed a kind of defilement on another tomb. What could be the meaning behind his action?

The truth is that that this short visit to Rennes-le-Château, which constituted a real discovery for me even though it included deep gulfs of perplexity, remains in my memory as an experience of pure enchantment. The beauty and calm of the village, the powerful simplicity of the castle, the mysterious gardens laid out by Father Saunière, the Magdala Tower that faces a horizon I imagine as completely bathed by the light of the red sun setting behind the mountains and mists—all of these imparted a sense of great comfort. Yes, I thought to myself, this is a place where anyone could live well. Of course, I was convinced that there was nothing to be found either by digging up the ground haphazardly or through shrewd calculations, each more false than the one before it. If I had been a resident of Rennes-le-Château, I would not have calmly accepted others coming to disturb the fullness and serenity of this area.

In short, I felt a complete harmony in this place—but not solely in Rennes-le-Château. The arid plateau around it resonates with ravines and a few insistent trees against the peak of Bugarach in the southeast, there to show that a mountain is still present to serve as an observation or surveillance post, much like the watchtower of a fortress. Actually, taken as a whole, this landscape gave the impression of a fortress. I knew this region had served as a safe haven for its former inhabitants, those of the time when the Razès ruled and during the time of the Visigoths, who are still considered to have been "barbarians," though they were simply foreigners blessed with a brilliant civilization. In addition, hidden somewhere in a valley was Rennes-les-Bains, that other Rennes, which to my sense formed an odd contrast with the aridity of this Rennes perched on the side of an abyss.

We left for Rennes-les-Bains that September by the most unlikely road that snaked across the plateau. It was more a path than an actual road, but nothing that my car had not seen before, having swallowed its share of dust and sun. This proved to be a marvelous pilgrimage during which we thought ourselves hopelessly lost on several occasions because of the dead ends we found at every crossroads and in all the hamlets we encountered. We slowly descended through the September heat into a valley that surprised us with its greenery and shade and a serenity that was totally different in nature from what we had experienced on the summit. This was a domain ruled by water. We quickly discovered on our arrival that the village of Rennes-les-Bains was an authentic thermal spa.[15] Among the first things I noticed there was a worn inscription on a defunct old-fashioned spa hotel: "Specializing in cures for *catarrh*." Rather amusing, I thought, in a region where the *Cathars* left an indelible imprint! This did not prevent the charm of this small town buried in greenery from affecting me fully.[16] I have always been fond of spa towns, not because I have wanted to take the cure myself, but rather because of the curious fin-de-siècle style I have always found in them, a triumph of *decadence* in the sense given to that word by the poets who succeeded the symbolists and helped vitalize the time of the Belle Époque.[17] I am not, however, a fan of the big spa cities. I prefer the small, sometimes half-forgotten stations such as Vals-les-Bains in the Ardèche, Néris-les-Bains in Allier, and even Saint-Honoré-les-Bains in Nièvre. Rennes-les-Bains had the same appeal for me, a spa that seemed to stand completely outside time and space, almost absent from the maps, succumbing to the torpor or heaviness of valley air swallowed while still charged with the aromas of all the herbs growing on the plateau.

The myth continues as well in Rennes-les-Bains. The Baths of Rennes, as they were formerly called, are mysterious in nature. They date from the time of the Romans, which means that the Romans renovated an establishment that was previously used by the Gauls. They are also subject to wordplay: The Baths of Rennes are also the baths of

---

15. Currently, this small spa has been given a new lease on life, thanks particularly to the sponsorship and assistance provided by the city of Rennes (Ille-et-Vilaine in Brittany).

16. [Here the author is enjoying some wordplay with *Cathar* and *catarrh*. —*Translator*]

17. [The Belle Époque was a time on the Continent that was equivalent to the Gay Nineties in England or America. —*Translator*]

the *reine* (queen). This pun was all that was required for local tradition to echo the rumor that Blanche de Castille, mother of Saint Louis, spent time there and, of course, buried—or discovered; there are several versions—a treasure, or documents. Both Rennes, whether the one on high or the one below, are definitely full of hiding places of this nature, which only adds to the mystery of a region that is already sufficiently mysterious as a result of its simultaneously wild and refined nature. It is a small bit of land lost in the Corbières where, as Rabelais once said regarding the years of drought, everyone must have a cool and well-stocked cellar—stocked with the fruit of the vine, of course.

Merely its souvenirs of the remote past are enough to guarantee the town's mysterious nature, but Rennes-les-Bains is also a mystical, almost magical place, if only because of the shadow left by Father Boudet, who was the parish priest there at the same time Father Saunière was officiating in Rennes-le-Château. He is another uncommon figure whose role, from what I know of his time, appears even more confusing than that of his colleague on the plateau. Father Boudet prided himself on being a writer, historian, expert on prehistoric times, and even a distinguished linguist. He wrote and published a work on the true Celtic language *(La Vraie Langue celtique),* which he reconstructed from the English language with the aid of an alleged cromlech that encompassed the entire region. Very odd. I attempted to read some fragments of this book and was forced to put it down each time because of the hysterical laughter it induced. I further believe that at the time of publication of the volume, which went unsold but was liberally distributed to learned societies and local scholars, no one took seriously Father Boudet's linguistic ravings. It required the resurgence of matters concerning Father Saunière to reawaken interest in Father Boudet and prompt the republication—on numerous occasions—of his work, augmented with prefaces that were equally delusional. Unless it could be . . . so many stupidities written in one book by someone who was obviously not an idiot does merit some examination. For instance, perhaps the work is concealing something. But if so, what?

Môn and I made sure to visit the parish church of Rennes-les-Bains. The building, quite sober in style, is ensconced in the old part of the town. Here I felt as though I was truly in a sanctuary that was authentic and intended for worship and prayer, despite the strange paintings that are the joy—and anguish—of mystery decoders. The church is dark and almost uterine in nature; it seems to protect those who enter from any malevolent influence from the outside. It is the kind of peaceful haven that each of us likes to find from time to time in the midst of travels that tire the eyes and irritate the mind. It is certainly no masterpiece of religious art, but it does not seem that Father Boudet, having been preoccupied with intellectual research, left his own mark on the walls. Nothing has been renovated here; the church reveals nothing shocking or disconcerting.

The cemetery, however, is a completely different story. Although the abodes of the dead generally have a reputation for tranquillity, rural cemeteries, especially when located in the middle of town next to a church (which is increasingly rare these days), definitely seem much more agitated. I am not talking about ghosts, those folk legends of all lands that draw abundantly from the fantastic world of phantoms. Instead I am confining my observations to the real world. Why, for example, are there two tombs for the same individual in the Rennes-les-Bains cemetery? Countless hypotheses have been offered to explain this strange anomaly. It is known that the individual in question "did good for his entire life," and it cannot be doubted that he belonged to a kind of Rosicrucian lodge when alive, as this inscription shows.[18] What, then, is the real story here? The possibility of a macabre hoax does not seem relevant to this particular case. There is another reason, and it is up to every individual to discover his or her own truth.

There is a point at which, as André Breton said in the *Second Manifesto of Surrealism,* the various aspects of reality cease to be *perceived* as contradictory. This is a very difficult notion to accept because life, as it appears to us, rests on this fundamental contradiction that I have demonstrated so many times, if only in the perpetual combat between the Archangel of Light and the Dragon of the Depths. Everything would be so simple if people did not try to make things complicated. But the human mind is "twisted," and permeated by

---

18. [One of the three commandments of Rosicrucians is to do nothing but good deeds. —*Translator*]

maleficent forces (by which I mean the forces of destruction and deconstruction inherent in the mind). During my first visit to Rennes-les-Bains I realized that there are so many heteroclite elements that human intelligence is no longer capable of discerning what is from what is not. In this sense the Rennes-les-Bains cemetery seemed to me a revelation of a certain state of mind, but I did not carry my speculations any further at that time.

Whatever the case may be, my intrusion into the "enchanted domain" of the Razès was merely an epiphenomenon with respect to what had chiefly captivated my interest at that time: the extraordinary adventure of the Cathars, and especially the relentless efforts made by those on high (the papacy and the Capet monarchy) to destroy a doctrine I consider to be the most wonderful in existence, a doctrine that asserts that the world cannot recover its original Light as long as the last human soul—an angelic soul, it goes without saying—has yet to be saved and refolded into its primal purity. Wouldn't sin then be defined as not helping others to save themselves? Wouldn't sin be a case of ignoring rather than giving assistance to someone in danger of dying?

I returned to the Razès with Môn after my book on Montségur was published. I still saw Montségur as the place from which to expand my field of vision and dive more deeply into an understanding of a tormented Occitania caught between the Mediterranean and the Atlantic; among Greek, Latin, and Germanic influences; between the megalithic peoples and the druids; between northern France and the peaceful kingdoms of the sun; between the mountains and the *causse*.[19]

Many things had changed in my life, or at least in my way of seeing the world through the mists of some disconcerting evening when everything goes out of focus, as if I were at death's door. So we did return to Rennes-le-Château, but only after having made the climb to Alet, which was once the seat of an important diocese. We had gone astray in the ruins of its cathedral (a former abbey), which, though in the process of being completely restored, still retained from the past its privilege as a sacred site both out of principle and due to the fact that it had been one since prehistoric times. When we travel through the

---

19. [The *causse* is the limestone plateau of southern France. —*Translator*]

upper Aude Valley, we are not just completing the leg of a journey. What we find there I call by its Celtic name, *nemeton,* meaning a completely natural sanctuary located in the middle of the woods near running water that circulates through the veins of the earth like blood through the arteries of the human body. Only here the water irrigates a mysterious heart whose beatings can be felt only by those who know how to pick out the echoes of telluric currents flooding the world.

I am not a druid, contrary to the claims of a few who seek to better highlight my contradictions. I cannot claim to have rediscovered the pale shadows of the priests of Celtic society—nor especially their doctrine and ritual—twenty years after their disappearance. In the priests' time all sacred function was combined with a social and cultural function, which would not seem to be the case today. I have never taken part in those masquerades in which individuals, by dressing in white robes and insignia that are bizarre to say the least (including the Aryan symbol, the swastika), seek to abrogate to themselves the right to officiate as priests in the name of eternal druidism. As we know, the last druids disappeared during the time of the Roman Empire not only because of persecution by Roman authorities, but also because they became Christian priests. So why look for them where they will not be found? Why claim to restore a jury-rigged druidism that has nothing to do with how it was truly experienced during the time of Caesar and Vercingetorix? I am fully aware of how crazy our era is about folklore, even that in the worst taste. But what credit can be given to people who declare themselves druids solely by asserting that heaven spoke to them and revealed to them the great secrets of their ancestors? It is true that a good number of these neo-druids have never claimed to be doing more than researching through the tradition. But they all fall into the same mash brewed up by the eighteenth-century Welsh scholar Iolo Morganwg, who was merely a brilliant "antiquarian," meaning a pre-Romantic intellectual with a dearth of sources. So I am not a druid, God help me! But I do know how to recognize druidic sites; I know how to sense them because they have been and will remain sacred sites for all time.

The town of Alet, with its ruined cathedral and medieval streets, its dreamlike alleys and impenetrable stillness, left an unforgettable imprint on Môn and me. I know and love medieval cities. I have spent much time dreaming on the slopes of Puy-en-Velay, behind the ramparts of Concarneau and Aigues-Mortes, on the upward slopes of Dinan and Baux-de-Provence, and around Rouen Cathedral. There was a time when the Middle Ages exerted an irresistible and fascinating force over me. I gifted it with all the novels I constructed, but, alas, this Middle Ages no longer exists, or else it emerges from the feverish and romantic mind of Viollet-le-Duc and his English counterparts. In the final analysis, what I truly prefer is the rough and wild beauty of the ruins of Glastonbury in England, the alleged site of the tomb of King Arthur and Queen Guinivere; Tintagel in England (actually, in Cornwall, a mere detail), where lurk the shades of Arthur, Merlin, Tristan, Yseult, and King Mark; or even the wrenching melancholy of the Clonmacnoise Monastery in the center of Ireland, the place where the majority of the great fundamental texts of Gaelic tradition were set down—by Christian monks, no less! I also prefer the harshness of Montségur, whose roughness expresses better than any restoration the drama that occurred there. But I also love Alet and its tiny streets. I felt as if I were in another world there, one similar to that Celtic Other World I have been hunting down with no respite for so many years.

Alet, however, with everything it evoked on a subconscious level, was not our goal. We returned to Rennes-le-Château, this time without visiting the church. It was the site we wished to contemplate and to allow to permeate us. We were not disappointed. We again experienced that same atmosphere that had impressed us so greatly the year before: a kind of incomprehensible stillness and a sense of absolute well-being. Yet the mystery remained intact, for I had in the meantime gathered more information about those details that stirred up this modest Razès village. We ate at the same place beneath the trees in a park transformed into a restaurant. We wandered a little in the town. Then we set off for Rennes-les-Bains, again by the same dusty roads. We stopped once at the cemetery, at the double tombs of the lord of Fleury, and then continued our journey northward and eastward in a futile search for the famous tomb not far from Arques that was allegedly the model for the one painted by Nicolas Poussin. This was the mysterious tomb surrounded by shepherds trying to decipher its inscription: *Et in Arcadia ego*. Of course, these shepherds would have been incapable of discovering the true meaning of this logogriph. Of course, the tomb near Arques is a "fake," erected after Poussin's painting was created (though we may still ask why). Of course, we didn't manage to find the tomb, but we nevertheless wished to go farther.

A new circumstance had arisen in Môn's life: She had learned that her father owned a house somewhere not far from Razès, in Mouthoumet, in the very middle of this same Corbières region with which neither of us was truly familiar. Now, because Môn's father had abandoned this house and, what's more, had to a degree forbidden his daughter to set foot in the region, curiosity was killing us, as you may well imagine. We had to visit Mouthoumet. That is why, leaving Rennes-le-Château, passing through Rennes-les-Bains, and then going back up by Serres, we were looking so desperately for the famous tomb on the road to Arques, the one immortalized by Poussin. Our road continued on through other green valleys and garigues that we guessed were full of snakes. We finally reached Mouthoumet, which proved to be a seemingly deserted, sunbaked village. What would happen in such a place? Feeling somewhat thirsty, we entered the only bar and restaurant in town. The clientele, somewhat jovial and probably a little too much under the influence of "Corbière,"[20] were embroiled in a discussion. In their midst there was even a uniformed gendarme speaking louder than anyone else. Needless to say, no one paid us the slightest bit of attention when we entered. We sat down in hopes of getting something cool to slake our thirst. It was a waste of time. We waited for at least a quarter of an hour without any sign of a hostess or waitress to take our order. The clientele continued to talk noisily without even glancing our way. We made a dignified exit from the establishment, which was no doubt highly rated by the Michelin Guide but was obviously reserved only for zombies, and yet . . . It reminded me of an old television movie whose plot took place in a Corbières village. I cannot remember the title; I recall only that the main actress was the wonderful Clothilde Joanno, who, alas, was taken from us too soon. It involved a couple who found themselves in a village completely cut off from all contact with the outside world. The telephone wasn't working

---

20. [Corbières is known for its red wine. —*Translator*]

and cars could not enter or leave the place, but the inhabitants acted as if all were normal, though they behaved like perfect automatons. In short, it was a nightmare in which the real world and the imaginary world were so close together that it was no longer possible for the couple to tell which world they were in. I truly had the impression on that June afternoon in 1986 in Mouthoumet (Aude) that I was in the Other World. I had a very sharp sensation that everyone I saw in the room of that restaurant-bar was only a seeming, what the Latin poets called the *silentes,* those people who, according to ancient Irish legend, dwelled in glass towers in the middle of the ocean. They could be seen, they moved and went about their lives (what kind of lives did they lead?), but they could not answer the slightest question that audacious sailors might ask them. A strange impression—a strange land.

We found ourselves strolling through the streets of Mouthoumet, where there was not a soul to be seen. We saw nothing but the sun and houses whose windows were frightfully empty of any human presence. Following the directions we had been given, we easily found Môn's father's house. It was just as empty and absent of life. Its roof was in perfect condition, but the house itself had obviously been abandoned. We continued wandering the streets, all of which led into scrubland. Somewhat out of sorts, we made our way back to where I had parked the car.

It was then that something happened. We heard the noise of a motor and spotted a van that had stopped on the square. It was a traveling grocer who gathered his customers together with some loud blasts of his horn. A miracle unfolded before our stupefied eyes, for at that very moment a crowd of women surged from all over, emerging from the same lifeless houses we had just passed. Cackling, they gathered around the van where the grocer had set up his stand. The women passing us greeted us amiably, as if we were old acquaintances. Needless to say, this scene intensified the vision I had of an Other World swallowed up like the city of Ys beneath the waves and regaining the surface on only a few rare occasions, at which time the inhabitants would take advantage of their freedom to speak and ask something of those who happened by chance to be there at that time.

Unfortunately, I have no idea what the people of Mouthoumet

might have asked of us on that sunny afternoon, the day after the summer solstice. We climbed back into our car and had no problem finding our way out of the village and onto the road west. But I wanted to change our itinerary. We then took secondary roads that threaded their way through narrow valleys and appeared to lose themselves in dense dark forests. I would never have expected to find that area so wooded. From one crossroads to the next, each of which demanded some hesitation, we made our way to the foot of Bugarach Peak, the mysterious mountain that seems to be a counterpart to Montségur in an area where the Templars and the "Bougres," meaning the ancestors of the Cathars, have both left some traces. Here I again knew where I was and we no longer needed to find our way by trial and error. We were in the very center of the Razès region, and from there we made our way directly to the town of Quillan and then back to our base camp of Montségur.

I have retained an ambiguous remembrance of that day. Just what happened then? Had some indefinable shadows lurking above Rennes-le-Château and Rennes-les-Bains decided to accompany us on this pilgrimage through a foreign world that was necessarily at the very border of the unreal and the impossible? The discovery of a country is never limited simply to recognition and knowledge of the visible. It demands that time be spent in the company of the intangible, in the presence of everything that is subtle yet forms the very soul of a region. We can report rationally on the visible, we can comment upon landscapes and monuments, we can assign a value to the events that took place here or there—but it is much harder to describe impressions, especially those born of an almost mystical contact with the soul of beings and things. We could say that the heat among those sun-scorched rocks caused hallucinations and even actual mirages. We could also point to the importance of the underlying myths and legend that formed the foundation of our approach. But one thing remains certain, to me at least: Rennes-le-Château and the Razès would henceforth nourish a rich and fantastic world.

2

A Fortified Encampment

Rennes-le-Château is part of a small region, the Razès, located in the foothills of the Corbières mountain range at the southern end of the Aude department[1] on the border of Roussillon. The Razès is a land of small mountains, plateaus, and deep valleys with, at its heart, the upper Aude Valley, toward which converge all the streams and rivers that begin in the mountains. Its most important town at present is Quillan on the Aude River, forming a crossroads from which stray the roads to Perpignan to the east, Carcassonne to the north, and Foix to the west. There is a heavy Pyrenees influence here, but this landscape is typically Mediterranean, as is its climate, although the southern wind ushers in cold temperatures during the winter. In principle the Razès is a place of transit, not a destination. Over the last few years, though, tourism—notably trips starting from Montségur to the so-called Cathar castles—has sparked noticeable interest in people who previously would have driven straight through the region. Of course, the Rennes-le-Château mystery has drawn to this remote spot huge crowds made up of the curious, the skeptical, and assiduous treasure seekers ever since a newspaper article on the church appeared in 1956.

The Razès is picturesque and would merit being better known for its beautiful countryside than for its somewhat dubious reputation. In

---

1. [France is divided into ninety-five administrative regions known as departments. —*Translator*]

accordance with the saying that there is never smoke without fire, however, we should acknowledge the reality of certain mysteries in the region. As we shall see, the better part of these mysteries is connected to the Aude countryside as well as to both the mind-set and the ancestral traditions of its inhabitants. Certainly there is nothing surprising to be found there; similar "mysteries" can be found in countless other regions, especially in what are sometimes referred to as "fortified lands" containing natural curiosities, architectural riches, and connections to both history and legend. In fact, there are so many such connections that those who wish to tell a story must first clearly establish its particular scene—even if the tale will turn fantastic, ultimately taking place outside of time and space.

Today Rennes-le-Château is a simple village of houses clustered around a castle and a church. It is hard to imagine that it was once the capital of an earldom—even one of reduced size—that played its own particular role in the Merovingian Dark Ages. Despite current belief, however, a capital is not necessarily a large city. It could simply be the residence of a leader; then, as in more recent historical times, a leader need not have been surrounded by all his people. Versailles, for example, was the residence of the king and his court but was removed from the true capital of Paris. There was probably never anything more at Rennes-le-Château than a fortress, albeit a well-equipped one that included a number of dwellings around the count's residence. This does not mean that there were no outposts in the surrounding area that were also fortified. In Merovingian times, it is likely that in the valleys there were additional populated communities where economic activities necessary to the survival of the group took place. There were countless examples of merchant and artisan towns located on easy paths of communication to a more fortified population center and within proximity to a waterway or fertile land or even mining resources. Their location apart from the fortified area in no way prevented the inhabitants of these towns from seeking refuge inside the fortress—generally situated on a height—in the event of war or other danger. It is with this understanding that we should consider Rennes-le-Château.

The village's position, high on a rocky promontory that dominates much of the horizon, is certainly ideal, allowing for excellent surveillance over the surrounding area. Furthermore, it is—or rather, was—located on an important communication path (no one takes it into account anymore). The village, in fact, sits on the site of the Roman road that connected Carcassonne to Catalonia by way of the famous pass known as the Pass of Saint-Louis, which served for a long time as a frontier post between Catalonia and France. But this ancient road, which must have been constructed over an older Gallic road, is no longer visible today except for a few stray remnants here and there in the countryside. We can best grasp the importance this town, perched over a veritable eagle's nest, must have had when we approach it by way of department road 52 out of Couiza. All the residences are in fact on the butte's summit, situated below the castle, which is very old but was renovated considerably during the sixteenth century. The castle dominates the north side of the promontory, which is the side most exposed to the attacks of possible enemies. Striking above all is the grouping formed by the church and the property converted by Father Saunière, which consists of the gardens, the Villa Bethania, and the Magdala Tower overhanging the magnificent landscape. This now famous site was also well known in Saunière's time from the postcards he printed of his "work," but in his time no one talked about cursed treasure or jealously guarded secrets held by a mysterious priory.

The rocky platform supporting Rennes has an altitude of about 1,540 feet, and largely overshadows the hamlets of the surrounding area that are nestled here and there in pockets on the plateau. When we look out over the countryside from the Magdala Tower, we can see below a small village whose name—Casteillas—signifies that a fortress once stood there. Farther down the valley, beyond some rounded hills, woods, and the outlines of the Pyrenees in the Ariège region, is the town of Espéranza. Toward the northwest are Couiza and Montazels, part of Father Saunière's native area. Toward the north are the Aude Valley and what is known as the Étroit d'Alet,[2] and a little farther northeast are the village and ruined castle of Coustaussa, perched among the rocks on a hillside that overlooks the Sals River. To the south are woody clumps that make up the Lauzet Forest, which extends to the town of Granes in the direction of Bézu. By all evidence a sacred site, Bézu was the domain of Templars, who enjoyed a very special status that allowed them to escape

---

2. [The Alet Straits. —*Translator*]

the persecution of Philip the Fair. The southeast is dominated by the *pech* of Bugarach, which is about 4,000 feet in height. To the east, in the direction of Rennes-les-Bains and hidden behind a wall of wooded hills, are a number of small hamlets that mark out a narrow, sharply winding road: Maurine, Lavaldieum Sourde, and le Pas de la Rocque—their names cannot help but bring to mind a past that still holds many mysteries.

This brief description provides some idea of the appearance of the immediate area around Rennes-le-Château. Beyond this, it is hard to describe. It is a world of its own, a closed world, and there are reasonable grounds for Father Boudet's talk of an immense cromlech existing here, though it seems he may have intentionally played on the confusion between natural features of the landscape and rudimentary human construction.

The village of Rennes-le-Château is picturesque with its narrow streets and the imposing mass of its castle. The oldest part of the castle dates back to the twelfth century and was built on the site of a Carolingian (and perhaps Visigoth) fortress by Guillaume d'Assalit, who was the steward of the counts of the Razès. Damaged over the course of the centuries, it was restored and renovated during the sixteenth century to include four towers that flanked the walls surrounding an inner courtyard. Until the Revolution the castle was the property of the Hautpol family, descendants of the Cathars. One member of that family, Marie de Négri d'Ables, who is buried in the Rennes cemetery, has become a figure of legend: It appears that her tombstone was, if not the starting point, then an important element in the mysterious activities of Father Saunière.

The garden in front of the church in Rennes-le-Château gives access to the cemetery where Marie de Négri d'Ables is buried and is quite odd in its design. A central path cuts diagonally across it and leads to the church door with the famous inscription *Terribilis est locus iste*. These are the words attributed to Joseph in the biblical text of the Vulgate, but what are they doing here and what could they mean in this context? To the left is the so-called Visigoth pillar (which is actually Carolingian, as its craftsmanship and decoration incontestably show) holding up a statue of Our Lady of Lourdes. The pillar is in fact an old altar stone that was found inside the church and placed in its present location, *upside down,* after being recut and recarved for the Mission of 1891. It originally measured a little more than a yard in height and is now a bit under two and a half feet tall. On its surface is a carving depicting a gemmate patty cross fitted at the end of a cabled molding and crowned by an alpha and an omega, which are the symbols of creation of the divine infinite universe, the beginning and end of all things, equivalent to the famous ancient symbol of the *ourobouros,* the serpent biting its own tail.

To the right of the pillar is a kind of false grotto—in no way similar to the grotto of Lourdes—and on the wall along this garden path is a depiction of a standing stone reminiscent of a menhir. Others have noted that this "menhir" can be seen in the wall descending from the Bethania Villa and the Magdala Tower. By all evidence, Father Saunière had something in mind when he laid out this garden.

Farther to the right of the pillar we find a circular path that goes around a Calvary cross inscribed with words that have inspired much analysis: *Christus A.O.M.P.S. defendit.* It is a version of the inscribed cross that had its origin in the Occitan cross (which itself was a distinctive symbol of the Volques Tectosages people of Gaul) and the famous Celtic cross. Farther along toward the cemetery there is a crater-shaped pool that was vandalized in 1979, and just beyond it is an altar for the dead arranged against the surrounding wall. The cemetery proper is entered through a porch above which Father Saunière had engraved the words pronounced by the officiating priest on Ash Wednesday services. Augmenting this inscription is a sculpted skull over two crossed tibias on a phylactery. The skull, which seems to be snickering, shows twenty-two teeth, corresponding to the number of cards in the Major Arcana of the tarot. This portal, which reveals extremely bad taste, and the altar of the dead are, by all evidence, a souvenir of those grand triumphal porches that are the glory of the parish property of Finistère. Here, however, we search in vain for any sign of beauty or the least evidence of the grandiose. Is this the result of a lack of means or a lack of artistic taste? Or was their creation an act of derision? Whether we want them to or not, these are the questions that come to mind in the garden.

The Rennes church, which is now known as the Church of Mary Magdalene, is the former castle chapel of the counts. The apse dates to the twelfth century, the time of the castle's construction, but was subsequently expanded and transformed, then finally restored and decorated by Father Saunière to meet his needs. It must be said that prior to Saunière's arrival, the state of the property was far from satisfactory. Several documents reveal the general decrepitude of this parish church long before 1885, the date Saunière assumed the reins of office. For example, in 1883 the vicar general of Carcassonne made an urgent plea to the Council of State for assistance to repair the building, which threatened to fall into ruin, and emphasized the fact that the populace of the village, lost on a high and dry plateau, was too poor to assume the costs of such work. Accordingly in his request he described "the deplorable state of the sanctuary, altar, and the two nave windows, whose frames have been broken and carried away by a hurricane." He went on to underline the danger this situation posed to the faithful, but it seems that the civil authorities, at the beginning of the quarrels of the laity, turned a deaf ear to this plea. We can easily see why Father Saunière, confronted with a sanctuary in ruins, did all he could to restore it. What could be more understandable or more honorable? The circumstances of this restoration, however, were very strange and its result quite startling.

The welcome given every visitor who enters the church (are there really any faithful who still attend this sanctuary?) is disconcerting. To the immediate left of the entrance is the horrible devil Asmodeus, with his grimacing face, his eyes—one has been replaced—popping from his head and staring demonically at the black-and-white checkerboard floor. His left knee is bent beneath the weight of the holy water stoup he is forced to hold. We might well ask if the water it contains is actually holy. The right hand of the devil is closed to form a kind of circle; it is said he originally held a trident, the kind the demons of hell used, according to medieval folk imagery, to prod their victims into their ovens. As a rule such representations were placed just outside of medieval cathedrals and churches, generally on the north (or *sinister*) side, better to illustrate that the sole means of escaping infernal torment was by *entering* the church. Perhaps Father Saunière knew of the famous fresco inside the Kernascléden church (in Morbihan), or even of the horrifying *taolennou* [paintings] that Breton missionaries, on the initiative of Father Julien Maunoir during the Counter-Reformation of the seventeenth century, displayed to the faithful of remote rural parishes after having subjected them to terrifying sermons and making them attend equally evocative dramatic performances. That the devil is forced to hold the holy water stoup is in itself an excellent idea, from the Christian perspective. In the church of Campénéac (in Morbihan), the devil is similarly obliged to prop up the rostrum from which the word of God emanates. All of this brings to mind Satan's fall into the abyss as it is richly and lyrically described by Victor Hugo in a posthumous work called *La Fin de Satan.* Yet it cannot be said that the sight of Asmodeus puts at ease the visitor to Rennes-le-Château.

Fortunately, he is not alone at the entrance. Above the devil and the stoup are four angels, each executing a part of the sign of the cross. On the pedestal we can read the inscription "By this sign you will triumph," which recalls the legend about Emperor Constantine, who, after seeing this inscription in the sky, overcame his enemies and issued an edict of tolerance that brought an end to anti-Christian persecution. Along with the angels on this pedestal are two monsters, which are perhaps basilisks, mythical animals borrowed from a medieval bestiary, as well as a circle surrounding the two letters *B.S.,* which can be safely assumed to be Béranger Saunière's initials. After all, the names of the donors are always preserved in religious buildings.

On the back wall of the church, which has no openings of any sort and against which the confessional is placed, there is a fresco that is intriguing for both its naïveté and the details that can be made out in it. It depicts Christ on a flower-covered mountain, surrounded by individuals who are difficult to identify. At the foot of this mountain of flowers we can clearly make out a grain sack that has burst; grains of wheat are spilling from it. What meaning should be given to this representation? Could the grains of wheat spilling from the sack be the words of Christ that have spread here, there, and everywhere, yet have not been understood? Or is it a partial clue about a "treasure"—one that, of course, is buried somewhere in the region? This last interpretation has inspired many enthusiastic searches, though it rests on no precise foundations. Sacred texts and the illustrations of episodes recounted in these texts appear here only with what is generally called "artistic license." Again, all that can be declared for certain is that Béranger Saunière had an idea in mind when he commissioned the depiction of this scene. It should be added that the details in this work are especially irritating. The background, in fact, consists of an odd landscape in which we can see villages and towns. Could this be Razès as seen, fantasized, and revised by Father Saunière, or else a vision of a paradisial world in which Jesus, through his parables, evokes the profound reality through the deceptive appearances of a world threatened by the ironic eye of Asmodeus?

On the opposite wall, beneath the altar, is a painting that, according to some unverifiable witnesses, Father Saunière himself created. There is nothing intrinsically surprising about its subject; it is simply a depiction of Mary Magdalene. But it has nothing to do with the Gospel story of the resurrection of Jesus, nor even with the Provençal legend about the Holy Balm. In it we see Saint Magdalene clothed in rich garments on her knees in a cave with her hands clasped and her fingers interlaced. She is staring fixedly at the top of a cross fashioned from some tree branches and stuck in the cavern floor. Next to her knees there is a human skull, and a little farther back there is an open book. Outside the cave we can see a barren landscape that is crowned by sketchy ruins stretching into a luminous but stormy sky. The cavern entrance seems to be framed by stone blocks fallen from the wall. This is certainly a very strange painting. Of course, the cave can bring to mind Christ's tomb, but what would this skull be doing there? It is also reminiscent of the cavern of the Holy Balm, but Mary Magdalene has more the air of a rich aristocrat here than of a poor hermit. Interestingly, the image of the skull reappears on a statue of Mary Magdalene in the church itself, as well as in the private chapel Father Saunière had constructed in Villa Béthania. This depiction of Mary Magdalene, the patron saint of the parish, must have been a matter of heartfelt importance to Father Saunière. But what could this strange painting really mean?

As for the other statues in the church, they all display a frightening artistic nullity. There are plaster saints similar to those that can be seen everywhere: Saint John the Baptist, Saint Germain, and Saint Roch. But why are there two statues of Saint Anthony, one of the hermit who resisted temptation and the other of Padua (who is the patron saint of lost objects and causes), each standing almost directly opposite the other? Here again, it is impossible that their presence is merely accidental. It is apparent that in positioning them opposite each other, Father Saunière certainly intended that viewers compare them and reflect on their symbolic significance. Given these oddities, is it so surprising to see people creating novels based on the "Temptations of Father Saunière" and seeking lost buried treasures in Rennes-le-Château?

There are still two more statues framing the altar. On the left—when looking at the altar—is Saint Joseph and on the right is the Virgin Mary. There would be nothing extraordinary about this if each of them was not holding an infant Jesus. It seems there are thus two Jesuses in Rennes-le-Château, one the issue of his putative father, the other the issue of his mother. Here is a notion that could hardly be any more heretical.

I have already proposed one theory on this subject that can be taken for what it's worth.[3] We find ourselves in a land where the Cathar influence has played a strong role. The strong presence of the devil in this church may be reminiscent of the belief of Cathars, at least the radical dualists, in a principle of evil incarnated by Satan, the creator of matter, an "almost god" of evil who opposes the God of good. It could almost be said, then, that the child held by Joseph on the left—or sinister—side of the altar is not Jesus but Satan, whereas the true Jesus is held by Mary on the right side. To use even further the theory of dualism expressed by some Cathars, *both of them, Jesus and Satan, are brothers,* sons of God the Father, the sole Creator; they are the two manifestations of a good and evil deity. Why not? Another hypothesis, this one put forward by Franck Marie, is equally interesting: The child held by Joseph represents the masculine element, that which is apparent, visible, and external, like the male sex organ. Conversely, the child held by Mary represents the feminine element, the subtle element of *what is hidden.*[4] Again, why not? We should not overlook the fact that the rostrum, source of the exoteric and from which the divine word emanates, is placed on the left side of the altar. The bell tower is a similar exoteric symbol that permits a sonorous outward manifestation of divine thought. But on the right side of the church is the door leading

3. Jean Markale, *Montségur and the Mystery of the Cathars* (Rochester, Vt.: Inner Traditions, 2003).

4. F. Marie, *La Résurrection du "Grand Cocu"* (Bagneux: S.R.E.S., 1981), 16–18.

to the small sacristy and, more important, from there to a secret room that Father Saunière had constructed. We should also remember that the Stations of the Cross are arranged in reverse order in this church (which is extremely rare), and that following the Stations requires beginning on the left side of the church and ending on the right. At Rennes-le-Château, then, everything is arranged as though someone wished to show us the importance both of not being taken in by appearances and of following the external, exoteric path to eventually discover the secret, esoteric path. What is written on the door of the church of Tréhorenteuc (in Morbihan)—"The door is on the inside"—appears fully justified in this church of Mary Magdalene.

A visitor to Rennes-le-Château cannot leave without a visit to the small museum there that has on display the mysterious Stone of the Knight. This "stone" is actually a bas-relief that was discovered in the church and which offers a difficult challenge to those who would interpret it. It has been claimed, without basis and with no proof, that this is an extremely significant piece of evidence regarding the presence in the Razès of a legitimate Merovingian descendant, a son of Dagobert II (who, we know, died at a very young age). Out of this grew the serial novel—which is still growing!—concerning the future "King of the World," who will be the recognized heir of the first dynasty, that of the "hairy kings." In fact, this bas-relief is no more Merovingian than the famous upside-down pillar is Visigothic. It is a very handsome Carolingian work dating to the eighth century and depicting two mounted knights beneath two arcades. The horse of the rider on the left seems to be drinking from a trough, and it is possible this rider may be a woman because of the hairstyle and the folds in the garments that she is wearing. As for the rider on the right, like other representations of this type and perfectly characteristic of Carolingian art, he is brandishing a spear and holding a round shield. It is, in all likelihood, a hunting scene, a profane work that the artist sought to Christianize by adding, as was proper, a grape representing the Eucharist and the Tree of Life made famous by biblical stories and Grail legends. It was Father Saunière who discovered this stone while overseeing work on the church, and it is certain that it was one of the constituent elements of the chancel, the separation between the nave and the choir. But whatever the truth may be and whatever may have been said about this representation, the work is a splendid testimony to the art of the late eighth century, and this alone merits its removal to the museum. Authentic works of art from this site are rather rare.

Rennes-le-Château was not the site of the first fortress in the Razès region. It is more than likely that the Gallic site would have been at the place called Le Casteillas, an enormous limestone mass that haphazardly emerges from the rachitic plant growth and can be easily seen by looking toward the southwest from the foot of the Magdala Tower. The name Le Casteillas indicates a very ancient fortification (*castellum* in dog Latin) and designates almost everywhere it appears in France (and in Britain) settlements of rocky promontories in Celtic times. It evokes certain hill forts that are particularly plentiful in the southwest portion of England. If Rennes-le-Château is truly of Celtic origin (and that is almost certain), then we should concentrate our search in Casteillas, on the small rise separated from the town of today by the curiously named Stream of Colors, which forms a depression that is difficult to cross. It is currently impossible to see anything there but rocks and vegetation, though during the nineteenth century the existence of "three blow holes" was discovered. "In fact," as noted by a geologist of the time, one may note "a kind of warm air that seems to emerge from the entrails of Casteillas, as the lower region is studded with galleries, a veritable spelunker's paradise"[5]—and, one might well add, a veritable paradise for treasure hunters and other fans of hidden mysteries. There have also been recent claims of the discovery of a column and the remnants of an extremely ancient portico. This information must be regarded with all the customary reservations, because if compared with all the better-known examples of this architecture, this Celtic-style castellum was only a summit encircled by ramparts consisting of a foundational layer of dried stones on top of which a wooden palisade was erected. The "dwellings" inside would have been constructed in the same fashion. All that could be discovered there, if systematic excavations were to be undertaken, would be various objects, weapons, and jewels.

If we leave Rennes-le-Château by the road that snakes across the

5. R. Bordes, *Rennes-le-Château* (Paris: Éditions Schrauben, 1985), 30.

limestone plateaus, we are transported through areas charged with history and legend. This is the Coume Sourde road, named after the isolated hamlet of the same name, which is Celtic in origin. *Coume*, sometimes spelled *come*, is simply the French and English *combe*, which appears so frequently in the toponymy of the Hexagon.[6] It comes from a Gallic root meaning "curve" but through semantic evolution has come to mean "a winding valley." There are countless variations on this theme, from Chateaubriand's beloved Combourg and Combrit in Finistère to the various Chambons in the Central Massif, with a side trip through Chambord ("the ford on the bend"), not to mention all the Combes that distinguish so many place-names. In this instance, Coume Sourde, according to the regional historian Father Sabarthès, means "sordid combe," an allusion to the poverty of this area. But according to a specialist in thermal spas, a Doctor Gourdon who wrote a scholarly work in 1874 on this subject, the region of Rennes's subterranean area contained "a basin limited to close to 5,000 feet" beneath the town, which would assume an expanse of groundwater (no doubt warm, if one refers to Casteillas), which would give this place-name the meaning of "Combe from which a dull sound emanates." Why not? But another entirely Celtic etymology can also be offered here. The word *sourde*, in this case, would derive from a Gallic root akin to the Latin *siccus*, "dry," which engendered the Gallic *sych*. In these circumstances, Coume Sourde would simply be "dry combe," which corresponds perfectly to the characteristics of the countryside. Who, however, can boast of having the last word in matters of toponymy?

There is another strange and desolate site that lends itself to analysis: Lavaldieu, which is not a typical name for this region. We find the ruins of an abbey of the Val-Dieu in the Réno Forest located between Longny and Montagne-au-Perche in the Orne region, and the extremely beautiful cloister of Lavaldieu near Brioude in the Upper Loire region, and in all these cases there is no doubt that the name refers to *Vallis Dei*, "Valley of God." The difficulty lies in determining whether this name dates from the Christian era or if it might be carried over from an

---

6. [The French often refer to France as the Hexagon because of its shape; it can also mean the area of Île de Sein proper. —*Translator*]

older time. According to a local legend recorded before 1874, long before the events relating to Father Saunière, Dr. Gourdon pursued his investigations on the thermal groundwaters of the region and came up with a curious hypothesis: There once existed "in this place whose name was sometimes corrupted into Bal-Dieu, a temple erected to the god Baal in which the inhabitants of the land gathered to make sacrifices. One is tempted to believe that this temple would have been founded by Phoenicians who created several colonies on the closest Spanish coast." This is not impossible; the Phoenicians might well have advanced into the backcountry of the Mediterranean, if only to exploit the gold and silver mines that were once so plentiful there. But perhaps it is not necessary to go looking for a Phoenician god. Couldn't the name have been a corruption of the Celtic Bel, an abbreviation of Belenos, meaning "Brilliant One" or "Shining One," a nickname given to different Gallic deities that have left numerous traces in place-names—most often confused with the French adjective *bel?* It should be pointed out that both Lavaldieu and Coume Sourde were, for a while, the property of those strange Templars of Bézu, who enjoyed a very special status, as mentioned earlier.

Locally the ruined castle sitting above the village of Bézu is still called the Templars' Castle. One legend claims that these Templars cast down a well the silver bell of their chapel in order to prevent it from falling into the hands of the king's men, and that this bell still lies there. The legend goes on to say, according to Father Mazières, that "it tolls a death knell every year on the nights of October 12 and 13." At that time, it is said, "a long column of white shades" can be seen "leaving the cemetery and climbing up toward the ruins." These are the dead Templars searching for their former church, where they wish to sing the office for the dead.[7] Certainly this region cannot be found wanting in the way of legends.

But Bézu prompts other questions. First, the Castle of the Templars is called the Ruins of Albedun on a general staff map from 1830. The name Albedun is incontestably of Celtic origin (Albo-Duno, "white fortress"). It can be found farther to the north, toward Rennes-les-Bains, in the

---

7. Abbé Mazières, *Les Templiers du Bézu* (Paris: Éditions Schrauben, 1984), 30.

Franco-Occitan form of Blanquefort, or Blanchefort, designating the ruins of a castle that was the birthplace of the famous Blanchefort family. Albedun and Blanchefort are therefore two identical names. It should be pointed out, however, that the name "white fortress" is common throughout the entire territory of ancient Gaul, where it designated an ancient fortified city, whether still flourishing, in ruins, or existing only in memory. This is the former name of Vienne (Isère), once known as Vindobona (*vindu,* from which comes the Breton *gwenn,* "white," and *bona,* "enceinte, wall"). Nor are we far from myth: In popular imagination, the "white city" is easily confused with the "city of glass,"[8] the marvelous city of olden days (the realm of Faery is always placed at the beginning of history) inhabited by people who belong more to the Other World than to the world of mortals. In Chrétien de Troyes's *Lancelot, or the Knight of the Cart,* Guinivere is brought to the "city of Gorre (or Voirre, meaning Verre) by Meleagant, another form of Maelwas, who, according to the most archaic Arthurian legends, was king of the Glass Tower, located on what is now Glastonbury Tor in Somerset, England. It is known that Glastonbury, following a false interpretation of the name (which is Saxon), passed for the city of glass and even for the Isle of Avalon.

It can also be noted that Bézu still retains all its mystery—as much for the savage beauty of its landscape as for the myths it evokes—and possesses just the right atmosphere for such "affairs" that have shaken the Razès not just over the last decades, but since the early Middle Ages. Contrary to what some authors maintain, however, it is phonetically impossible for the name Bézu to derive from Albo-Duno. Furthermore, the name Bézu is extremely widespread in the names of villages and in place-names throughout the domain once occupied by the Celts. Accordingly we find a Bézu-la-Forêt and a Bézu-Saint-Éloi in the Eure region, not far from Gisors. It also appears frequently in the country of Wales in the form of Bedd. Its meaning is ambiguous, though, for it means both "birch" (a Celtic root akin to the Latin *betula*) and "tomb," as in the famous Grand Bé of Saint-Malo, where Chateaubriand's tomb is located. This is its most current meaning in Wales, where we find, not far from the village of Tre-Taliesin, the remnants of a dolmen called

---

8. ["Glass" is *verre* in French. —*Translator*]

Bedd Taliesin, the Tomb of Taliesin. Taliesin was a semi-historical, semi-legendary bard of the sixth century. Local tradition claims that anyone who sleeps on this dolmen will wake up as either madman or poet. The same tradition exists in the Central Massif, in Pilat, not far from the so-called Merlin's Rock. But with regard to the Bézu in the Razès, haunted by the Templars and the Cathars and still, by all evidence, a sacred site, should we prefer the etymology of birch or tomb? The legend of the Templar ghosts would seem to weigh in favor of tomb, a meaning supported by the neighboring White Fortress, which evidently is the fading recollection of ancient beliefs and archaic rituals.

This distinctive atmosphere reigning over Bézu and its immediate surroundings, which is due as much to nature as to the historical and legendary auras connected to it, is only partially present in the neighboring parish of Granes. Yet here again we find Celtic tradition intact. It has been correctly said that Granes has something in common with the Latin *granum,* and that the name of the village of Sougraine alludes to this. This would imply a land rich in grains, yet apparently nothing could be farther from the truth. In fact, the name Granes, like the name Grand in the Vosges, as well as the former name of Aix-la-Chapelle (Aquae Granni, hence the German Aachen), is built on the agnomen, or rather one of the agnomens, attested to during the Gallo-Roman era: Grannus of the Celtic Apollo, who Caesar, in his *Commentaries,* placed second after the Gallic Mercury in popular veneration. This Apollo is primarily the tutelary deity and initiator of healing springs, and it is as a god of medicine that Apollo entered Indo-European mythology before being incorporated into a solar deity, in reality before usurping the place originally held by a solar goddess (Artemis for the Greeks, Diana for the Romans). One thing is certain: All the inscriptions mentioning Grannus relate him to medicine and the healing of illnesses through sacred waters. It so happens that Granes is quite close to Bains-de-Campagne and Rennes-les-Bains, and that the subterranean region beneath the Rennes-le-Château plateau is occupied by a large pocket of thermal waters—hot waters, as the name indicates, known from earliest antiquity and exploited for medicinal purposes (and medico-religious purposes, it goes without saying, given that in long ago times medicine, magic, and religion were all connected).

Because the solar aspect of Grannus cannot be overlooked, the reference in the name Granes to one of the most honored Celtic deities creates a counterweight to the alleged temple of Lavaldieu that may have been a sanctuary for Bel-Belenos. In the healing of illnesses the sun complements the water gushing from the earth. In England's city of Bath, a dedication to the goddess Sul has been discovered on the site of a famous thermal spa of the Victorian era that was built on the site of ancient Roman (therefore British) baths. The name of this goddess clearly indicates her solar characteristics and makes reference to very ancient times, when the solar deity and the deity of medicine were female. Likewise in Ireland, even though there was a god of medicine, Diancecht, it seems that his daughter played the principal healing role if we are to believe the many mythological variations on this theme.[9] It should also be pointed out that the name Grannus most likely derives from the same word that gave us the Irish *grian,* "sun"—the word also found in the shape of the heroine Grainne, one of the most obvious prototypes of Isolde the Fair, the last medieval translation of this former solar goddess.

There can be no doubt as to the Celtic paternity of Granes; the toponymy of the Razès contains numerous Celtic elements. We may detect the Gallic in the name Rennes and in the name Razès itself. In addition, we may note the Gallic word *bec,* meaning a "point," in Saint-Julia-de-Bec, and the Coume de Bec, *coume* being likewise a Gallic term. The name of the village Artiques comes from the Gallic root *arto,* meaning "bear." Cassaignes is derived from the Gallic word *cassano,* "oak," from which the current French word for "oak"—*chêne*—derives. The name for the peak of Chalabre contains the radical *calo,* which means "hard." In the name of Limoux (as in Limoges, Limours, and Lake Leman), we recognize the Gallic word *lemo,* "elm," and in the name of the stream Verdouble, it is not hard to make out the ancient *Vernodubrum,* or "water course through the alders."

There is a site in the Razès that poses problems as much by the configuration of its terrain as by the origin and symbolic meaning of its name through a kind of haphazard sacred geography that we can begin

---

9. See Jean Markale, *The Druids* (Rochester, Vt.: Inner Traditions, 1999), 69 ff.

to perceive in this region. I am speaking of Bugarach—both the peak, which reaches close to forty thousand feet in height, and the village. Does the village take its name from the peak or vice versa? Nobody knows, though we do know for certain that the village has been called Bulgarach since the tenth century if we go by a charter from 889 that confirms the ownership of this parish by the abbots of Saint-Polycarpe in the Carcassonne diocese. The value of these monastic charters is, of course, always subject to caution, for the monks of the Middle Ages were quite skillful in the forging of documents that confirmed or expanded their privileges. Whatever the case may be, the name appears in this charter under the Latinized form: Burgaragio. We find the same name designating the same place in 1231 in the form of Burgaragium. In 1500 it appears as Bigarach, in 1594 as Bugaraïch, and in 1647 as Beugarach. Its current spelling did not appear until 1781. It has been noted that this place-name is not unique to this particular site; it is also found south of Toulouse in the form of Bougaroche and near Bourdeaux in the very close spelling Bougarach. In any case, the word appears only in what was once the Occitan domain.

What, then, is the origin of this word that is as mysterious as the Razès site that it names? It is tempting to see it as a derivative of the Germanic radical *burg,* which designates a fortress (the equivalent of the Celtic *duno*) and which passed into the French language as *bourg*. But this term was never used in the lands that formerly spoke the Occitan language. It is more likely to have originated in the ethnic word that has given us, among other words over the course of the Middle Ages, *bulgari, bugares, burgars, bougrais,* and the modern Bulgarian. We know that the Bougres or Bulgarians generally pass—and rightfully so—as the direct ancestors of the Cathars.[10] We should agree, then, that the name of the peak of Bugarach refers to a place where, for a certain unspecified period of time, heretics from the East found refuge. These heretics had a great influence over the region's inhabitants and thereby led them to adopt so-called dualist ideas. Bugarach would therefore have a direct or indirect relationship with the Cathar matter.

---

10. See Jean Markale, *Montségur and the Mystery of the Cathars* (Rochester, Vt.: Inner Traditions, 2003).

There is in fact an obscure relationship between the *pog* of Montségur and the *pech* of Bugarach. Fernand Niel, once one of the top experts in the field of Cathar studies, built a hypothesis worth keeping. According to the very precise calculations taken by this railroad engineer who was impassioned by the dualistic heresy, the builders, or rather rebuilders, of Montségur around 1200 would have consciously aligned the Cathar fortress on the average position of the sunrise:

> [T]his east–west direction falls over the pech of Bugarach, the terminating point of the Corbières, which has an altitude that is quite close to that of Montségur and a latitude, 42° 52', that is the same as well. To the extent they [the builders] followed their east-west direction precisely, they would have seen the peak of Bugarach standing out at the end of their alignment. Thus spurred, they would have definitely adopted this reference point offered by nature.[11]

In short, Bugarach was a kind of double of Montségur, or it was its opposite. No one can deny there was a correlation between the two peaks, at least from the symbolic perspective and, as Fernand Niel said, from a perspective that used the reference points offered by nature. If a sacred geography does indeed exist throughout the world, it should certainly be admitted that this Razès region offers a gripping example of it. Relative to this, it should no longer be a cause for surprise if Father Boudet thought he could see in the environment of Rennes-le-Château a gigantic cromlech, the code of which he claimed to hold.

There are coincidences that are no longer such when everything tallies together. The solar aspect of the castle of Montségur can no longer be subject to doubt once the strange phenomenon that occurs there during the summer solstice has been witnessed. At that time the rays of the rising sun enter the windows of the fortress's mysterious medieval hall, a room analogous to those "chambers of the sun" so plentiful in Celtic

---

11. F. Niel, *Les Cathares de Montségur* (Paris: Seghers, 1976).

tradition.[12] None can avoid comparing the ensuing effect to what transpires at megaliths such as New Grange in Ireland, Stonehenge in England, and the Dissignac Mound in Saint-Nazaire when the rising sun of the winter or summer solstice strikes the center of the monument.[13] But the neighboring Granes and Lavaldieu, the latter of which may well be an ancient sanctuary of Belenos and both of which are tied to the presence of thermal springs, show us that this sacred geography of the Razès is not merely some phenomenon hatched in the addled mind of a journalist looking for a story. Whether you believe or reject this notion in no way eliminates the observations that people have been induced to make. Yes, the cromlech at Rennes really exists, but in *an intellectual and symbolic form,* propped up by natural features of the landscape. It is the rest—in other words, the interpretation of tangible and visible realities—that is the imagination's domain.

It has been said that the pech of Bugarach was a landmark for "extraterrestrials." The idea has been floated that the sides of this mountain house caverns where these extraterrestrials hide out while conducting missions on our planet. Taking advantage of this idea of hidden caverns, some have declared that the mountain holds fabulous treasure. Why not, then, that of the Cathars, the Temple of Jerusalem, or Delphi? It is always possible to invent stories, and it seems that no one has held back. Yet a century ago Jules Verne took a close interest in the Razès and the Bugarach peak in particular. Why?

Jules Verne is not only an author of novels for the young. Because we now know that he left coded messages in all his works, concealed in tales of pseudoscientific and fantastic adventure, we are aware of his interest in a certain kind of esotericism. We are also aware of his membership in

---

12. I have given this subject a thorough examination in my book *Montségur and the Mystery of the Cathars.* The Chamber of the Sun, or the Crystal Chamber, is an image that appears frequently in Celtic legends, particularly in the story of Tristan and Isolde. It should not be forgotten that Isolde represents, in a fictionalized and Christianized form, an ancient solar goddess. The Chamber of the Sun is a kind of sanctuary where regeneration by sunlight takes place, especially when the sun is at the height of its summer or winter strength.

13. See also Jean Markale, *Carnac et l'énigme de l'Atlantide* (Paris: Pygmalion, 1987).

a "philosophical society," a term used to designate an initiatic brotherhood, of course. Which brotherhood in particular hardly matters; what is important is that Jules Verne was perfectly familiar with the Razès and the traditions lurking in this land, *long before the "affairs" of which Father Saunière was more or less the intentional hero.* There is in fact a little-known novel by Jules Verne, published under the title of *Clovis Dardentor,* in which the Razès and the peak of Bugarach play a fundamental role, even though they are presented under the cover of a very different region, exotic North Africa.

The plot of the novel is centered on the hunt for a treasure hidden somewhere on the coast near Oran. We can immediately detect the wordplay here: Oran equals *or en* ["gold in"]. It has even been thought that the hero's name, Clovis, evokes the Merovingian legend of the Razès and that the name Dardentor can be read in several ways, one of which is erotic but all of which are connected to the hunt for treasure. Verne even goes so far as to call Oran the "Gouharan of the Arabs," which immediately brings to mind the village of Gourg d'Auran in the commune of Quillan. The heroes of the adventure, furthermore, eventually find themselves at the Vieux Château, in the quarter of the Blanca [whites]. This last allusion is clear cut; it involves the ruins of the Blanchefort Castle. In the novel, near Mers el Kebir, there is a small thermal spa (imaginary, of course) that is called the Bain de la Reine [the Queen's Bath]. Now, we know that the former name of Rennes-les-Bains was les Bains de Rennes and that one of the springs, actually called the Queen's Bath, comes complete with a legend concerning Queen Blanche of Castille. Jules Verne even made sure to specify that the waters of the spring in his tale had a "clearly salty" flavor, with a "light odor of sulfur," which is characteristic of the thermal waters of Rennes-les-Bains. The similarities are curious, to say the least. One final, absolutely convincing aspect of the novel is that the captain of the ship, an authoritarian figure who takes charge of the entire expedition, directs everything, and knows the plan leading to the treasure, bears a name that Verne did not invent: Captain Bugarach. There can be no possible doubt: The peak of Bugarach, which is the highest peak in the region and thus exceeds all others, is the mandatory landmark for all successful quests in the Razès. *At least, that is what Jules Verne is saying.*[14] But whether we take this presence of Captain Bugarach as mere geographic allusion or look for a sacred resonance in it, it is nonetheless true that Jules Verne is telling us an odd story that takes place inside a camouflaged Razès that the novelist seems to know quite well.

Fundamentally these "coincidences," these traditions whose authenticity no one can verify, only reinforce the attraction that the pech of Bugarach exercises on its own. An indispensable element of the Razès landscape, it remains, despite everything, a haven of peace and serenity, overlooking from its great height a region that has experienced its full share of historical events, many of which remain confused and inexplicable. Yes, "Captain" Bugarach is the master builder of every quest in the Razès, even if this quest is simply the search for a magnificent landscape where the good life can be found.

The good life can also be found in Rennes-les-Bains. This village, with its ancient houses and antiquated hotels, lost at the bottom of a lush green valley traversed by the salty water of the Sals River, is a charming sight. What's more, the virtues of its waters are recognized not only for healing rheumatism, head colds, and other "catarrhs," but also for simply restoring health to the overburdened and "stressed-out" people of our time.

The most interesting spring in Rennes-les-Bains is one commonly known, complete with wordplay, as the Bain de la Reine. Local tradition claims that Queen Blanche de Castille was the mother of Saint Louis and that she actually stayed in Rennes to take the waters. This is far from proved, but it is known that, shaken by the expeditions against the Albigensians, Blanche de Castille did play a considerable role during the beginning years of the thirteenth century. From a strictly northern French perspective, she could even be faulted for her excessive indulgence of Raymond VII of Toulouse, who was ever ready to help the heretics and join the camp of the enemies of the king of France. It could be assumed that Blanche de Castille, at the time when the famous Trencavel sought to regain his earldom of Razès, had secret negotiations with certain Occitan lords regarding mysterious documents that

14. For more on this topic, see the excellent book by Michel Lamy, *Jules Verne, initié et initiateur* (Paris: Payot, 1984).

would have been stored in the area of Rennes-le-Château. This unverifiable part of the story has helped, as one might guess, to fuel the famous hypothesis of legitimate descendants of the Merovingians finding refuge in the Razès. But it also means that it is not impossible that Blanche de Castille visited Rennes-les-Bains.

The problem emerges when we note that the Reine Blanche (White Queen) primarily designates a mythological entity that is well known everywhere, but most particularly in the Pyrenees and their immediate surroundings. The White Queen, or the White Lady, is a translation of the fairy of folktales and the White Goddess of ancient mythological tales. She often appears in riverside caves[15] that are located near springs, which she is said to have caused to appear. Could something similar have occurred at Rennes-les-Bains? In this case the springs would not have been called forth by Blanche de Castille but instead would be from a bygone age when a White Goddess—a healing goddess, of course, who bestowed life and health with the waters she caused to gush forth in the valley—was worshipped there. As for the homophony between Reine and Rennes, it has been thoroughly played, multiplying the mythological components of the theme.

In any event, we know that springs, especially those with recognized curative properties, have been highly frequented places of worship since the earliest days of antiquity. There was a famous temple dedicated to the springs of the Seine during the Gallo-Roman era. As noted earlier, the goddess Sul was worshipped in Bath, England. In Vichy curious traditions speak of fairies who were once the benefactors of the land. The Gauls were perfectly cognizant of the use of thermal waters, especially because druidic medicine was one with the religion of druidism and the druids themselves were both priests and doctors (as well as many other things). The Romans had only to follow the example of the Gauls, and they renovated springs that were already in use. They were particularly interested in saline springs because salt (especially in regions far from the

---

15. Without seeking to cast doubt on the appearance of a White Lady to Marie-Bernarde Soubirous in the Lourdes grotto, it is worth noting an astonishing similarity between these "apparitions" that are recognized by the Church and the faithful the world over and the numerous versions of the White Lady that are said to have been seen throughout the Pyrenees.

sea) was an indispensable element for the vital equilibrium of the populace—and for that of animals. This explains the importance of the thermal establishments of Fontaines-Salées in the Burgundy town of
Saint-Père-sous-Vézelay, or even Salins in the Jura not far from the real
Alésia, which was a fortress-sanctuary. There is a lack of documentation
on the ancient baths of Rennes-les-Bains, but the Roman presence there
is widely confirmed. And once again, the word *thermal* implies worship
given to healing deities, Apollo in particular under the names Grannus
and Borvo ("boiling," hence the name Bourbon), and also solar goddesses often presented in triads (the Three Mother Goddesses), which
obviously brings us back to the traditional theme of the White Ladies.

The water of the spring called the Queen's Bath stands at about 41
degrees Celsius and contains a high amount of sodium chloride—but there
is another spring in Rennes-les-Bains that is worthy of attention. It is called
either the Magdalene or the Gode. Of course, the first name is intriguing
when we consider the worship of Mary Magdalene in the Razès and Abbé
Saunière's apparent understanding of it. Furthermore, in the legend of her
piety that is told throughout Occitania, Mary Magdalene is connected to
the theme of the grotto, which also explains the painting beneath the altar
of the church in Rennes-le-Château. The Magdalene spring is also quite
salty with some sulfurous elements—in the literal sense of the word—
mixed in. The second name for this spring, the Gode, is very interesting.
Father Boudet, author of *La Vraie Langue celtique* and, secondarily, priest
of Rennes-les-Bains at the beginning of the twentieth century, probably
came up with the idea of rediscovering the Gallic language through the
English language here. The word Gode seems quite close to the English
word *god* (or *goddess*), which connection would demonstrate that this
spring was placed under the name of a deity, a Fairy of the Waters similar
to the Irish Boyne or the Vivian of Arthurian tradition.

As noted by Franck Marie, however, "[I]t is surprising to see that
Father Boudet, so quick to interpret every word by the English language, transcribed Gode as 'to goad,' meaning 'to needle, incite, urge
on.'" Why did he avoid the translation of Gode as "God?"[16] The question is an interesting one. Franck Marie goes further by suggesting that

---

16. F. Marie, *La Résurrection du "Grand Cocu"* (Bagneux: S.R.E.S., 1981), 106.

the appellation of la Gode refers to a traditional local custom, specific to Bugarach but closely tied to the famous Limoux Carnival in which, during the festivities that are spread throughout the Razès region from Limoux to Axat by way of Alet, Couiza, Quillan, and both Rennes, we can see processions of masked figures called *fécos* and *goudils*. According to Marie the fécos are "ones nauseous on wine lees" and the goudils are "ragpickers." The goudil, however, represents the hermit (man or woman) who lies low in a cave and appears in the world only on certain occasions, namely during Carnival. Couldn't this be a remote recollection of the Celtic feast of Samhain on November 1 that became the Christian All Saints' Day and is highlighted in Anglo-Saxon countries by the carnival-like parades of Halloween? Couldn't the goudil be one of the deities that the Irish called the Tuatha de Danann, who lived in the mounds (megalithic monuments) and emerged on the surface of the earth on the eve of Samhain?

There is something unsettling about this interpretation, still connected to the White Lady because the fairy women of the mounds, who sometimes shift-shape into white swans, are extremely important figures in early Celtic mythology. Under these conditions it is tempting to interpret the spring called the Gode as the spring called the Woman of the Mounds, after she who awaits the propitious moment to appear to humans but who, in any case, protects them and gives them the water necessary for life and health. So what, then, is the connection to Mary Magdalene, who, let us not forget, is one of those whom we currently call the Three Marys? Everything seems to be linked in this sacred geography of the Razès.

But this sacred geography is not as simple and precise as it may appear. Fantastic novels on the Razès have been built out of totally authentic elements. Accordingly, the White Ladies and other goddesses could very well be no more than the redrafting of various facts. Louis Fédié, who remains an incontestable historian of the Razès, points out a local folk legend that would explain the myth:

> Once, some time ago, a queen of Spain named Blanche de Castille took refuge in the castle of Pierre-Pertuse (Peyrepertuse) to escape dangers that threatened her very life. The governor of the fortress

treated her with all the respect due one of her rank and misfortunes, and she passed her sorrowful days sometimes praying in the chapel and sometimes taking walks in the countryside near the castle. The inhabitants of the neighboring villages worshipped her like a saint and watched her from afar with a curiosity blended with even greater respect when she went down to the fountain that flowed at the foot of the ramparts. And there, seated beneath an old weeping willow whose branches leaned over the crystalline waters, she spent long hours emitting her plaints of exile and bemoaning her fate as a woman without a husband and a queen without a crown.

One day, distracted by her painful memories, she let slip from her hand a silver goblet that rolled over the precipice and was found much later by a shepherd who sold it to the lord of Rouffiac. This goblet, bearing the coat of arms of Castille, was in the possession of the royal treasurer of the Fenouillède region[17] before the Revolution. He resided in Caudiès and guarded it as a most precious relic.[18]

The historian continues his story, or legend rather, with the mention of an illness that Blanche de Castille contracted, probably the famous scrofula. To relieve her affliction and gain her cure, she had herself carried by litter to the Locus de Montferrando et Balneis to take the waters. Hence the name given to this spring was the Queen's Bath, according to Louis Fédié. The problem is that the Blanche de Castille in this story seems to have nothing in common with the mother of Saint Louis. Perhaps this queen was a chatelaine from the area and a Spaniard. Local tradition no longer seems to distinguish reality from fiction, and it seems that the story of Blanche refers to beliefs that are much older than the thirteenth century.

The mystery remains. And what do we make of the declaration of Dr. Gourdon, who, in his research of hot springs in the Razès, claims that the "source of the Madeleine" [Madeleine is an alternative French spelling for the name Magdalene] simply comes from a certain Miss Madeleine who used this spring around 1871? What happened to the

---

17. The region south of the Razès. It also neighbors Roussillon.
18. Louis Fédié, *Le Comté de Razès et le diocese d'Alet* (1880).

myth of Mary Magdalene from that moment onward? There is one incontestable fact: Over the course of the centuries, numerous Roman remnants have been found near the springs, particularly statues, some of which depict a feminine figure. Was this the goddess of the Rennes springs? This small thermal spa was well known, for even in the fourteenth century Rabelais cites in his *Pantagruel* that among the springs frequented in his time there was a Liomons, an obvious alternate name for Limoux. Because there are of course no springs in Limoux, this must be a reference to Alet or Rennes-les-Bains. Did Rabelais personally visit the Razès? Perhaps. According to Father Boudet's testimony, an anthropomorphic sculpture was removed from the springs in 1884 to protect it from vandalism. Identified by the priest as the head of Jesus Christ, the sculpture had been found on rocks bearing the name Cap de l'Hommé [Head of Man] (the spelling of Father Boudet, who even speaks of *menhir!*). In fact, it seems that everything in this account is thoroughly confused. A male head was discovered in Rennes-les-Bains in 1884 and a female head was found in 1889. Both of these items have been mixed together by storytellers. The female head is described as follows by the archivist René Descadeillas, the great demystifier of the Saunière affair: "This sculpted head could be of cult origin if it represents the face of a female deity jutting from a rock emerging from the water. And in this case, she would be the deity of a spring or stream." What could be more common in a Romanized thermal establishment that dates back to the earliest days of Gallic prehistory? The myth of the Lady of the Lake is still present and sometimes materializes in the form of sculptures. In any case, the craftsmanship of the sculpture is Gallo-Roman, which is not surprising given that those in Gaul before the Roman conquest never depicted their gods in animal or human form. This simply shows that Rennes-les-Bains was a place of worship at the same time that it was a thermal spa.

But the Magdalene spring and the Queen's Bath are not the only springs that exist there. The Rennes-les-Bains Valley has five cold-water and five hot-water springs in all. There is the Spring of the Gentle Bath, which is 33 degrees Celsius and is also known as the Spring of the Skinflints because of its reputation for treating leprosy. Among the cold springs there is the Fountains of Love, which has inspired more than one regional commentator to give free rein to his speculations. All those seeking to explain the importance of the Queen's Bath from the time of antiquity are free to explore this choice terrain. They will find not only water, but also obvious remnants of the prolonged use of the site and its longstanding sacred nature.

Yet it should not be thought that Rennes-les-Bains is only a thermal spa. It is also the parish over which Father Boudet reigned during the end of the nineteenth century and the beginning of the twentieth. This is the priest who thought himself both a linguist and an archaeologist and who studied his region from a curious perspective. He was also, it is said, the discreet inspirer and mentor of his colleague in Rennes-le-Château, Father Béranger Saunière. It is thus perfectly legitimate to take a look at his parish church.

We enter the church through a vault offering the distinct feeling that we are truly in a sacred place and that this sacred place includes the village of which this church is an integral part. It does not give the impression of entering a bazaar where everything is for sale, as is unfortunately the case in Rennes-le-Château. Instead, it is truly a place of prayer, a sanctuary that will never give anyone the idea that a "backward Mass" could take place there. This site, however, does pose some questions of its own. The parish church of Rennes-les-Bains has a complete simplicity that verges on Jansenist austerity. It has been restored without any affectation and projects a sense that the local people, who are proud of their sanctuary and periodically gather there, maintain it in good repair. And it is a good thing to gather in a nemeton, a sacred ancient druidic clearing in the middle of the forest, in communion with nature but also in communion with everything that exists in that great fraternity of beings and things to which all Creation aspires.

There is definitely something in this church that, while not an anomaly, is still a curious detail: a painting of mediocre value, artistically speaking, but that has proved to be quite mysterious. Entitled *Christ and the Hare*, it is a Pietà, like those found in so many other Christian sanctuaries. It was donated to the parish at the end of the eighteenth century by Paul-Urbain de Fleury, the local lord and owner of the Queen's Bath, who was considered to be one of the benefactors of the church. *Christ and the Hare* would certainly not attract any attention if it were not a somewhat modified—and, *more important, reversed*—copy of a work composed in 1636 by Van Dyck, the original of which is on display in the Fine Arts Museum of Anvers. We could hold forth endlessly on certain details of this painting, and it surely conceals a special meaning, but what is it? Treasure hunters in the Razès have not failed to analyze it from every angle, but apparently without result, unless those who found some answers have refrained from letting this be known publicly. The difficulty with objects that are invested with a tradition of secrets is that sincerity and falsehood are automatically intertwined in any interpretation of their symbols. If someone were to discover the solution to a given mystery, he or she would certainly refrain from revealing it to others first because of self-interest, then because the solution to a mystery is valid only if it has been achieved by following what is pompously referred to as the path of initiation. But how can we find the central chamber of a mound, for instance, if we do not first cross the stage of *initiation* or, in other words, the *entrance* into a domain where obscurity, out of principle, rules as absolute master?

Every visit to the parish church of Rennes-les-Bains necessitates visiting the adjoining cemetery. The site is calm, peaceful, and definitely less tormented than the cemetery at Rennes-le-Château. Here no tombs have been defiled, though it is the story of a tomb here that is troubling in a number of ways. Again Paul-Urbain de Fleury, donor of the painting *Christ and the Hare,* figures into the story, this time in circumstances that are, to say the least, bizarre. Paul-Urbain de Fleury has *two tombs* in this cemetery. In addition, the set of dates of birth and death inscribed on these two tombs are *different from one another.* Make of that what you will. As for the epitaph—"He departed while doing good"—what are we to make of it? Perhaps it constitutes a Rosicrucian signature. The questions this raises are obvious: Why these *intentional* errors in the dates? Why two tombs for the same individual? Which of these two tombs is the *real* one? Every "quest" in the Razès definitely passes here, and any who find the answers will be rewarded by some surprise. By all evidence the cemetery of the church in Rennes-les-Bains is not a *neutral* zone. It should never be forgotten that an ancient Gallic sanctuary was located there long before the Roman invasion. It seems that even in the eighteenth century some individuals, as shown by the Rosicrusican Paul-Urbain de Fleury's two funeral monuments, knew what the real story was. They have left behind its imprint. It is up to each of us to take the test or, if you prefer, the *initiation.* All the rest, including the scholarly decoding of the true Celtic language by Father Boudet, is only sensational literature.

The exploration of the mysterious Razès does not end in Rennes-les-Bains, though that place does present itself as the pivotal point of a sacred geography that is sketched without showing its exact contours very clearly. If we head north before angling eastward in the direction of Mouthoumet, we first pass through the village of Serres. Long before reaching Arques in the commune of Peyrolles, we find the hamlet of Pontils. Not far from here is an authentic menhir known regionally as the Peyro Dréto (Standing Stone). Finally we reach the Tomb of Arques. As Pierre Jarnac rightly said in his magisterial work on the affairs of Father Saunière:

> Despite its great antiquity, its prestige has suffered through the presence of a more recent monument customarily called, though incorrectly, the Tomb of Arques. This tomb, almost hidden by the trees, was placed there on the edge of a peak level with a small bridge crossing a stream, the Cruce, that has run dry now. . . . It has the appearance of a parallelepiped topped by a truncated pyramid.[19]

This monument has lent itself to the most diverse and truly delirious commentaries. It is in fact a replica of the tomb depicted by Nicolas Poussin in his famous painting *The Shepherds of Arcadia,* a work that has been heavily embroiled in the Rennes-le-Château affair. It is said that Father Saunière, while visiting Paris to have someone decode the documents he discovered in his church, made a special visit to the Louvre to study the painting and even bought a reproduction of it. By all evidence it is the tomb in Pontils that is a copy of the monument painted by Poussin. We know through supporting documentation that it was built at the beginning of the twentieth century by a certain Louis

---

19. Pierre Jarnac, *Histoire du trésor de Rennes-le-Château* (Paris: Éditions Bélisane Cazilhac, 1998), 400–401.

Galibert, who buried his grandmother in it. Later, a new owner of the property, Louis Bertram Lawrence, an American, renovated the tomb. The actual landscape behind the monument resembles that seen in Poussin's painting, an enigma made more mysterious by the phrase inscribed on the tomb in Poussin's painting, *Et in Arcadia ego,* that brings to mind the comparison certain authors have made between the Razès and the Greek Arcadia. Lending further mystery to the enigma is the river that winds through the Arques Valley, the Réalsès, which means "royal water." (This is also the name of a large national forest in the south.) Still another mysterious detail is the seeming correlation between the shepherdess depicted in Poussin's painting, resting her hand on the neck of one of the shepherds, and the name of a mountainous pass seen from the actual tomb: Col d'Al Pastre.[20] It is certain that Nicolas Poussin wished to depict this landscape. But why? That is indeed the question. We may also ask why someone deliberately had a tomb built at this location around 1900. Are we really in that mysterious and more or less mythical Arcadia where the underground Alpha River flows?

These coincidences were all that I needed to start inquiring into the name of the village of Arques. It has been seen as a derivative of *arca,* "arch," but also "secret," as in the word *arcane.* This was enough to make the tomb and the painting by Poussin (of which a reversed replica exists in England) the key to all of the mysteries in the Razès. Unfortunately, up to the present no one has succeeded in deciphering the meaning of the painting or the inscription, unless those who have been successful have not boasted about it. As for Arques, the fans of secrets risk being disappointed when they learn the real etymology of this name: It derives from the Latin *arx* (plural *arces*), which means "citadel" or "fortress," and is a souvenir of a castle that was once located in or near the village. There is nothing surprising in this; farther west on the side of the same mountain the ruins of the castle Coustaussa rise. The toponym Coustaussa comes from the Latin *custodia,* "guard" or "guard post," a provenance that is not belied in any way by its geographical configuration, for the castle literally guarded the Sals Valley.

-----

20. [This means Shepherd's Pass or Shepherd's Collar. —*Translator*]

The Christian town of the Razès is Alet, currently a simple, rustic town nestled at the bottom of the Aude Valley, between Limoux and Couiza. The regional historian Father Lasserre described it as "placed like a basket of flowers in a delightful valley that God took pleasure in enriching with all the gifts of nature."[21] The medieval village, which has been tastefully restored and perfectly maintained, is admirable, and the surrounding landscape is full of charm. Water gushes everywhere, which no doubt gave this site its ancient reputation: The earliest information available about Alet concerns a thermal establishment there during the Gallo-Roman era. It is still a town of waters, which contributes to making it a place heavily frequented by both tourists and visitors taking the cure.

The village sits on the left bank of the Aude and is bordered on the west by a bend in the river and on the north by a stream called the Cadène. These two natural defenses combine with ramparts that almost completely encircle the village's houses and gardens in a kind of pentagon. There are six large streets in Alet, all arranged in a star pattern around a central square. One of the streets connects the square to the north entrance of the abbey, which occupied the area nearest the Aude. At one time another street crossed Alet from north to south—from the Porte Cadène to the Porte Calvière—until 1776, after the monks ceded part of their lands. A new route was then created (the current Departmental Road 118), separating the village from the abbey and connecting to the seventeenth-century bridge that allows access to the right bank. This bridge replaced an older medieval bridge that had been located farther north.

The houses of Alet are notable for their stylistic purity. Those facing the square have corbeled, half-timbered facades with sculpted beams. In one of the narrow streets there is one notable structure called the Romanesque House on the rue du Séminaire. It consists of a ground floor with an entrance door in sections and six surbased arches, and a second story built of corbeled wood and lit by two magnificent windows whose semicircular arches are supported by small columns with leafy capitals. It is a very beautiful and very rare example of civil architecture from around 1200.

---

21. T. Lasserre, *Recherches historiques sur la ville d'Alet et son ancien diocese* (Paris: Carcassonne, 1877).

The abbey was once huge, but only fragments remain. The cloister has disappeared entirely, and the remainder of the abbey-turned-cathedral is nothing more than some protected ruins. The aisles and part of the nave can still be seen on the north side, which is the best preserved. This is where a door opens out onto what were once monastic buildings, including a very handsome capitular hall. Around the remnants of the Gothic choir, which was built when Alet became a bishopric in 1318 in place of Limoux, the magnificent Romanesque apse remains almost intact. It opens onto the nave by way of a triumphal arch set upon two columns with finely worked capitals and abaci and decorated with modillions with floral motifs. The lower part of the semicircular vaulting in the apse is interrupted by deep-set windows with interior splaying that rest at the height of the walls over a string course depicting a row of pearls and ovals with floral motifs. This Romanesque chevet is strikingly original and foreshadows the chevet in Saint-Jacques de Béziers. In addition, the original Romanesque abbey of Alet seems to have served as a model for Saint-Just in the city of Carcassonne, though its renovation has been subject to the influence of Saint-Sernin in Toulouse. The entire edifice, although belonging to two different eras and styles, has retained a remarkable unity. It stands out as a rich and powerful conglomerate for both the daring of its construction and its abundant decoration. It is highly regrettable that this ancient monastery-cathedral has been subject to so much abuse at the hands of time and men. It would otherwise likely be one of the most beautiful medieval religious monuments in the Languedoc, which is not lacking in exceptional sanctuaries.

As consolation, however, we can still wander through the ruins. Often the remnants evoke a past whose presence can be keenly felt in the smallest stone and the tiniest sculpture. Alet was once the center of Christian spiritual life in this area of the Razès, for while the "affairs" connected to Father Saunière and Father Boudet seem to place a greater emphasis on the pagan elements that preceded Christianity or on what has been improperly labeled heretical, it should not be forgotten that there is always continuity in beliefs and worship. Attempting to understand Rennes-le-Château without referring to this abbey bishopric of Alet would be like looking for a treasure lost in the deepest abyss of the seas.

3

The History of the Earldom of Razès

The earldom of Razès is practically unmentioned in French history textbooks. It should first be made clear that the Razès is located in Occitania, a country that, before the time of Saint Louis, had nothing in common with the Capet kingdom, which emerged from the overthrow of Frankish Merovingian usurpers and strove relentlessly, all factions united, to empty Occitania of its cultural and spiritual identity and to despoil it materially. It is not at all surprising, then, that textbooks of national (in fact, nationalist) history have ignored this modest territory located within a Catalonia that was more Spanish than French before it was partially incorporated into the Capet kingdom. While history cannot be made over, we should respect the historical events that it comprises. The earldom of the Razès does not really appear until the Visigoth era, at the time when Germanic "barbarians" fell upon the Roman Empire. This, the textbooks say, was the era of the Pax Romana, and as authentic documents show, it was a troubled time filled with palace coups, murderous wars, and a decadence so complete that it prompts us to ask why it has been passed over in such complete silence.

But the earldom of the Razès, and thus the region of Rennes-le-Château, did not wait for the Visigoths to arrive to establish itself as a cultural and territorial entity. In fact, the presence of megalithic monuments—not Abbé Boudet's imaginary cromlech but authentic menhirs and pieces of dolmens—proves that this area had been inhabited most likely since the Paleolithic era, which is more commonly regarded as the time of the cavemen. The geology of the area consists of heavily creviced limestone, and though there are no visible remains of these times, there is no doubt that the Razès provided a peaceful dwelling place for very ancient peoples. Where this turns into "folklore" in the pejorative sense of the word is when contemporary authors, who otherwise fulfill a valuable role as historians regarding the so-called temptations of Abbé Saunière,[1] start wildly exaggerating when their discussion turns to the ancient population of the Razès. In these cases, it is better to refer to local historians such as Louis Fédié and René Descadeillas, who have contributed to demystifying the legend of cursed treasure of Rennes but have also shown evidence of their objectivity by presenting in a clear way pieces of a dossier that have been intentionally surrendered and foggily represented by others, thus allowing for the wildest kinds of speculations. When seeking to exploit a mystery, it is necessary to thicken it in order to disorient any potential seekers. This is a tactic as old as the world, going back at least to the time when the work of Thucydides caused Herodotus's mythological narratives (already filled with essential information) to become histories that took pains to respect actual facts.

The first problem that arises is both historical and linguistic in nature. It concerns the names Razès and Rennes, formerly Redhae or Reddae, which no doubt have come from a common root. The words of an author (whom we need not name) regarding these two words may induce us not merely to smile but to laugh outright: "The names Razès and Rennes come from Red, god of lightning and storms, whose temples were underground." How could anyone have come up with such an interpretation? The ground of Rennes is riddled with caves, that's

---

1. I am thinking here of Pierre Jarnac, who, in his book *Histoire du trésor de Rennes-le-Château,* presented some very convincing documents related to Abbé Saunière and conducted an extensive inquiry into the sites that have been shamelessly exploited by certain serial-novel builders. May Pierre Jarnac forgive me, but his evocation of the primitive Razès and his imagining of its original Celtic inhabitants simply recycle some of the wildest fantasies of serial novelists whom he quite frankly denounces elsewhere.

certain. It is also a fact that Abbé Boudet—author, let me remind you, of a priceless work on the true Celtic language—believed that the Celtic language could be explained only by modern English. Let's also recall that at the beginning of the nineteenth century, the Breton grammarian Le Brigant, following in the footsteps of Théophile-Malo Coret de La Tour d'Auvergne, first grenadier of the Republic, declared in all seriousness that the low Breton dialect was the language spoken in Eden long before the unfortunate adventure with the apple tree. And if the names Razes, Rennes, and its former name Reddae did descend from Red, god of lightning—a figure who is completely absent from Celtic mythology—it is because in English Red also means the color red. But it is useless to "see red" when confronted by such ineptitude. Instead we are going to take a snake's-eye view of the situation: We know that ophidian worship has been a great delight to the esotericists of every stripe and that the megaliths have inspired numerous interpretations of this nature, notably in Carnac (in Morbihan) and Stonehenge (in England). It is, in fact, easy to visualize a long procession of priests and worshippers winding among countless standing stones. Why not? Not even Hollywood has presented such an image.

It was by means of this that the following explanation was found. "The name Reddae is also related to the entity of the Gallic sun god, Aereda the serpent. It comes from the term Her Red, racing snake who stretches out." It would be extremely difficult to detect any trace of this sun god–serpent in relevant mythological documents, unless our only recourse was to turn to the well-known Gallo-Roman representation of the Knight of the Anguipede in the shape of a warrior riding or fighting a monster with a human head and the tail of a serpent. But this snake interpretation appears elsewhere: "The name Reddae comes from Aer-Red, the racing snake or mystical Wouivre." The etymology is certainly Celtic, as is suggested by the Wouivre, the woman serpent who later became the Melusine of Poitou. As for *aer,* it really does mean "serpent," but in modern Breton. So how could a modern Breton word provide an explanation for an ancient name appearing in southern France? The Gallic language, which must have been the tongue of the ancient inhabitants of the Razès, is almost entirely lost; we know only a few words from it, thanks to Gallo-Roman inscriptions, glosses in certain

Greek and Roman manuscripts, and the study of place-names. It is perilous, therefore, to peremptorily declare meanings of Gallic words without attempting to find their oldest versions.

But we should not let this hold us back! There is no shortage of possible interpretations for the two words we have been discussing here. When the Celts established themselves in the Razès and when "their speaking was raucous," they gave this region the name Rhed, Rhid, or Rith. In the Welsh dialect Rheiddum means "spear" and the verb rhuid-il means "to cast or throw with force." We would have a great deal of trouble finding these last two words in a dictionary of the Welsh *language* (rather than the *dialect*). As for Rhid and Rith, they can be found under the form of Rhyd, still in Welsh, and meaning "ford," or Rhydd, which means "free." We might have better luck with Rhed as the Welsh *rhedeg* and the Breton *redek,* both meaning "to run" or "to flow quickly" (as in a watercourse). It is in these latter terms that we find the derivative of the assumed Gallic root word *red,* a root that we also find in the name of the rivers Rhine and Rhône, which actually are two fast-moving rivers.

This, in fact, is where we should focus our search for the meaning of Razès, Rennes, and Reddae. This radical *red* is also found in the name of the Gallic Redones people, who had settled in what is now the department of Ille-et-Vilaine.[2] Redones is therefore "those who run" or "the quick ones," a description well suited to an adventurous people. Because the Gallic word for "chariot," *reda,* has also been confirmed, the Gauls could also be considered "those who travel in swift chariots." This etymology based on *reda* has not been regarded with indifference by the fans of esotericism and astrology, and the Razès was easily turned into the Land of the Chariot, which also refers to the constellation of the Big Dipper. From here, it's not too far a leap to envision the Razès as a central region or kind of terrestrial pole equivalent to the Pole Star, with all the analysis that goes along with this.

Whatever the case may be, it is probable that the names Razès, Reddae, and Rennes come from Redones. The evolution of the French language eventually transformed it into Rennes as in Ille-et-Vilaine. The name Razès is the result of the Occitan phonetic evolution of the word,

---

2. [This is one of the departments of Brittany. —*Translator*]

similar to what took place in Brittany, where the modern Breton form of Rennes is Roazhon, which corresponds quite closely to Razès. The names Rhedae and Reddae are merely different variations following Celtic colonization in a land where there was considerable blending of different languages as a result of invasions. Under Roman rule, which had strong centralizing tendencies, Gaul itself as well as all the territories of the ancient Gallic peoples were integrated into the new administration. These fairly large territories became *civitates,* "cities," whose largest settlement often took the name of the people themselves instead of retaining its original name. For example, the Rennes in Ille-et-Vilaine took on the name of the Redones, whereas it was originally called Condate, meaning "confluent." Later, as part of the imperial structure, these cities became dioceses, which were then grouped in provinces, divisions that, as we know, remained in the administrative apportioning of the Christian Church. Within this system the smaller territories remained *pagi,* "countries,"[3] and their inhabitants, generally left untouched by Romanization and later Christianization, became Pagani in the current sense of the word *pagans.* The Razès corresponds exactly to one of these "countries."

Given the fact that this part of the Languedoc region was the domain of the Gallic people called the Volques Tectosages, it is appropriate to ask what role the Redones played here when they were apparently tied to their region in the Armorican Peninsula. There is, after all, a significant distance between these two groups. We should not, however, exclude their influence on this basis; all the people of Gaul came from the Harz region on the other side of the Rhine, and in their westward march what had been one people may have split into two or more groups, each of which retained its original generic name. In addition, there were later migrations: The Helvetians' requested passage through Gaul in order to reach the sea is another proof of this. This was also Caesar's pretext for invasion, which marked the beginning of the Roman conquest. One group of Helvetians, the Vivisci, who have left their name in Vevey on the shores of Lake Leman, eventually ended up in the Médoc region, where they became the "guests" of the dominant

---

3. [In this use "countries" refers to rural districts. —*Translator*]

people they found there. The Atrebates, who could be found in both the Pas-de-Calais (Arras) and England, also migrated through Gaul, as did the Osismi of the western Armorican Peninsula, who could be found in what is now the Orne Department, in Exmes. The Boïens ended up in both Bohemia (that region takes it name from them) and the region of Arcachon, where they have left their name at the Teste-de-*Buch*. The Gablaes settled in the Cévennes and could also be found in Gavaudun (Lot-et-Garonne), in the land of the Nitiobrigi. Such small groups were either absorbed by the peoples of the host countries or tolerated as ethnic units and made into vassals. Something of this nature must have been the case for the Redones who settled in the western part of the Corbières, in the vast domain of the Volques Tectosages.

We know almost nothing about this Celtic period of history in the Razès. No doubt there was a castle in Casteillas below Rennes-le-Château to keep watch over the plateau and especially the ancient road that once came from the north and made its way toward the Iberian Peninsula by way of the famous Pass of Saint Louis. We can also guess that this mountainous, forested, and somewhat out-of-the-way region (though it was located at a comfortable altitude) was a choice site for druidic worship. Yet because the Celts before the Roman conquest never constructed temples and did not sculpt in stone, it is difficult to locate their original sites with precision. The lack of archaeological finds, however, does not imply that the Celts and particularly their priests, the druids, did not engage in a vast amount of activity here. After all, the Celts were excellent metalworkers, and even though the mines in the Razès are not profitable at present, they were once both common and significant. The same is true regarding the "medicinal waters" of the abundant springs in the region. The Redones of ancient Reddae must have contributed, to the extent of their means and talents, to the grandeur of the large confederation of the Volques Tectosages, assuredly the most powerful people of the Occitania of their era. Legend enters the mix as well. After all, isn't it said that certain survivors of the expedition of the second Brennus in Greece and Delphi (the others having formed the Galatian kingdom in Asia Minor) had managed to settle in Occitania, where they buried the treasures they pillaged in Greece, especially the famous "cursed gold" from the temple of Delphi?

It was in 121 B.C.E. that the Romans made their appearance in a Languedoc that still bore a heavy Celtic imprint. The Romans, seeking to arrange their supremacy over all of the Mediterranean's shores, plied its waters in confrontations with the Phoenicians, who contested this supremacy. This was also the time when the first vague invasion attempts by the Germans appeared. The Cimbrians and Teutons, peoples who were incontestably Germanic but were heavily influenced by the Celts (their common names provide the proof of this), were stopped by Marius in what is now Provence. The occupation of southern Gaul became necessary to ensure the security of the Roman state. Little by little, moving in from the coast, the Romans won the interior lands by either reducing them to small islands of resistance or keeping watch over peoples who did not inspire their confidence or exploiting—or rather, having their slaves exploit—the numerous gold and silver mines in the Occitan Midi. In this way, at the impetus of the proconsul Domitius, a Provincia Romana—in other words, a "conquered territory"—was created. Narbonne (Narbo-Martius) was designated its capital. This is why from the time of Augustus's reign this part of Gaul, Gallia Togata, would be called the Narbonnaise.

The Romans never totally occupied a country. They were content to establish camps at strategic sites and reconstruct the existing paths into roads suitable for vehicles and for allowing an entire army with arms and baggage to move quickly from one place to another. They also created Romanized centers chiefly through founding schools (to gradually reduce the influence of the elite of a conquered people, such as the druids in the Razès, who were forbidden to teach), pushing their own ideology to the foreground, and practicing religious syncretism. The numerous so-called Gallic temples date from this time, though they are really merely Roman temples that haphazardly absorbed the Celtic deities and incorporated them into the somewhat disparate pantheon characteristic of the Roman Empire. Having thus "squared" the terrain, the Romans could permit themselves to go ever farther so that Rome, both in *civitas* (cities) and *urbs* (towns), was truly the center of the world.

This tactic is very visible in the Razès. There are virtually no Roman remnants on the plateaus. There is nothing Roman in Rennes-le-Château. But in the more vulnerable places—that is to say, in the "bolts" or paths of communication that are the valleys, such as Alet—the Roman presence was felt more strongly. This was also true of Rennes-les-Bains because the Romans appreciated the benefits of the thermal springs. In the process of Roman conquering, the Razès became a pagus: It was governed in Roman fashion but retained its archaic character and its own lifestyle.

It was at the end of the Roman Empire, with the first great invasions, that the Razès emerged from obscurity. This is the basis of the belief of numerous historians that the Visigoths founded the city of Reddae. It was the Visigoths who, unlike the Romans, left an indelible imprint on this territory, though this fact has unleashed a series of unsupportable assumptions. In truth the Razès was no more Visigothic than the rest of Septimania, those seven Occitan lands that distinguished themselves during the Merovingian era. The fact does remain, however, that the "fortress" of Reddae certainly appears to have been if not founded, then reorganized and expanded by the Visigoths.

But just where was this "fortress" of Reddae? In Rennes-le-Château? This is what some are desperate to have us believe, but nothing could be less certain. First, we know that the original location of the Rennes fortress was Casteillas. Next, the situation of the site and its surface area do not allow for a city as populous as Reddae appears to have been. It is claimed, based on local tradition, that Rennes had a formidable enceinte wall, but no remnants of it, except for some extremely modest substructures, have been found. It is also claimed that the town possessed two castles, which is far from being proved, and that it included two churches, one dedicated to Saint Peter and the other to Saint John (the latter almost certainly being the seigneurial chapel). There is no mention, however, of Mary Magdalene's name. It has been stated that the town numbered some thirty thousand inhabitants, which is strictly impossible, and seven butchers' stalls. The fact is that if all this was true, then the fortress of Reddae would by necessity have been located somewhere else. Rennes-le-Château would have been only a surveillance post on the road from Carcassonne to Iberia.

Then where was the location of this formidable fortified city that documents suggest was on the same scale as the actual citadel of Carcassonne?   Logic would suggest that Limoux was its location. The name Limoux suggests an ancient settlement dating from the Celtic era. It sits in the bottom of a valley, where a fortress would be easy to build, easy to expand, and easy to fortify. Thirty thousand inhabitants certainly could have lived there. This does not mean that the seigniorial residence could not have been located in Rennes-le-Château. Our error arises from the confusion caused by the word *city:* It now designates a precise site—such as the city of Carcassonne—but during the Roman Empire and long after, the word designated only a moral entity in the etymological sense, which is that of the Latin civitas, or "community of citizens." Never in ancient times would it have been possible to confuse city—a community of law and as such a grouping together of citizens of one ethnic group—and a town, or *urb* in Latin, perfectly situated in a precise location and truly a place of habitation, activity, and group defense. For the same reason, there could be no possible confusion among city, town, and citadel, *arx* in Latin, which was the equivalent of the medieval castle fort and could be located either inside or outside a city or town.

In his work *Le Comté de Razès et le diocese d'Alet,* Louis Fédié pulls out all the stops in his attempt to show that Reddae was Rennes-le-Château. His imagination is stronger than his eyesight, however, when he claims that "the fortified enceinte occupied the entire plateau." But perhaps because he realizes that this assertion is somewhat strange, he goes on to add, "However, large spaces remained unoccupied on the perimeter." These empty spaces may well have existed during the Gallic era, but, in this case, the castrum was never a town, only a temporary meeting place, a place for assembly, exchange, and also protection during times of war: "Following the example of Roman towns, the Visigoth cities, even when they were sites of war, remained true to their special allocation, forming one or two towns inside the enceinte of a town, one or two citadels within the citadel. An example of this can be found in Carcassonne." He pursued this idea, declaring that Reddae was divided into three quarters, still recognizable in the village, and that "the fortifications surrounding the citadel of Reddae have not completely disappeared." Given that the entire plateau must have included surveillance posts at various times, the opposite would be more surprising. Yet how are we to believe that Rennes-le-Château, which had only two hundred inhabitants in 1709 (some fifty homesteads), could have had thirty thousand during the Visigoth era, some twelve centuries earlier? During this era the population was not great in the territory of the former Gaul, and people were widely scattered as a rule. Only large urban centers, which are laid out for easy supplying, could hold that many people. This is definitely not the case for the dry plateau of Rennes-le-Château, incapable of supporting the needs of even a reduced population on its own and quite poor in comparison to other centers located on the plains or in the liberally watered, fertile valleys. Reddae did exist, that is certain, and though it was not inhabited by thirty thousand people, a number that is certainly exaggerated, it did have a significant population. Therefore, it could only have been located on the site of present-day Limoux or perhaps Alet or Quillan.

Whatever the actual location of Reddae may have been, the Visigoths did surely invade the Razès and turned it into a kind of lair, reorganizing the region as if to have it in reserve. When King Reccared, who had recanted Aryanism (the Visigoths were Aryan Christians, don't forget), wished to reorganize the bishoprics of Septimania and proposed naming a bishop for Reddae, the bishop of Carcassonne opposed him, because until that time Reddae had been one of his dependencies and this nomination would have significantly reduced the size of his revenues. Then, by an ironic twist of fate some time later, during the reign of King Wemba in 680, the Episcopal seat of Carcassonne became occupied by an Aryan bishop who forced the orthodox bishop to flee and seek refuge in Redda, from which he might perform his functions over the whole of his diocese. It must be noted that these quarrels between Aryan and Orthodox Christians have fueled many speculations that were quickly transformed into legends. This was also the time when a large number of Jews fleeing persecution immigrated to the Razès, where, it seems, they were warmly welcomed, especially in Alet. Today we can see some traces of their presence in the architecture and ornamentation of the abbey. This, of course, became the starting point for another story having to do with the ancient Jewish origin of the Merovingians, in particular the "legitimate" root stock hidden by the Carolingian usurpers who, as we know, sought refuge in the Razès!

The certain extended presence of the Visigoths in Rennes-le-Château had other effects on the legendary history—or historical legend—of this region. It is in fact claimed that the contingents who accompanied Alaric in his capture and sack of Rome brought back much of the treasure they had divided among themselves and carefully hid it in a secret location in the Razès. This treasure would, of course, be the same treasure that the Romans under Titus and Vespasian would have brought back from the sack of Jerusalem. So here we are, having come full circle: Rennes-le-Château is holding a treasure in some mysterious cave or grotto. It does not necessarily consist of gold and jewels, but is more likely made up of documents of primary importance because they concern the end of Jewish independence and the "sect" of Christians. This legend, which may be merely a distortion of certain facts (why wouldn't the Visigoths have brought back valuable objects and documents from Rome?), was not overlooked by those who, during Saunière's life but especially since 1956, have exploited the theme of the odd "millionaire priest." It is likely that he was in contact with the most zealous occultists of his day due to his position as the keeper of "secrets," which the Vatican wanted to buy from him so that they might be kept safe from unhealthy public curiosity. This is the way stories are grown. But then again, there is never smoke without fire, which is why the Visigoth history of the region, especially everything touching on the possible presence in the Razès of treasures or documents that were stolen several centuries earlier from Jerusalem, should not be ignored—even if at first glance it may appear incredible. Isn't history, after all, constructed of black holes that we strive to fill for better or worse?

The Visigoth empire represented a threat to the Franks, Clovis in particular, whose conversion, albeit obviously opportunistic, set him at odds with all things Aryan. Political interests and religious interests always go hand in hand, as would be shown again in the thirteenth-century Albigensian Crusade. The Crusades not only offered the opportunity for eternal salvation; for some, they also contributed to a more temporary, terrestrial happiness. More enterprising and primarily more cynical than the other Frankish leaders, Clovis saw to their removal through either ruse or hired killers (who were executed immediately after the job was done) to prevent them from becoming obstacles to his personal ambitions. After concluding a treaty with the lone powerful authority remaining on the soil of the late Roman Empire—the Church—he attacked the Visigoths, defeating Alaric II near Vouille in 1507. This triggered a rush of Franks immigrating to the south, where they could easily take possession of domains and sinecures. On their arrival at the Pyrenees, they established a kind of protectorate over all of Occitania, but it seems the Razès escaped their covetuousness, no doubt because the Franks considered it to be of little importance. In short, the Visigoth presence still endured for some time in Rennes-le-Château and the surrounding area.

It was during the troubled Merovingian times that the "marginal" nature of the Razès was thoroughly confirmed. In fact, this region remained outside the incessant internal wars waged wholeheartedly by the descendants of Clovis, who were worthy heirs of their ancestor, experts in every kind of crime, yet nonetheless immortalized in French history textbooks by authors who never managed to read Gregory de Tours's chronicles all the way through. Then arriving on the scene were the "lazy kings," who have been the delight of French academics. We now know what to make of the ridiculous stories that allege that these last Merivingian monarchs were transported in specially outfitted carts so they could enjoy a well-deserved nap: The fact is these kings were *made into nothings*[4] thanks to the palace mayors, the formidable family of Pippin d'Heristal, who were just as cruel and more cynical than those who preceded them. To this piece of history has been grafted the legend of a descendant of Dagobert II, who was assassinated on Pippin's orders. This descendant is said to have found refuge in the Razès, where he had a family, which therefore makes him the ancestor of an authentic Merovingian line whose offspring still exist. Of course, this legend has been spun with the help of illicit genealogies and alleged "secret documents" that have miraculously—and anonymously—been deposited at the National Library in Paris. It is part of the myth of Rennes-le-Château and the mystery of the cursed treasure. The fact remains, however, that under Carolingian domination, the Razès would

---

4. [This is an untranslatable pun on the French name for the "lazy kings," the Rois Fainéants. "Made into nothings" is *faits neants,* a homonym of Fainéants that would be more literally translated as "made nothing." —*Translator*]

continue to exist in that same marginal land that is its chief distinguishing feature.

In contrast with his predecessors, though, it appears that Charlemagne took a keen interest in the region. To keep himself informed of events there, he sent the bishop of Orléans, Theodulfe, as his envoy. The bishop reported in the form of a poem on what he had seen, citing for the first time the cities of Carcassonne and Reddae. We should note that he refers to them as cities [*cités*] and not towns [*villes*], making Carcassonne and Reddae more or less equal. We can easily understand the Razès clergy's insistence on the creation in their region of a bishopric that would be independent of the Carcassonne seat.

Charlemagne had good reason to keep close surveillance over the Razès. "Saracens" who had spilled over the Pyrenees from the Iberian Peninsula were constantly threatening Septimania. Of course, contrary to popular opinion, Saracens were not Arabs at all. There were never enough Arabs to conquer nearly the entire Mediterranean basin in two centuries' time. As is well known, the Muslim Arabs practiced the technique known as *telescoping:* They began by subjugating their nearest neighbors and converting them to Islam, then sent them to continue the same task in regions farther away. It can be certain that the Arabs defeated by Charles Martel in Poitiers were essentially Iberians accompanied by some Moors—that is to say, Maghrebi [North Africans]. The same was true of those who ceaselessly infiltrated Occitania and who at times invited a martial expedition on behalf of the emperor and that of his vassals who were most directly involved. This was the basis on which was built the great epic of the chansons de geste in which Charlemagne is portrayed as the great defender of Christendom—which he truly was—engaged in a merciless struggle with the Saracens. Though they do not resemble Arabs, what can be said about the Saracens is that they symbolize *all the pagans* opposed to the task of converting Europe to Christianity, which the Frankish emperor was undertaking with the explicit accord of the papacy. Charlemagne, wishing to turn the Razès into a kind of citadel to keep watch and possibly prevent Muslim raids, named a trustworthy individual to govern the region, bestowing upon him the title of count. Thus the earldom of the Razès was born.

The first earl was a most notable individual, William of Gellone, a great military leader and a Christian of conviction. After having devoted a large part of his life to successfully fighting the Saracens, William of Gellone came to spend his remaining years at Saint-Guilhem of the Desert, an abbey whose construction he had ordered. Part Carolingian and part Romanesque, it remains one of the most handsome examples of Occitan abbeys. William of Gellone died, shrouded in the scent of sanctity, hence his canonization *vox populi* and the attribution of his name to the monastery.

William of Gellone is claimed by some to have been a descendant of the Merovingians through the son of Dagobert II, who had taken refuge in the Razès and is said to have wed the daughter of the count. This overlooks the fact that the first count of the Razès was none other than William of Gellone. It also overlooks the fact that Dagobert II's son, if he truly escaped the Carolingian assassins, would have been a very young child when he arrived in the Razès. Here again, although nothing can be firmly concluded, it seems that William of Gellone's family tree was somewhat "rearranged" to serve the needs of the cause.

It is true that this holy man was a figure of legend. In fact, in what is known as the cycle of Garin de Monglane in the chansons de geste, he was the model for the extraordinary figure of William of Orange, called William of the Short Nose (*curb nez,* not *court nez,* which means "hooked nose"), protector of Louis the Pious and great destroyer of Saracens. The cycle of Garin de Monglane incorporates real historical elements into a mythological framework from a clearly archaic tradition (as revealed by the Indo-European social structures within it). This William (Guilhem/Guillaume) of Orange, husband of the former Saracen Orable, who becomes Guibourc, forms a kind of fantastic duo with his nephew Vivien (Vezien) that is comparable to the ones formed by Charlemagne and Roland, Arthur and Gawain, and all those kings and nephews of Celtic tradition (with the nephews being, of course, the sons of their sisters, which signals a matriarchal line of descent).

William of Gellone's destiny, both real and imaginary, was thus quite amazing! In addition, he contributed to an event of considerable importance for the Christian West by aiding his friend Saint Benedict of Aniane in his reform of the original Benedictine Order, established three centuries earlier by Saint Benedict of Nursia, through integrating into it elements from the rule of Saint Columba, the Irish saint who helped in the restoration of Christianity on the continent. This led Louis the Pious, son of Charlemagne, during a large gathering of monks and abbots in Aachen in 817, to command all the monasteries in the empire to follow the reformed Benedictine Order.

Shortly before this time, an abbey had been founded in Alet under a name that was still rare at that time: Our Lady. It was Benedictine, of course. The charter of donation dates from 813 and was issued by Bera IV, count of the Razès, though, as is the case with the majority of monastery charters from this era, it is quite suspect, especially because of the error mentioned in it: The charter places the monastery under the pope's protection, something that never occurred before the end of the tenth century. The construction of the abbey did take place, however, and the counts of Razès took pains to ensure it the means to exist. A century later Alet was part of a kind of monastic confederation under the aegis of the famous monastery of Saint Michael of Cuxa at the foot of the Canigou. In 993 Abbot Garin controlled Saint Michael of Cuxa, Saint Pierre of Mas-Grenier, Saint-Hilaire, Pierre de Lézat, and Our Lady of Alet. Upon the death of Garin, this confederation dissolved in 998, at the time of the development of the Cluny Order, which would contribute to another reformation of the Benedictine monasteries, the most significant to occur before the rise of Saint Bernard and the new Cistercian Order.

William of Gellone gave the earldom of Razès to one of his sons. There were accordingly several generations of counts named Bera who protected the Razès until 870. On this date the line of succession passed into the hands of the noble house of Carcassonne, after which, for a number of years, its ownership was disputed between the counts of Carcassonne and the counts of Barcelona. Throughout all, it remained a very important center and the meeting place of all the lords of the surrounding area. Meanwhile, the development of the abbey in Alet continued apace. It even claimed to own a fragment of the True Cross, which enormously increased its prestige as well as the number of profitable pilgrimages made there. In 1090 the Saint Polycarp abbey fell under the control of the abbot of Alet, and on June 16, 1096, the abbey of Our Lady of Alet received a visit from Pope Urban II, who came there on a visit to Toulouse and Carcassonne. This gesture demonstrated the pope's sudden interest in the development of the monastery on the banks of the Aude.

In 1067 Countess Ermengarde sold her sovereignty over Carcassonne and the Razès to her relative Raymond-Béranger, count of Barcelona, for the sum of one thousand ounces of gold. Catalonia's ownership of the region would have certain consequences for the status of some monastic orders, in particular the branch of the order of the Templars established in Bézu, which would not be under the sway of the king of France, Philip the Fair, but would remain in the sphere of the count of Barcelona, allowing it to escape French royal persecution.

A period of obscurity then began for the Razès. This was the time of the Cathars in Occitania. This group of "heretics" had spread with amazing speed, benefiting from the strong support of local lords. Religious problems mirrored political difficulties; the Occitan nobles knew full well the ambitions of the northern French, particularly the Capet family. The Occitan Midi has always been a land of heresy and protest, as though these were integral parts of the Occitan mentality. Catharism, which first appeared in France in the Troyes region, found very fertile soil for its blossoming in Occitania and more particularly in the region of the former Septimania (including the Razès).

At this time, the Razès had fallen to the rank of viscounty. In 1194 it was under the flag of Raymond Roger Trencavel, viscount of Carcassonne and Béziers, a hero of the Albigensian Crusade who was basely betrayed by Simon de Montfort and perished in a dark dungeon in his city of Carcassonne in 1209. His son quickly picked up the torch of revolt. As a boy, he had been entrusted to the count of Foix and raised in his court where swarmed—and this was no secret to anyone—heretics of all stripes who had only one thing in common: a profound hatred for the French and their king.

For while the prevailing heresy of the time was that of the Cathars, there were quite a few others. Never has any time been as rich in sects, dissident churches, and strange cults—some openly diabolical—as the twelfth and thirteenth centuries. While the Inquisition was officially created to fight with both word and fire those respectfully called the good men in the countryside and Dualists in the ecclesiastical courts, its task was also to check the rising tide of various resurgent and syncretic traditions unfolding over Christian Europe. Tolerance was not an option in a time when in fact no one knew what it was. All discussion was impossible, for from the perspective of the Roman Catholic Church nothing could cast doubt on the word of the Scriptures and those of its official commentators. The principle of relativity was completely unheard of and the major refrain of the time was, "There is no salvation possible outside the Church!" Yet artistic and literary works of the time show many deviations from orthodox belief—though an equal number of heretics were left to rot in prisons or were burned at the stake.

There is an explanation for Roman Catholic aggressiveness: The Cathars as well as a certain number of other sects were casting doubt as to the prominent and necessary role of the priest. This was an intolerable situation for a system based on a society divided into three classes: those who prayed, those who fought, and those who worked. Furthermore, even though the clergy was not only uneducated but also often living in wretched conditions, at least in the poorer rural regions, never before had the Church been richer in worldly goods. If the Church were to go along with the Cathars, who claimed that the priests served no purpose, it would cut itself off from the abundant resources procured through the performance of worship and obligatory tithes. Fear gripped the orthodox Occitan clergy due to the rise of Cathar ideas at the onset of the thirteenth century combined with the ambition and bitterness of the northern nobles, ever ready to enter a struggle to the death if they might win some lands. This fear was obviously masked by the crusade against heretics of any kind as well as the Occitan nobles who had the gall to side with such miscreants. Cathar Occitania was destroyed in the name of a God who is never wrong and in the name of the material interest of the king of France and his vassals.

It is impossible to turn a blind eye to the injustices and atrocities of this Albigensian Crusade, which overturned the rights of all humans; contradicted Christian charity; satisfied a most monstrous egotism; and amounted to spiritual and cultural genocide and, finally, pure hypocrisy blessed by a papacy that did well by the whole affair. It is impossible to overlook the massacres of Béziers. It is impossible to excuse the "sadism" of Simon de Montfort and the least of his henchmen. But it is also impossible to remake history.

Thus, Trencavel the younger went to live at the court of the count of Foix, where he was brought up on the anti-French and anti-papist refrains of his companions in exile. As a victim of the intolerance that killed his own father, he could not listen to these refrains indifferently. Despite his young age, he loudly declared his desire for vengeance and swore to whoever would listen that his life's purpose was the reconquest of the heritage stolen from him—that is, the earldoms of Albi and Carcassonne and the viscounty of the Razès, which was a region especially dear to his heart.

Trencavel is a curious figure. He was not a typical adventurer like those that were plentiful in this troubled time, but was instead a kind of Grail quester, a knight who tilts against windmills. It is because of these characteristics that some have not hesitated to claim that he was the real model for Perceval, the discoverer and king of the Grail according to the German version of the Perceval story by Wolfram von Eschenbach. The sad fact, however, is that the young Trencavel was not yet born when Chrétien de Troyes introduced the figure of Perceval in the Arthurian epic in 1190. Perhaps the opposite occurred: Perhaps the young Trencavel had known about the work of Chrétien de Troyes (generously completed and expanded by skilled writers of the early thirteenth century), who sought to use as his heroic model a fatherless boy who fulfilled his vengeance against his father's murderers and became the king of an ideal kingdom.

As for actual history, while Trencavel was buried in his dreams, his official guardian, Bertrand de Saissac, who was desperately striving to save what remained to be saved, had difficulties in the Razès, mainly in Alet. Following the death of Pons Amiel, abbot from 1167 to 1197, the monks of Our Lady of Alet had elected as his successor Bernard de Saint-Ferréol, who was already the abbot of Saint Polycarp. Bertrand de Saissac rushed to Alet and seized the new abbot, ordered the body of Pons Amiel disinterred and placed upon his abbatial throne, and then ordered the monks to hold a new election. The monks, seemingly either won over to his position or out of fear of him, did not dare refuse. They chose a certain Bozon, who hastily sent a large sum of money to the archbishop of Narbonne to gain both his approval and his blessing of this coup. But Bernard de Saint-Ferréol, the dispossessed abbot, spent his time instituting ecclesiastical proceedings and let it be known that a violent act had occurred. Bertrand de Saissac, himself a partisan of the "good men," did not trust Bernard de Saint-Ferréol, whom he deemed too "orthodox" and overly devoted to the papacy.

The affair would drag on for some time. On July 21, 1222, at the council of Puy-en-Velay, the pope's legate, Cardinal Conrad, nullified Bozon's election and ordered the monks to leave the abbey immediately. It would be secularized and placed under the direct authority of the metropolitan archbishop of Narbonne. But the monks who had supported neither Bozon nor the coup that put him in power made an appeal to the pope. Gregory IX appointed two abbots to examine the request for adjudication and eventually the abbey was restored to the monks, who hurriedly elected a new abbot. By then Trencavel was occupied by concerns other than keeping watch over the abbey of Our Lady of Alet, for he could not return to his domains. The abbey never fully recovered from the crisis.

Trencavel soon became the heart and soul of the revolt of the *faidits,* which was the name given to the lords who had been stripped of their lands as a result of the prosecution of heresy. The faidits prepared to win them back. In 1239 and again in 1240, at a time when there was severe repression of the Cathars, Trencavel and his vassal Olivier de Termes, who still held the Corbières, the Temenès, and the fortresses of Quéribus and Peyrepertuse, launched expeditions that were more akin to guerrilla raids than military operations. They operated incrementally, and Trencavel, who was welcomed everywhere as a liberator, had some immediate successes. He did not follow up on them, however, which allowed his adversaries to regroup and react. It seems, moreover, that Trencavel had received promises of aid from Raymond VII, the count of Toulouse. Raymond VII was known to be on the side of the heretics, but was in a very delicate position; by dint of his hesitation, he did not intervene in time on behalf of Trencavel, and the situation turned sour. Olivier de Termes made his submission to the king of France following a vigorous French counteroffensive—he was no doubt bought by the Capets and betrayed Trencavel outright. The result was checkmate.

Trencavel then had to make his official submission to the king as well, but his lands were not returned. Brooding about his dark designs, he resolved to stay in Aragon, where he hoped to find some understanding listeners as well as money to resume the fight.

The Razès was now occupied by the troops of the French king, who devoted themselves to an all-out hunt for heretics. God knows there were plenty to be found in these isolated mountains! The year 1225 had seen the creation of a veritable Cathar diocese in the Razès separate from the Cathar diocese of Toulouse and entrusted to Benoît de Termes, a relative of Olivier. We know that Cathars did not recognize a priesthood, only deacons who were more or less preaching brothers. (The prefects within Catharism were not priests but rather believers who had attained the highest level of spiritual development and who administered only the consolamentum.) Nor did they see any value in ecclesiastical organization. For the cause, however—mainly to confront repression—they had been forced to set up a kind of clandestine counter-church with a hierarchy and leaders who were given the rank of bishop. There was, then, a Cathar "diocese" in the Razès, and because Cathar worshippers were many, this hierarchy managed to limit arrests and find refuge in inaccessible places.

In the Razès, oddly enough, it seems that the Templars concluded an alliance with the Cathars. As we know, the Templars were solidly established in the Rennes-le-Château region. Some were located in Campagne-sur-Aude and Lavaldieu, dependencies of France, and others, who were no doubt more powerful, had a fortress in Bézu and were dependents of Aragon. According to documents that may be none too reliable but do testify to a certain de facto status, the Bézu Templars would seem to have concluded an accord in 1209 with the Aniort family, who owned almost the entire region of Rennes-le-Château. This accord is said to have consisted of the fictive cession to the Templars of the Aniort family properties that were open to seizure by royal authority. What this clearly says is that the Templars willingly aided heretics, in this instance the Cathars of the Razès. We should note that they acted almost identically during the previous century with respect to the Jews; a document explicitly states that in 1142 the fairly numerous Jews of the Razès who owned lands had turned them over to the Templars as tenant farms. These seemingly unnatural alliances may be surprising to some, yet it should be understood that the Templars had always played a fairly ambiguous role in the Albigensian Crusade. In fact, they never took any part in this war, either directly or indirectly. There are certainly grounds for suggesting that the Templars were the secular arm of the Cathars, whose religion forbade the use of weapons. Why not? Whatever the case regarding armed support, the collusion of Cathars and Templars seems to have been fully operational in the Razès.

The Templars clearly conducted operations in this mysterious region. In 1156 they elected as their grand master a man named Bertrand de Blanchefort. Contrary to what some have declared without verifying their sources, however, he was not a member of the Blanchefort family of the Razès. Bertrand de Blanchefort, grand master of the Order of the Temple, was from a well-known family in Guyenne. There can be no doubt about this. But this did not prevent him from giving the Razès very special attention. During this time the Templars of Bézu brought in a veritable colony of German workers—smelters, to be more precise—to work in the area's mines. The lead, silver, copper, and gold mines of the region were quite numerous but not very rich, largely because they had been heavily exploited during Roman times. What is rather confusing, though, is that the Bézu Templars called on *smelters* and not *miners,* as would have been expected. We are therefore obliged to question the "work" these Germans were asked to perform. Furthermore, why hire foreign workers who knew not a word of either French or, more important, Occitan? It seems that the intention was to use foreign laborers who could not speak to the local inhabitants. Under such circumstances it is understandable that so many legends have spread concerning Rennes-le-Château's buried treasure, secret mines, or gold guarded by the devil, not to mention its hidden treasure of Delphi, treasure from the Temple of Jerusalem, or treasure of the Templars or the Cathars. Indeed, why wouldn't one of these caches include the Holy Grail?

The mysterious work of the Germans whom the Templars employed and the apparent collusion between the Templars and the Cathars obviously bring us back to the Albigensian Crusade and the unresolved mysteries it has presented. It is now established that the negotiations between the Inquisitors and the last defenders of Montségur, Pierre-Roger de Mirepoix and Ramon de Perella, were conducted under the surety of Ramon d'Aniort, lord of Rennes-le-Château and Rennes-les-Bains. It is also accepted that following the escape of four prefects charged with transporting the famous "treasure" (whatever it was) several days before the capture of Montségur, a fire was lit on Bidorta Mountain to let the besieged know that the operation had been a success and the Cathar valuables were safe. As it happens, Escot de Belcaire, a man who was a special envoy to Ramon d'Aniort, lighted this fire. Given all these circumstances, it is reasonable to assume that the Cathar "treasure" was hidden, at least initially, in the depths of the Razès.

The noble families of the Razès at times acted out their strange destinies, and all were more or less in league with the "heretics." After 1231 the king of France entrusted Limoux and the Razès to the seneschal Pierre de Voisins, a minor noble from the Île-de-France and a companion of Simon de Montfort. His most urgent task was to dismantle all the fortresses in the region, but later, oddly enough, the seneschal's grandson, Pierre II, made dogged efforts to rebuild them and even saw to the building of Rennes Castle. (It was renovated again at a later time.) Following the disappearance of the Cathars, the majority of nobles regained their holdings and hastened to refortify those structures that had been dismantled, foreseeing future troubles and possible future heresies as well as the need to reckon with the bandits of all kinds who lurked in the area. For example, a band of Catalan brigands invaded Rennes-le-Château and pillaged the castle, the church, and numerous homes, thereby bringing about the ruination of the village.

A long time had passed, however, since the Trencavel family had renounced all their holdings in the Razès. Harassed by the northern French and betrayed by his own people when they saw he was pursuing an ambiguous objective, the unlucky Trencavel decided to abandon his struggle. In 1247 he ceded all his rights to the Razès to the king of France, Louis IX. He still managed to pull out of it rather well: It is claimed that Saint Louis was quite upset with Trencavel and wished to imprison him, but Blanche de Castille defended him with much zeal and demanded indulgence for this impenitent rebel that the French king, good Christian that he was, did not display to his enemies. Certainly

Blanche de Castille did all she could to dispossess Trencavel of the Razès—and she succeeded—but we must ask what was the currency of exchange in this compromise. Did Trencavel know a secret, or at least of a trail that could lead to a secret? Let's not overlook the fact that the name Blanche de Castille is linked to a spring in Rennes-les-Bains, yet even if we take into account the well-known legend of the White Lady, guardian and protector of the springs, we might still hesitate before denying any grounds for this affair in which a nonnegligible role was played by Trencavel. Wasn't Trencavel a Cathar himself? What was he really searching for? What were the Templars of Bézu looking for? What would Colbert be looking for later in these same places? And just what did Abbé Saunière find in his church or elsewhere? Posing these questions can be quite helpful in building stories with multiple episodes—but it is also a way of shining light into certain murky zones.

In any case, the d'Aniort family appears to have held a fairly compromising position in its entire business with the Cathars. By all evidence it was on the side of the heretics at the time of the crusade in 1209. The four d'Aniort brothers—Géraud, Othon, Bertrand, and Ramon—joined by two of their cousins, were violently opposed to Simon de Montfort. They were all excommunicated, of course, and their castles confiscated, but shortly afterward, curiously enough, the excommunications were lifted and part of their domains were restored to their possession. D'Aniort Castle was slated to be razed, but at the last moment Louis IX sent a messenger to countermand that order. A short time later Ramon d'Aniort was received by Saint Louis, who showed him a courtesy that was quite exceptional and somewhat disconcerting, considering the role he had played as both rebel and ally of heretics. Why this indulgence, or at least these retreats, on the part of the king? Was he motivated solely by a desire to pardon the guilty party? We might well wonder what price was required from Ramon d'Aniort in order for him to purchase his pardon, for everything in politics has a price tag, even for kings who are later canonized. As we have asked of Trencavel, what did Ramon d'Aniort know?

All the mysteries of the Razès seem to crystallize around the Aniort family as well as the descendants of Pierre de Voisins, who was entrusted with guardianship over the territory to Trencavel's detriment. The

Voisins were also on very good terms with the Templars and later, following the persecution triggered by Philip the Fair, one of the family made arrangements to help a good number of the fugitives escape to Spain. It is Philip the Fair himself whom we find visiting the Razès in 1283, before he assumed the throne, though he was merely accompanying his father, Philip the Bold, son of Saint Louis, on a trip through the Languedoc region. The king stayed at the home of Pierre II de Voisins, the lord of Rennes and guardian of the whole of Razès on behalf of the kingdom. The purpose of Philip the Bold's trip was to obtain the benevolent neutrality of the local nobility, some of whom, because of the complex ramifications of feudal power, were vassals of the king of Aragon. He wanted to take some precautions in view of the war he was planning to wage against Aragon; thus there was a very good explanation for his visit to Pierre de Voisins. Yet he took advantage of this sojourn also to visit Ramon d'Aniort, who, along with his wife, Alix de Blanchefort, and his younger brother Udaut d'Aniort, warmly welcomed the monarch and his son. It even seems that a solid bond of friendship was formed at this time between the future king of France and Udaut, with Philip suggesting to Udaut that he become his comrade in arms. Udaut, however, had other ideas in mind. He wished to become a Templar.

This visit could not be any more suspect or strange. Two of Ramon's uncles had been diehard Cathars, and the d'Aniorts had always stood up to protect the "heretics." Alix de Blanchefort was the daughter of a faidit noble and the sworn enemy of Simon de Montfort. The designs of a king, however, are often impenetrable. It is possible that the purpose of this visit was to arrange a marriage. In fact, Pierre III de Voisins, a widower, subsequently wed Ramon's cousin Jordane d'Aniort. In this way the two families were united. But to what end? To keep watch over the d'Aniorts through the Voisins or to rehabilitate the d'Aniorts?

Ultimately, the Templars found themselves beset by unfortunate circumstances. As we know, they were hounded all over France at the will of Philip the Fair, hauled before ecclesiastical tribunals, and finally, after some strange confessions—not all of which were extorted by violence—they were condemned,[5] and the Order of the Temple disappeared,

---

5. For more on this subject, see my book *The Templar Treasure in Gisors* (Rochester, Vt.: Inner Traditions, 2002).

absorbed into the Hospitaliers of Saint John of Jerusalem. But their persecution by Philip the Fair's henchmen and his minion Nogaret did not
extend beyond France's borders. The Templars, though not spared
totally, were absorbed into other kingdoms, and we know that many of
them, forewarned in time, were able to escape, while others, like those
of Bézu, benefited from a special status that temporarily sheltered them
from all persecution.

In an Occitania that had shown itself ever willing to support the
least orthodox kind of doctrines, it was necessary to ensure, along with
the purification of bodies and minds, an increased surveillance of souls
and consciences. This was why in 1317 the French pope of Avignon,
John XXII, on the advice of the king of France, which he was obviously obliged to take, made the decision to create new dioceses. This
action would provide a better means to isolate problem areas and also
provide a slight check to the omnipotence of the metropolitan archbishop of Barbonne and the bishop of Toulouse. New bishoprics were
thus established in Limoux, Saint-Pons de Thomières, and Saint-
Papoul. Immediately the pope received a violent protest from the nuns
of Prouilhe, who, for more than a century, were paid significant fees by
the religious establishments of Limoux and the surrounding area. The
papal decision threatened to ruin them, and because they had such
influence over the archibishop of Narbonne, he obtained from the pope
a revocation of the bull that had created a seat in Limoux. The pope,
however, did not abandon his desire to establish a new bishopric in the
Razès. In 1318 he created the Episcopal seat of Alet, which explains
how the Abbey of Our Lady of Alet became a cathedral. Barthélémey,
the last Benedictine abbot, became the bishop of Alet shortly thereafter.

This was the beginning of a new life for the old Romanesque abbey.
It was too small to be a true cathedral, but was extended on the east with
the addition of a Gothic choir, some of which remains. At the same time,
the village of Alet was transformed into a veritable small city surrounded
by ramparts and provided with a new parish church, Saint-André, which
still exists on the southern side of the abbey. The bishopric of Alet lasted
until the French Revolution, though of course it experienced its share of
difficulties before that time, especially during the Religious Wars, during
which the cathedral was pillaged. In the sixteenth century, the Episcopal

seat was in the hands of the Joyeuse family, and the bishopric—which was then an abbey-bishopric, with the bishop acting as both bishop and abbot—was definitively secularized. In the seventeenth century, Bishop Étienne de Poverel decided to create a new cathedral church oriented from north to south in the former buildings of the monks. In memory of the Benedictines, it was called Saint Benedict Cathedral.

In 1637 a young bishop named Nicolas Pavillon took control of the Alet diocese, from which position he played a significant role. Along with Saint Vincent de Paul and the abbot Jean Ollier, founder of the church and seminary of Saint-Sulpice in Paris, he was the driving force of the famous Brotherhood of the Holy Sacrament, upon which plenty of light still remains to be shed. There are known ties connecting the Brotherhood of the Holy Sacrament to the family of Nicolas Foucquet, the superintendent of finances who was judged and imprisoned iniquitously by Louis XIV under conditions that are obscure, to say the least. Nicolas Foucquet was an incredible megalomaniac who had at his disposal certain means of pressure that he was unable to turn to his use and which were ultimately used against him. Shortly after his imprisonment, his victorious adversary Colbert ordered that excavations and document searches be undertaken in the Razès. Why? The most realistic reason is that Colbert was seeking to exploit the few gold mines on the Rennes-le-Château plateau that might still have had some value. But there are far too many coincidences in this affair, and those discreet investigations seem to have had a direct relationship to "the secrets known by Mr. Foucquet," to borrow an expression of the time. That combined with the mysterious letter from Nicolas Foucquet's brother concerning Nicolas Poussin, painter of the famous *Shepherds of Arcadia,* only increase the shadows that lie over the Razès. Whatever the truth may be, Nicolas Pavillon, bishop of Alet, along with the other members of the Brotherhood of the Holy Sacrament, strove to aid Foucquet, which spared him from simply being put to death, as was the king's desire. And whether we like it or not, the Nicolas Foucquet matter spills over into the Razès.[6]

None of this stopped Nicolas Pavillon from attending to work in

6. For more on this, see Jean Markale, *La Bastille et l'énigme du Masque de Fer* (Paris: Pygmalion, 1989). In it I develop the hypothesis that Nicolas Foucquet was the Man in the Iron Mask, or at least "one of several Men in Iron Masks."

his diocese. He created a seminary for the instruction of young priests in Alet on the advice of Saint Vincent de Paul, who, after becoming aware of the intellectual poverty of the clergy of his time, displayed the greatest zeal in finding a way to remedy it. During the entire time he held the bishop's chair, Pavillon had frequent contact with Abbot Ollier, who was himself the founder of the seminary of Saint-Sulpice. Given these circumstances, why is it surprising to encounter so much speculation about the subtle relationship that existed between the church of Rennes-le-Château and the church of Saint-Sulpice in Paris?

But times change. The Razès slumbered in a kind of torpor, as if wrapped in a summer mist. Certain incidents did occur, though discreetly. The few dominant families who seemed to watch over this territory almost fiercely witnessed their financial strength shrink over time. The aristocracy was no longer what it used to be, and land, especially that of this scorched region, no longer took in the kind of revenues it once did. In 1422 the heiress of the Voisins (and thus of the d'Aniort family), Marcafava, married Pierre-Raymond d'Hautpoul, heir of one of the oldest and most illustrious families of Occitania. The founders of his line had been named the Kings of the Black Mountain, a title that was somewhat indicative of their propensity "to go underground" and to mock from their mountain fortresses the legal authorities who claimed they should submit to the laws. At the time of the Albigensian Crusade, they obviously favored the "heretics" and found themselves stripped of their castles and lands. In short, in the fifteenth century the Hautpoul, were still worthy representatives of those faidits lords who left such an indelible imprint on the Cathar region and its immediate surroundings. It was the Hautpouls who would later become the lords of Rennes-le-Château.

In 1732, long after the troubled affairs of the reign of Louis XIV, François d'Hautpoul married Marie de Négri d'Ables, who also had rights to the inheritance of the d'Aniort family and who, it appears, owned this family's archives. François d'Hautpoul and Marie de Négri d'Ables had three daughters. One of them, Elisabeth, lived and died a spinster in Rennes-les-Bains. The second, Marie, married her cousin d'Hautpoul-Félines, and the third, Gabrielle, married the marquis of Fleury, who seems to have been a member of various secret societies, most notably the Freemasons and Rosicrucians.

When it came time for the succession of their parents to be settled, Elisabeth quarreled with her sisters concerning the allotment of property, refusing to give them the family papers and titles on the pretext that it was dangerous (we may wonder why!) to consult these documents and that it would be more appropriate to "have deciphered and distinguished which were family titles and which were not at all." Perhaps this could mean that the Hautpouls, full heirs to the d'Aniort family, possessed in their archives documents *that were not the family's* but which they held for safekeeping and no doubt did not have the right to dispose of as they saw fit. It is quite obvious that we will never know what these papers were, but we can agree that it is possible they were compromising—but to whom? That is the real question.

We must further take note of the very strange story whose events took place a full century later, in 1870. It appears that the notary with whom the Hautpoul-d'Aniort family papers were stored refused to turn them over to Pierre d'Hautpoul, descendant of this illustrious line, on the pretext that it would be terribly imprudent to relinquish such important documents. What are we to make of this obviously unverifiable anecdote? Some have imagined that among these documents were genealogies marked with the seal of Blanche de Castille, proving the permanence of the Merovingian dynasty. She would have signed these genealogies during her stay on the Razès in exchange for the submission of the principal nobility of the region, which would explain her extreme indulgence of Trencavel and the d'Aniort family. It is impossible to confirm such an assumption, however, because the notary never passed on these documents and *no one has ever seen them.* It seems that the theory of the permanence of the Merovingian dynasty smacks not only of fantasy but of the purest form of fraud as well. All of this is, in fact, quite irritating. From one coincidence to the next we are buried ever deeper in shadow, until we end up with whatever it is that Abbé Saunière discovered in his church when he was renovating it. He actually did find something, which was then claimed to be—and is now even more strenuously claimed to be—the "treasure" of Blanche de Castille. But what treasure is this?

At the time of the disagreement between Elisabeth d'Hautpoul and her sisters, just before the Revolution, someone did know of the existence and perhaps the contents of the mysterious documents: Abbé

Bigou, priest of Rennes-le-Château. Antoine Bigou was the nephew of a priest who had also served in Rennes. Once he had joined the priesthood, in 1176 he succeeded his uncle in Rennes-le-Château, enjoying, as René Descadeillas tells us, "the respect and esteem of his parishioners." At this time Marie de Négri d'Ables was living an impoverished existence with her daughter Elisabeth d'Hautpoul in the Rennes castle, where she died in 1781. She was buried in the small cemetery behind the church beneath a tomb that bore the inscription that has since received serious study, especially recently, for it appears to have been defaced by Abbé Saunière, though we may ask why. The inscription contains mistakes that have drawn the attention of cryptogram fans, but as René Descadeillas says again in his work *Rennes et ses derniers seigneurs* and in his *Mythologie de Rennes-le-Château,* there is nothing surprising about these errors. "In these remote villages of the seventeenth century education was not widespread and the person who knew how to handle the chisel was ignorant of the letters and words he was carving . . . Cutting another stone and carving another epitaph were out of the question. This work was not free, and we know that the Hautpoul[s] of Rennes were not very rich." Yet this does not negate the provable fact that Abbé Saunière inventoried this tomb of Marie de Négri d'Ables and then made sure the stone disappeared in 1906—but why was he getting mixed up in this?

Following the death of Marie de Négri d'Ables, Abbé Bigou continued to take an active interest in Hautpoul family matters. His uncle had already assumed to some extent the role of proxy for the Hautpouls, and there was no reason for the nephew to discontinue fulfilling that function. This, then, is how Abbé Bigou truly knew the contents of this strange family's documents. With the arrival of the Revolution, however, there came a wide array of troubles, including those triggered by the Civil Constitution of the Clergy. On November 29, 1791, a decree of the Legislative Assembly declared that all priests who had not given an oath to the new government would be suspected of revolt, would have their pensions taken away, and would be exiled or punished with two years of detention. Before this edict, on February 20, 1791, Abbé Bigou swore the oath but coupled it with such conditions that it was refused. Considered henceforth a refractory priest, he soon saw himself on the verge of being deported per the law of August 26, 1792. During the first days of September that same year, however, he slipped clandestinely over the Spanish frontier, as did the majority of the refractory clergy of that region. At this time Antoine Bigou was seventy-three years old. He found lodging with several other priests from his diocese in Sabadell (in the province of Barcelona) or its immediate surrounding area. This was where death found him on March 21, 1794.[7]

Abbé Antoine Bigou, who in all likelihood knew much of the subject of the documents in the keeping of the Hautpoul family, died in exile, taking his secrets to the grave. Is this truly so certain? Events taking place close to a century later show that before leaving the country Abbé Bigou made sure to conceal in the Rennes church valuable cultural objects and currency belonging to him that he could not take with him into exile. This stash is incontestably what Abbé Saunière discovered during the restoration of his church. But this still leaves the mystery of the possible manuscripts that were allegedly found in a hollow pillar holding up the altar. The inventories made in 1793 show that in fact none of what was hidden had been found. This was a disappointing result and the subsequent sale of objects of worship brought in almost nothing. We should note that the same was true for most parishes then, and if in our time the "treasuries" of many churches can boast of extremely beautiful precious objects, it is owing to this practice of hiding them, which was all to the greater good of our cultural patrimony.

After the Revolution and the Napoleonic Wars, the Razès fell back into its torpor. At this time wealth was no longer measured by land surface. The Industrial Age had begun, and the Razès escaped that furious blaze of activity that characterized the nineteenth century. The lands that were outside the new centers of activity were quickly forgotten. The plateaus of the Corbières, the valleys that had quickly became overgrown with vegetation, the towns in which the houses slowly crumbled because the owners could not afford to pay for the necessary repairs: All of this remained slumbering peacefully in the mist of the past.

Political regimes succeeded one another as each found itself challenged. New ideas were spreading, but because the multiple channels of

---

7. Pierre Jarnac, *Histoire du trésor de Rennes-le-Château*, 114–15.

communication automatically distorted them, no profound changes occurred. The Razès merely became one of those regions that no one ever mentions and which serve to shelter a kind of human being who is on the verge of vanishing. Hence the dilapidation and great dissolution within a society that no longer knows what will become of it. The old families tried to survive—poorly, more often than not—this mutation of the species, knowing full well that they would not last much longer and that everything would have to be sold to the commoners who had been enriched by the sale of national properties.

There was one exception, however: the Hautpoul family, heirs to the d'Aniort over whom hovered the shadow of Trencavel. It should be remembered that Gabrielle d'Hautpoul de Blanchefort married the marquis Paul-François-Vincent de Fleury, a figure at home in the Enlightenment and a member of so-called philosophical societies. Several children were born to this couple, one of whom, Paul-Urbain de Fleury (born in 1778), had the good fortune not only to survive this hunt of former aristocrats but also to earn a considerable fortune under strange circumstances. This was how he found the means to buy back the properties—the Rennes castle, in particular—that had belonged to his and his wife's families and which had been sold as national properties. He then wed a representative of the fallen nobility, an immigrant who was nonetheless perfectly at home in this new society. He died on August 7, 1836, at the age of fifty-eight and was interred in the cemetery of Rennes-les-Bains. It is he who has two tombs, one of which bears the inscription "He has departed while doing good," an obvious symbol of his membership in a Rosicrucian organization. Two tombs for one man is excessive, especially when the dates carved upon them are incorrect.

The Razès is definitely a disconcerting land. Nothing happens here as it does elsewhere. Until this time, it was figures like King Arthur and Merlin the magician who had the honor of multiple tombs. Would Paul-Urbain de Fleury therefore be part of the lineage of one of these mythological characters who have long been a part of Western Europe and, more significantly, the human collective unconscious? We may be tempted to think so. But we should not overlook that in all these lost regions, as one generation takes the place of another, traditions remain as if they constitute the essential structure of reality. While we can indulge ourselves with a detailed nomenclature of anomalies, oddities, and anachronisms that can easily be seen in such regions the world over, there is a great risk that the task will take a long time. Why, then, has there been such interest in the Razès and particularly in Rennes-le-Château and Rennes-les-Bains? There is nothing that substantially distinguishes the history of the Razès from other regions of this kind. Really, no one should have anything more to say about it.

Yet in 1885 an ecclesiastic native to the region, Abbé Bèranger Saunière, was named priest of Rennes-le-Château, and it was through him that the scandal erupted.

Part 2

HE WHO BRINGS SCANDAL

4

The Abbé Saunière Legend

It was the summer of 1885. The heat was intense in the part of the Corbières that looks down over the Aude Valley. In Paris the Republican government was expediting its daily business in an atmosphere of torpor and expectation. The ministers had only a single idea in mind: to get back to their districts, not only to take a vacation but also to properly prepare the voters to reelect them by a comfortable majority in the coming elections scheduled for October.

Life was good for the servants of the Republic. Their sole difficulty was getting reelected. Here the future was not always certain, particularly because of the Roman Catholic Church. Thanks to the Concordat, not only did the clergy receive seventy-five gold francs a month, but they were also permitted to criticize as they pleased the policies of those who were governing. This was truly a case of "biting the hand that feeds you." None of this would have occurred if the first Napoleon, the great one, had not had the ill-advised idea of concluding such a pact with the pope. Thus it was necessary to support the ecclesiastics, repair their churches and their presbyteries, and do them a thousand favors— at least on the surface, for there was no lack of very subtle plans being drawn up to contrive the separation of Church and State. There was even thought of seizing the property of the clergy, something achieved by a good number of sovereign authorities elsewhere, more or less successfully. All this is simply to say that during the year 1885 anticlerical campaigns were multiplying among the Republicans and that these campaigns often found a favorable echo in the Aude, which as every-

one knew was a *leftist* department, a *red* department, ever ready to follow the lead of a revolt or a heresy. Wasn't this the land of the Cathars,
after all?

At this time the Episcopal seat of Carcassonne was held by
Monsignor Felix Billard, whom all witnesses described as a good, discreet man in love with justice. He had recently named a new priest to
Rennes-le-Château, the rotting parish that still managed to avoid dis-
appearing despite the poverty of its inhabitants and the harshness of the
sun, and which brought in nothing for the bishopric. The inhabitants of
Rennes did not have a reputation for being fervent Christians; it was
even rumored that some of them indulged in the practice of sorcery,
something that was not so rare overall in the Carcassonne diocese. But
because the town had to have a spiritual leader, Monsignor Billard had
recently assigned a priest there who was thirty-three years old and still
full of illusions, a native of the region who understood the local mentality and who for several months had been suffering from melancholy
in a minor parish of no interest. This priest was Béranger Saunière, a
native of Montazels and a member of an honorable and fairly well-off
family. His younger brother was also a priest, but of the kind to alarm
religious authorities. It would be all to the greater good if Abbé
Saunière found himself back in his natal mountains, where he would be
sheltered from the bad influences he might be subjected to through his
brother whose daily life, it was guessed, did not conform to what was
expected of an ecclesiastic.

Thus, full of joy and trusting in his future, Abbé Béranger Saunière
arrived in Rennes-le-Château on a hot day in June 1885. The village
was a familiar sight, for it resembled all the other villages he knew in
the region, with its houses holding up each other in an attempt to create cool havens from the torrid weather. The colors of their
Romanesque tile roofs, determined by age, ranged from a bright red to
a brown that combined with the color of the moss withering on the
tiles. "This village," writes Louis Fédié, a witness of this time, "offers
large empty spaces that take up almost two thirds of the plateau's surface. Neither time nor the efforts of man have changed in any way the
shape of this rocky mass that, cut and carved in the shape of a truncated
cone, dominates the plain in every direction."

Abbé Saunière felt a sense of pride on his arrival. From this eagle's nest he would have a dominating position. He would be observer of the universe and master of the elements. Wasn't this what he, a priest, was made to do in the service of God and humanity? Certainly, he had some weaknesses: some health complaints and a weak heart of which he was aware. But he was young, and this ailment did not prevent him from looking—even staring—at women, especially the younger ones who passed close by. He was sensitive to feminine charm and knew quite well it was not only for aesthetic reasons. The body has its needs. For proof of this, try to live without eating and drinking.

But disenchantment rapidly set in. His first visit was to his church. It was a desolate site: The roof was threatening to cave in. There were no panes of glass in the window frames. The vault was on the verge of collapsing—at least he thought so—and the dilapidation of the rest of the building matched that of the interior. Béranger Saunière asked himself if his bishop may not have sent him here for penitence and not as a promotion. Such case occurred frequently in the Holy Roman Church, which is just as deft at giving out punishments as it is rewards. But what grave sin could he have committed? His faith was sure, as he had shown on many occasions. He was scrupulously devoted to his work. Could he have been paying for the sins of his brother? Whether this was true or not, he asked himself this question. After leaving the church he went on to the presbytery meant to serve as his home. Another disappointment, it too appeared on the verge of collapse, suggesting that the commune of Rennes-le-Château, which was obliged to ensure the church's upkeep, was instead devoted to the devil—in this instance, the anticlerics who truly wished to see the Republic abandon the Holy Church to its sorry fate, and who would even take potshots at the ambulance carrying it to its fate.

In reaction to the dominant leftist political tendencies of this commune, Béranger felt a reawakening of his monarchist impulses. He was a Republican only to the extent necessary for those resolved to accept a *fait accompli*. But in his family, tradition was everything—and above all else, tradition was the Church. Who could defend the Church if not the monarchy, the sole regime that could still safeguard the alliance between priesthood and empire and harmonize the relationship between the sacred and the profane? Abbé Saunière told himself that he would change what he found before him. He was a fighter. Despite his weaknesses he was physically resourceful and basically intelligent. He wished for change and made the commitment before God and himself to contribute to making his parish the most beautiful in the entire diocese. He felt perfectly capable of achieving this. With a little time and a great deal of energy, he would show all these peasants and his bishop that his was not the soul of a slave. Patience . . . He well knew that in his family no one had ever been held back by a defeat and no one had ever been bested by adversity, whether man-made or devil-made.

In this instance the devil was present, but Béranger Saunière knew how to conjure away the devil. He even imagined that it would be the devil himself who would welcome the faithful at the door of the church—but in a terrible position of inferiority, holding up a stoup full of holy water, which everyone knows the devil cannot touch without experiencing great suffering. Was the devil looking for him? Béranger Saunière knew how to make him bow down. Aren't there folktales everywhere, after all, that tell of the great saints of this world who have forced the devil to erect buildings, bridges, and even cathedrals[1] without having to give anything in exchange because the devil can always be "conned" by those who are pure of heart? So Béranger Saunière's decision was made. He had been given an inhospitable rock. He would attach himself to it and make it the most beautiful rock imaginable. It became essential to find the means to reach this goal.

The first task was to get the situation in order. Saunière therefore went in search of the mayor to register himself (his salary depended on this) and to belabor the town official about the sorry state of the church and presbytery. The mayor could respond to his complaints only by saying that the commune was not rich and did not have the means to make the necessary repairs, but that they would look later at what could be

---

1. This is notably the case in Tréguier (in Côtes-du-Nord), where local legend maintains that Saint Tugdal made a pact with the devil, who was to build him a magnificent cathedral in one night and in return could take possession of the souls of all those who died between High Mass and Vespers the following Sunday. But Saint Tugdal immediately began singing the first chant of Vespers as soon as High Mass was over. There are countless variations on this theme.

done. He advised the new priest to take up temporary lodging with one of the parish's inhabitants. In this way Saunière found room and board with a woman of the village and ran up some debts at the grocer's because he had not yet received his wages and his savings were meager.[2]

The summer passed quietly. Saunière tried to deal with basic necessities—that is, he cleaned out all the debris that had accumulated in the church and asked the devoted parishioners to do the routine housework. He therefore managed to present an honorable place of worship. One fine day he received a visit from his closest colleague, Abbé Boudet, priest of Rennes-les-Bains. Boudet approached Saunière with an air of condescension; he was sure of himself and slightly self-infatuated, as though he was holding confidential information. He convinced Saunière that some of this information was intended for the priest of Rennes-le-Château, but that he, Boudet, would dole it out piecemeal on the condition that Saunière prove cooperative.

What kind of cooperation did he mean? It is a real mystery. The sly old tomcat Boudet refrained from confirming anything; he was content to make suggestions and give advice to his colleague. Saunière, who was younger than Boudet, was impressed. Boudet's stand-out reputation preceded him: He was a scholar who had published journal articles and even books and who, moreover, was connected to very influential people who were quite capable of providing the funds to undertake the restoration of the Church of Saint Mary Magdalene in Rennes-le-Château. Saunière began to ruminate. How was it that a modest priest from Rennes-les-Bains could have such influence? It was important to conform to what his elder told him. *It was even more important to try to grasp what he was being told in such sibylline terms.* In short, what we have here is Abbé Saunière's first temptation. It would not be the last.

Abbé Boudet had invited his young colleague to come visit him in the parish of Rennes-les-Bains. At this time people traveled by foot, by horseback, or by cart. It was a long way between Rennes-le-Château and Rennes-les-Bains, and unlike Abbé Boudet, not everyone had the good fortune to own a cart. Nevertheless, Abbé Saunière managed to

2. I am recounting the Abbé Saunière legend here as it has been contrived since 1956. There is no need to say that the reality was completely different.

make his way down into the valley, thanks to a peasant from the neighborhood. Here he was in Rennes-le-Bains. The presbytery there was a complete change from the wretchedness of his own. It was handsomely furnished with paintings and a bookcase full of books, for Abbé Boudet was a distinguished intellectual, and Saunière was given a meal that would normally be served only on special occasions. Though a cook without peer, Abbé Boudet's servant may not have been very pretty and had long ago reached canonical age. Béranger Saunière didn't pay her any more attention. How could Abbé Boudet, who at that time ministered a population of only 447 inhabitants (which does not mean 447 faithful), live such a life of creature comforts? How could he have collected so many books and beautiful objects? Perhaps he came from a well-to-do family. But this was not the case. So what can we make of the display that Boudet, somewhat cynically, brought to his colleague's attention? Saunière wondered what kind of place this was. After all, both Abbé Boudet and he were only modest servants of poor parishes. The priest of Rennes-le-Château wondered what was the source of the affluence of his colleague in the valley.

Boudet clearly refrained from telling him, but he did all he could to excite his curiosity, and consequently his envy. Saunière told himself that he too, after all, could treat his visitors with just as much magnificence. He felt like the poor relation, who was welcomed warmly enough certainly, but also with a certain amount of condescension. Now, one of Saunière's weaknesses was pride. He knew that one day or another he would have to return Boudet's invitation and that he ought to return it a hundredfold. A storm of emotions was raging in the mind of this country priest. Boudet, who leisurely extended his display of wealth . . . Boudet was the image or incarnation of the tempter whom Balzac described in *Le Père Goriot,* wearing the features of Vautrin. Saunière could have read the book while still in the seminary, but secretly of course, for Balzac was blacklisted as a craftsman specializing in the perversion of souls. It was obviously forgotten in the higher ecclesiastical spheres that Honoré de Balzac, worthy student of the Oratorians of the College of Tours, had described in his *Louis Lambert* the states of the soul of a young man who was prey to the demons of spirituality, not to mention spiritism. Finally, Béranger Saunière cast aside his literary recollections; they incited a disturbance that was too similar to the adolescent agitation once inspired by the description of the Jewish beauty Esther Gobseck. He listened to what Boudet was telling him, which blended with these temptations very welcome considerations about the local oddities, strange rocks, and caves that held secrets or treasures. His host ended by saying that certain people were firmly counting on Saunière to perform a mission that could be entrusted to him. Saunière was astonished. How could a poor country priest such as himself be able to serve the designs of the powerful people of this world? Boudet reassured him that in life everyone has a role to play and no one is useless. It is often the most humble who are promised the greatest destinies. In the words of the Gospel, "the first will be last" and vice versa.

Béranger Saunière no longer knew where he stood. The servant bustled around him and poured after-dinner drinks. His head was spinning. He wished he was back up on the plateau, where he was sheltered from the somewhat shady delights Boudet was proposing. After all, what did he really know about Boudet? It was said that he would seal himself up in his study for days, where he would consult old grimoires. It was also said that he wandered the countryside, maps in hand, looking for God knows what but surely not the Good Lord. True, he was an irreproachable priest and a person could listen to his sermons attentively without having to fortify him- or herself beforehand with a drink at the closest bistro. But why the insistence to Béranger Saunière that he, the new priest, was asked to complete a mysterious mission? Saunière eventually returned to Rennes-le-Château in the cart of the peasant, who had waited patiently for him. Back in his village that night he slept the sleep of the just, it seems. But the devil had his eye on him.

The summer died. Elections took place in two tiers, as usual, on October 4 and October 18, 1885. But before the polls opened on October 18, Abbé Béranger Saunière addressed his congregation in the Saint Magdalene Church of Rennes-le-Château, and what he said was rather disconcerting. He praised the fact that the first tier had provided satisfactory results but indicated that victory was not complete. On this occasion he invited the parish women—who were obviously the only ones attending Mass—to exert all their power over their men to "make the right choice"—that is to say, to convince the ill-informed electorate to vote for the defenders of religion. During his address he made comments that have been scrupulously reported: "The Republicans, they are the devil to be defeated; they are to be brought to their knees beneath the weight of religion and the baptized. The sign of the cross is victorious and with us!" It was as if the ornamentation of the Magdalene church was already visible, complete with the devil Asmodeus and the famous inscription: "With this sign you will be victorious." So what was eating the priest Saunière? Was there something in the excellent wine that Abbé Boudet had given him? This is just one more mystery in the Razès, where customary logic does not always seem to apply. In fact, with this inopportune sermon, Béranger Saunière was openly biting the hand that fed him, for his monthly salary was granted to him by the French state, which was as Republican as could be.

This sermon, in fact a political speech that he had no right to make, was an assault on the detachment he was expected to observe as a civil servant. His aggressiveness against the Republicans, who were seriously contemplating action against the clergy in 1885, was equaled only by his lack of awareness. He was preaching the vote for the conservative if not reactionary right. It so happens that the Occitan Midi at that time, Aude in particular, was veering to what was then called the red and what we might today call pale pink. The Radicals triumphed almost everywhere, and Saunière, as a priest of a parish supported by state funds, was denounced to the Aude prefect for inciting disorder and asserting electoral pressure. It is certain that the law and the rules were against Saunière. He was caught in the wrong. The Aude prefect could only conclude that he was guilty and sentence him to a salary suspension, which was put through immediately by the Ministry of Cults. Poor Béranger Saunière! Later he would be *suspens a divinis* by his own bishop, but for the moment his salary was suspended by his prefect.

This situation was serious, for the priest had no resources. Monsignor Billard clearly understood this and in an attempt to remedy the annoyance named Abbé Saunière to the position of professor at the small seminary in Narbonne. Most important, however, was his loan to Saunière of two hundred francs out of his own pocket, a considerable sum of money at that time. Should we believe that Béranger Saunière was protected by Monsignor Felix Billard?

Here the story reaches new heights, and the versions, differing in their details and conclusions, are all in agreement on one point: Abbé Saunière was manipulated by Monsignor Billard, who was not only bishop of Carcassonne, but also an eminent member of a mysterious sect. The purpose of this sect was to rediscover a treasure and documents hidden in Rennes-le-Château in order to use them toward reestablishing on the throne of France a legitimate representative of the original dynasty, meaning the Merovingians, who were themselves heir to an even more prestigious dynasty, no less than the House of David by way of Jesus and Mary Magdalene.[3] It was the poor abbé Béranger Saunière, a native of the region, who had been chosen for this extremely delicate mission. Monsignor Billard could not leave him in need, for Saunière had found himself in this situation as a result of obeying his orders, albeit those conveyed by the ambiguous words of Abbé Boudet, who was himself an influential member of this same sect.

As we know, quarrels between various authorities do not last long. After a period in which each side displayed intimidation tactics, a compromise was finally reached. In July 1886 the Aude prefect, feeling that the punishment had been long enough (and no doubt having had enough of the pressures put on him to end it), withdrew the suspension and restored Béranger Saunière's administrative duties, along with his monthly stipend. The priest could now return in triumph to Rennes-le-Château.

"In triumph" is stretching things quite a bit, however. The few women in the parish who were accustomed to his preaching were delighted, but their husbands, all of whom voted Republican, were much less so. Here again within their walls was a foe of circle dances, a person known to be an ardent enemy of democracy and one who needed to be set straight if they were to avoid future problems with the prefecture as well as the bishopric. The people of Rennes-le-Château were profoundly anticlerical, which they had been proving since the time of the Cathars. They would keep the priest under surveillance while giving him to understand that they would accommodate him on points that would not offend anyone. This would be the municipal policy during Abbé Saunière's ministry.

---

3. Again this is the story, and not historic fact, that I am citing here.

But Saunière did not return empty-handed from Narbonne. He had the considerable sum of three thousand gold francs at his disposal, an amount that was generously given to him by the countess of Chambord, the widow of the count of Chambord, a legitimate pretender to the French throne who lived in exile in Austria. If Saunière ever gave thought to the words of Abbé Boudet, it seemed he had proof now that highly placed individuals expected something of him. Curiously enough, according to the documents at our disposal, the total cost for the most urgently needed repairs at the Saint Magdalene Church proved to be 2,797 francs. The coincidence is too perfect to be fortuitous. By way of Abbé Boudet and with the blessing of Monsignor Billard, Abbé Saunière seemed to have been given a mission to accomplish something he may not have grasped entirely, yet realized was essential. Though he could not recall certain words of Boudet, he may have been under the spell of his colleague's aged Armagnac: "There is a fortune in it for you if you know how to catch it." These are the kinds of words we might not believe at first hearing, but when a packet of three thousand francs falls into our lap, then we might begin to be interested. What other option was there than to order the urgent restoration work for the parish church of Rennes? This is exactly what Saunière did, remembering his vow to make Rennes-le-Château the most beautiful parish of the diocese.

Béranger Saunière had his hands free for this restoration. The laws were in fact drawn up in such a way that when it was seen that neither the church council nor the commune could act, it was up to the parish priest to act. Of course, the commune of Rennes was too poor to undertake even the smallest kind of construction work, and the church council had only a small sum at its disposal, bequeathed to it by a former priest. Saunière therefore assumed almost all the repair costs, thanks to the gift that the countess of Chambord sent his way. His immediate concerns were the missing window panes, the cathedra (which was dilapidated), and the altar (which was threatening to collapse). To address these concerns he turned to craftsmen and settled on prices and job schedules with them.

It was at this time that he received a visit from a young girl who presented herself to him on behalf of Abbé Boudet. She told him that the priest of Rennes-les-Bains had asked her to come look after his needs so that he could fulfill his ministry under the best possible conditions. This girl had been working as a hat maker and her name was Marie Denarnaud.[4] Saunière, who had moved into the presbytery after "plugging up the holes," accepted Marie Denarnaud as his servant, but the presence of this young, fairly attractive woman caused him a certain amount of understandable torment. Thus, several days later, Marie Denarnaud went from being a modest servant to being the mistress of the robust and spirited priest of Rennes-le-Château. She remained in this role for the rest of her life, proving an exemplary fidelity to the man to whom she devoted all her time—despite the acts of infidelity he committed against her. For as was often repeated in the region, Béranger Saunière was "hot-blooded," and Marie Denarnaud was not the first to cause him to veer onto the path of sin.[5] In addition, the example of his brother, the Jesuit rejected by his brotherhood, who would soon live in a notorious relationship, provided some kind of encouragement for him. Of course, what a beautiful love story it makes, this passionate adventure between a modest parish priest and his young servant. Obviously she was not of canonical age, meaning the age required by ecclesiastical rules.[6] But who cared about this in Rennes-le-Château? After all, as the common saying goes, "A priest is a man just like any other man!"

So Abbé Saunière had set up a household, even if this household exuded a somewhat sulfurous odor. Because no one complained about it, though, why not continue and even openly display this uncommon liaison? Saunière was increasingly in contact with Abbé Boudet, who seems to have expressed his delight at the fine understanding that had grown between Marie and Béranger. After all, why couldn't Marie

---

4. This is an entirely invented episode. This possible liaison—which would have begun later but has not been proved—between Saunière and Marie Denarnaud owes absolutely nothing to any introduction by Abbé Boudet, which is quite regrettable for our story's creators. But that's just how it is.

5. The members of the lay clergy, including parish priests, took a vow of celibacy but not of chastity. It was the members of the regular clergy, therefore, monks and nuns, who took the vow of chastity.

6. [Meaning the age required to be mistress to a priest, usually the age of a postmenopausal woman. —*Translator*]

Denarnaud be a pawn—and one of great importance—in the game played in the parish of Rennes-le-Château? In the world of make-believe, female spies and secret agents still enjoy great success and inspire a somewhat murky respect. In fact, if Marie Denarnaud did become Abbé Saunière's mistress, it was at the orders of a higher-up. She was a dedicated, poor girl, but she was ultimately well rewarded, for Saunière subsequently left all he owned to his servant.[7] Here is more food for thought for those more sensitive souls.

This unexpected love affair did not prevent Béranger Saunière from pursuing his work. He came to an agreement with the municipality, the owner of the sanctuary, don't forget, and set up the first phase of construction. The members of the municipal council realized that this reconstruction of the Mary Magdalene Church was in the public interest and voted to provide a modest subsidy at the priest's disposal. The relationship between the mayor and the priest, strained at the onset, became much more amicable. The mayor strove to make things pleasant for the priest, who in return made efforts not to be disagreeable to the mayor. This nuance was huge, though, for Saunière had in no way abandoned his reactionary ideas and still displayed before the world at large his desire to see France become once more a monarchy ruling by divine right. The sermons of the priest were very clear: They all referred to the old medieval distinction of three classes, which oddly enough corresponded to the famous Indo-European tripartition revealed by the works of Georges Dumézill. This tripartition was common to all the peoples of Western Europe, and medieval Christianity incorporated it admirably.

To get his projects off the ground, Béranger Saunière did not hesitate

---

7. This is absolutely true. At his death Saunière owned nothing. Everything was in Marie Denarnaud's name. Under these circumstances, why imagine a scene in which Saunière leaves all his earthly possessions to his beloved servant? The reality is much more prosaic. Following the seizure of church property and the separation of Church and State, it was not in the interest of any member of the clergy to own personal property. Many resorted to figureheads or organized associations, such as those established by the law of 1901, to hold their property—a practice that is still relevant today. If by chance the State decided to seize the property of the clergy today, there would be nothing to seize; officially members of the clergy own nothing (outside of salaries and personal family possessions).

to carry the good word to certain individuals whose acquaintance he had made. For example, he persuaded a café owner by the name of Elie Bot,[8] who lived in Luc-sur-Aude and had a good deal of free time, to attend to the most critical construction on Saturday afternoons and Sundays. He also secured the help of a fourteen-year-old boy named Pibouleau, a native of Bézu. With his unqualified but devoted manual labor, Abbé Saunière began to turn the interior of the church upside down.

Why was there this ardent focus on the interior of the church when the most urgent work concerned the roof and windows? The answer is very simple: Abbé Boudet had let Saunière know that *those who took an interest in Rennes-le-Château* wished the priest to essentially concern himself with the inside. It would be the result of whatever he discovered here that would enable him to undertake other, much more profitable searches, which some in *high places* were essentially expecting him to make. Definitely the master builder was the priest of Rennes-les-Bains and not the priest of Rennes-le-Château. Béranger Saunière never undertook a step without the advice—or the order, who knows—of his colleague who lived in the valley below. This was no doubt because Boudet had promised him great wealth that would allow him to transform his parish—unless we should consider the more discreet whispers of Marie Denarnaud. "Pillow talk" is sometimes quite momentous, and while the locals generally accepted that the priest was sleeping with his servant, people were beginning to take umbrage at the exceptional importance young Marie was assuming. Every time anyone went to visit the priest, he had to first go through Marie Denarnaud; she seemed to be acting as the boss not only of the presbytery but even of the church. Tongues were wagging. People were wondering what these two, along with Elie Bot and the young Pibouleau, were really up to and they imagined all kinds of odd scenarios. Some would remind whomever would lend an ear that priests of all kinds had the reputation of practicing magic—white or black, but black more often than white!—which increased the parishioners' respect for their pastor on

---

8. In certain versions of the story, Elie Bot is portrayed as a Jew holding the secrets of the Kabbalah and as a man linked to a mysterious priory that was pulling all the strings in this matter.

the one hand, but also increased their fears. Because it could never be known for sure, it was better to be on his good side rather than suffer curses of inexplicable origin.

It was true that the priest often remained alone in his church. People doubted that he was there only to pray. It was thought that he was sounding the walls and floor, and was sanding away layers of plaster and other coatings to try and find out what might lie beneath them. What could he be looking for? By all evidence Saunière knew that the Saint Magdalene Church was hiding something and that if he succeeded in finding it, he would be able to transform the sanctuary and adorn it as he pleased. He was hoping—a very human hope—thereby to leave his mark on this place where destiny had led him, with some help from the Episcopal authority. He told himself that the best way to begin the renovation was to replace the old altar. Thus he ordered a new terracotta altar from Maison Monna in Toulouse, and it was now necessary to move the old one and clear out a space for the new.

The decisive moment was at hand. One day, when he was working with his two assistants to lift up the altar stone, he noted that the pillar, the famous pseudo-Visigothic pillar, was hollow and filled with ferns. Saunière fished inside and pulled out two or three wooden spools around which were rolled some parchments. He unrolled them in front of his two witnesses, but the documents proved incomprehensible; they were written in script that they could not read. Only a paleographic archivist or at least an expert in ancient script could decipher them. This discovery, however, made Abbé Saunière think: He knew that his predecessor from long ago, Abbé Bigou, had left something in this church at the time of the French Revolution, before he went into exile. Surely there must have been other hiding places. He began pursuing his work, concentrating on the places that appeared hollow when he tapped them. He even enlisted boys of the village to help him in his task.

One Sunday after Mass Abbé Saunière asked his choir boys, at least those who were nine and ten years old, to perform a small job for him on the following Thursday after catechism, promising them a nice treat as a reward. On that day Saunière locked the church from the inside. On the floor of the nave, not far from the choir walk, iron bars were arranged near a single large flagstone, which had been freed from the floor around its entire circumference. The priest and the boys pushed the iron bars under the sides of the flagstone and tried to lever it up. Finally everyone's good will and efforts began to pay off: The flagstone was lifted slightly. They shifted it over a little, which allowed several steps of a stairway to be seen. Unfortunately it was dark, despite the sunlight that was illuminating the nave. Because it was now noon, Saunière thanked the boys, saying: "Listen, we will stop working. Go out and amuse yourselves, and in four hours come and get your treat . . ." And that is what happened.[9]

But the boys had time to see that at the bottom of the pit there was an *oule,* a large pot, and that inside it were shining objects that looked like gold coins.

Of course, no one knows what the priest did between the hours of twelve and four. It is more than likely that he made a thorough exploration of the underground room. He would have unearthed the pot and carried it away. He may have discovered other objects or even documents. He never made any mention of it. As for the flagstone that had been pried up from the floor, it is known today as the Flagstone of the Knight and is displayed in the adjoining museum of the Rennes church.

The rumor quickly ran through the village that the priest had found a treasure, and all tongues wagged nonstop. No one, however, asked him what the treasure was. The inhabitants of Rennes-le-Château had long known that hiding places had been fashioned throughout the area over the centuries, and it was a sure bet that some of these caches held objects of value. Some were even found, but their discoverers made sure not to alert the crowds, preferring to keep their discoveries to themselves and cash them in discreetly when the opportunity presented itself. Thus, no one was about to reproach Saunière for doing what any one of them would have done in his place. Several days later, with the help of Elie Bot and several others, Saunière began to clean out the location

---

9. Testimony collected by Pierre Jarnac and published by him in his *Histoire du trésor de Rennes-le-Château,* 140–45.

of the high altar. Here another oule filled with shiny objects was discovered. On the pretext that it was time to eat, the priest sent away the workers and again remained alone in the church.

Béranger Saunière's life was turned completely upside down by these discoveries, which did not occur through happenstance. Certainly it had taken a long time through trial and error, but he was always searching in the correct locations. He must have been given some clues—and who better to supply him with these than his colleague Abbé Boudet, in the name, of course, of that mysterious brotherhood that hid behind the priest of Rennes-les-Bains? Of all the treasures, what intrigued Saunière the most were the manuscripts, though he was incapable of reading and understanding them. He thus sought out Boudet, informed him of his various finds, and asked his advice. It is at this point that the story veers in its murkiest and most suspect direction.

Abbé Boudet began by congratulating his colleague on the excellent work he has achieved and revealing to him that the "treasure" he has unearthed is his compensation, his "salary" to some degree, and that he can keep it for himself so that his sanctuary might benefit from it. But he warned Saunière that he would have to be careful. He should strike an agreement with the municipality so that it would not accuse him of dishonest actions. The town could not refuse the agreement because part of the "treasure" was to go toward repairing a communal property. As for the manuscripts, Boudet asked Saunière to entrust them to him for the time being so that he could try to decipher them. He then sent his colleague back to Rennes-le-Château, telling him that he would soon be giving him other instructions.[10]

Saunière actually did inform the mayor of his discoveries, though it seems that he downplayed their importance. He especially emphasized the manuscripts and obtained an agreement of principle from the

---

10. A number of inconsistencies can be noted in the story at this point. The discovery took place in 1886 but it was not until 1893 that Saunière was in Paris with the famous manuscripts. Why did he wait so long? There is not a shred of proof that Abbé Boudet had knowledge of these parchments. Given the fact, however, that Boudet had the reputation of a scholar and prided himself on his archaeological knowledge, it is not impossible that Saunière asked him to examine them. In this case we may question why Boudet would have been so long in advising Saunière to have them deciphered in Paris.

municipality allowing him to sell them should there ever be any sort of offer for them. Meanwhile, the interior refurbishment of the church continued. In 1887 the new terra-cotta high altar was installed and two months later stained glass was installed in the windows of the choir and the nave. Saunière then had the walls reinforced. Finally, he placed an order with Giscard Statuary of Toulouse for a bas-relief, intended for the entrance door, embellished by a statue of Mary Magdalene, patron saint of the church. The work was finished in 1891 and that same year Saunière asked authorization from the municipal council to enclose at his expense the public square adjacent to the church so that he might erect a religious statue there. This authorization was given with certain conditions: The key to the door that allowed access to the square must always be at the municipality's disposal, for the square was communal land open to all; further, the municipality did not give the priest any property rights to the places that had been renovated.

Béranger Saunière wasted no time. The so-called Visigothic stone was moved and cut to become a support for a statue of Our Lady of Lourdes. On the stone was carved Mission 1891 and on its capital were inscribed the words *penitence, penitence*. On June 21, 1891, in the presence of all his parishioners, numerous clergy from the surrounding area, and Father Ferrafiat of Limoux, who had come to preach the Mission for a week, Béranger Saunière performed the inauguration and benediction of all the church's exterior renovations What could be more orthodox than this pious display? The priest of Rennes-le-Château began to be known throughout the region for his incessant activity on behalf of his sanctuary, and no one had any complaints.

But what of the manuscripts? Saunière had not forgotten them. Boudet had confessed his inability to interpret them, so Saunière had taken them back. Because the mayor had asked him to entrust them to the town's archives, the priest provided him with copies—at least this is the story, for it is quite obvious that Béranger Saunière would have been incapable of making suitable reproductions of something he did not know how to read. On the advice of Abbé Boudet, Saunière sought out his bishop, Monsignor Billard, and explained the problem to him. The bishop considered these documents with great interest. It seemed to him that three might have been prayers and that the fourth could have been a fairly complicated genealogy, but Monsignor Billard was not a paleographic archivist and ultimately was also unsuccessful in decoding the documents.

Next, of course, Saunière should have turned to a qualified expert. The simplest solution would have been to visit the Departmental Archives of the Aude, where they surely could have found a specialist in this ancient script. But no, Monsignor Billard refused to consider the archives of the Aude. They were run by men who were much too Republican and thus anticlerical. It was impossible to entrust them with documents that could be used in their propaganda to promote the laity. After all, these documents might have held secrets that were dangerous to divulge. It would be much better to keep them among themselves. Monsignor Billard therefore suggested to Abbé Saunière that he go to Paris to find more trustworthy individuals. He gave him a letter of recommendation to a strange bookseller by the name of Ané, who produced religious books and had a connection to Abbé Bieil, the director of the Saint-Sulpice Seminary. Abbé Bieil would be able to take the county priest under his wing, examine his documents at leisure, and give him an opinion. In addition, the bookseller Ané had a nephew who was studying for the priesthood and who specialized in ancient languages and everything having to do with cryptography. This nephew, Émile Hoffet, could be of great assistance to Abbé Saunière. Monsignor Billard, who was definitely extremely considerate of Saunière after having secured the priest's commitment to leave his parish for three weeks, gave him fourteen hundred francs to pay not only his travel and room expenses, but also those incurred in his investigative work, including any expenses incurred for transcription of the manuscripts.

This attitude on the part of the Carcassonne bishop clearly indicates his great interest in the parchments unearthed by Abbé Saunière.[11] But the priest of Rennes-le-Chateau knew quite well what to expect of Billard, for Abbé Boudet had revealed to him the existence of the secret brotherhood to which allegedly the monsignor belonged. Saunière had been awaiting instructions; now here they were. With no further delay, he left for Paris.

---

11. There isn't a shred of evidence to confirm this discussion between Saunière and his bishop, nor are there any documents concerning the mission entrusted to the Rennes-le-Château priest.

It is hard to imagine Abbé Saunière alighting from the train in the middle of Paris in his old-fashioned cassock, prey to some very understandable misgivings. Paris was truly a foreign world to him, especially in a time when the people from the provinces rarely traveled. For this poor country priest it was a world apart. Nevertheless, on his arrival Abbé Saunière found the bookseller Ané, who gave him lodging at his home and promised to introduce him to Abbé Bieil the next day. He also told him that his nephew, Émile Hoffet, would be arriving in several days. Indeed, Saunière did see Abbé Bieil and showed him the parchments. The director of Saint-Sulpice waxed enthusiastic over these precious documents and warmly thanked the priest for coming in person to show them to competent and discreet people. He also told him that he could place complete trust in Émile Hoffet to successfully complete the delicate task of transcribing and interpreting them, and he advised Saunière to entrust him with the documents so that Emile could give them a detailed examination either by himself or with the help of specialists that he knew well.

Abbé Bieil, do not forget, was the director of the Seminary of Saint-Sulpice, and thus the remote successor of Abbé Jean Ollier, founder of Saint-Sulpice and an influential member of the all-powerful Brotherhood of the Holy Sacrament in the seventeenth century. Because Abbé Ollier and Nicolas Pavillon, the bishop of Alet, shared a tight-knit relationship, and because the decoration of the Church of Saint-Sulpice echoes that of Rennes-le-Château, we find ourselves once more in the Razès. We are back at the beginning and Abbé Saunière was in familiar territory.

At this time, toward the end of the nineteenth century, when different groups blossomed around various famous Parisians, Saint-Sulpice and the bookseller Ané's shop were at the center of an intense religious and *spiritualistic* activity. The least that can be said about these groups is that they were not very Catholic. In fact, they could be openly labeled occult. Here, then, we find Béranger Saunière plunged into an atmosphere that he may not have foreseen but which would reveal itself to be particularly favorable to him.

In truth, all of this is somewhat unsettling, for here is where "the temptations of Abbé Saunière" truly began. The devil came cloaked in many guises, some of which were quite pleasant and hardly conformed with the medieval image of the enemy. It was Émile Hoffet, who pursued his studies not at Saint-Sulpice in Paris but in Lorraine, who is considered to have been the person responsible for introducing Abbé Saunière to the occult milieu of that time. This "Father" Émile Hoffet (who was not yet a priest) is a curious figure. He had spent his entire life decoding old grimoires; taking an interest in more or less secret sciences; primarily devoting himself to intensive studies of numerous "fraternal" and "angelic" societies and other associations whose true purposes can never be distinguished but which exist all over the world; and "infiltrating" the intellectual elite in order to spread odd messages, usually under the seal of secrecy. When he died in 1946, Émile Hoffet had put together an extraordinary library, which is greatly coveted but which to the present day is open only to a few rare and privileged individuals, who must be ecclesiastics and who have provided proof of their intellectual honesty. None can deny that there is a Hoffet mystery just as there is an Abbé Saunière mystery, and the figure of Hoffet fully merits deep interest for more than one reason: Who was his inspiration? To what secret society did he belong? Did he really have a religious vocation? All of these questions go unanswered, but it can be confirmed that he had entrance into all the circles of that *decadent* era and apparently found himself perfectly at home in them.

In any case, according to the story that has been constructed around the Saunière matter, Hoffet and Saunière got along famously together, taking into account the fact that it was Hoffet (to Saunière's benefit) who assumed the role of the "introducing brother" in the worldly and occultist salons to which he hastened to bring the country priest. "His conversation was always interesting . . . Passionate and impassioned discussion went on long after the after-dinner drink and coffee were served, with an unsettling note that disturbed the strait-laced atmosphere of the right-thinking gatherings."[12] Thanks to Hoffet, Béranger Saunière was introduced to the very closed circle of Jules Bois, where he met Claude Debussy and other celebrities of the time.

Jules Bois is another person on whom much light remains to be shed. He was friends with all the symbolist poets and with those who

---

12. Jean Robin, *Rennes-le-Château, la colline envoûtée* (Paris: Guy Trédaniel, 1982), 24.

would later become known as the Decadents. He also frequented the sects of the Illuminati, the Rosicrucians and the Freemasons of various persuasions, which did not prevent him from being the guru of a group with clearly "Satanic" tendencies, though not necessarily in the "black" and destructive sense of the word.[13] He was the author of several books such as *Le Monde invisible, L'Au-delà et les forces inconnues,* and *Le Satanisme et la Magie,* the titles of which are revealing enough. He was also famous for his participation in several affairs that provide a good illustration of the world Abbé Saunière encountered during his stay in Paris, at least if we believe those who have invented the Saunière myth.

One of these affairs is particularly interesting for its involvement in the duel between Jules Bois and another occultist, Stanislas de Guaita. The motive for this duel was the mad and sordid adventure of Abbé Boullan, a perfectly orthodox priest who had become deranged by his passion for a nun of La Salette, whom he made both his disciple and his mistress. Together they founded a kind of bizarre community in which sexuality and magic set up shop with a theology guaranteed to cause even the most radical Christians to tremble. Here is how Jean-Luc Chaumeil described this "affair."

> Occultist and friend of Maurice Barrès, the marquis Stanislas de Guaita, had accused another occultist, Abbé Boudan, a defrocked priest and friend of Huysmans, of having devoted himself to black magic. He called together a "tribunal" to condemn Boudan and

---

13. It should be known that Satanism is not necessarily an erotic-obsessive perversion of the Christian ritual. In the mind of authentic Satanists, it does not involve blaspheming for pleasure, as vulgar atheists are apt to do. Quite the contrary, it consists of glorifying the Being and the Shadow—in other words, Satan unjustly dethroned by God and who, in the Darkness where he is enchained, represents for his adepts the hope of a world redeemed and renewed, for Satan is the original god and God the Father is the usurping god. To some extent it is a kind of reversed Catharism. The victim is the Fallen Angel while the origin of evil (metaphysical and otherwise) is to be found in this divine usurpation. Through Jules Bois's Satanism we can also see the broad lines sketched from the myth of the King of the World, who is subject to the cruelest imprisonment in the shadows, but will return one day to restore balance to a universe gone mad. Mythological justifications are not lacking in Satanist doctrines.

the result was a "magician's duel" between the two men that Barrès reported in these terms: "One evening Guaita modeled a small wax figure that he pierced with a needle to enchant the priest, who used the secrets of the Kabbalah in his evil designs. The priest, in response, cast a spell on his adversary's eyes to make him blind. Guaita took his measures, and the spell, through a return shock, was cast back upon the priest, whose death put an end to the battle." In fact, on January 3, 1893, Abbé Boullan died, having been struck in some inexplicable manner. Immediately Jules Bois picked up his journalist's pen and wrote, "I have been told that the Marquis of Guaita lives in fierce solitude, that he manipulates poisons with great science and marvelous certainty, and that he volatilizes them and directs them through space. What I am asking, without incriminating anyone, is that some light be shed on the causes of this death." As soon as the article appeared, Stanislas de Guaita sent his witnesses to Jules Bois.[14]

It goes without saying that none of this took place under normal circumstances. Jules Bois had two accidents, both of which were bloody and deadly, before arriving at the duel. Two bullets were exchanged without result and honor was thus saved. All this is is to illustrate that Béranger Saunière found himself at once in a strange milieu. But didn't similar affairs take place in the faraway Corbières, right in the middle of the department of the Aude?

In fact, as a priest Abbé Saunière was necessarily aware of certain magic practices that were still common currency in the mountains and valleys. It is not known if he was an exorcist himself, for this role—a formidable one—was reserved for certain priests who were stronger and more resistant than others, but he was not unaware of what really went on in the hamlets of his parish and the surrounding area.

The Aude has always been a receptive land for magicians and wizards, and it will not be the bishop of Carcassonne who will belie me if I declare that the forbidden arts (at least those forbidden

---

14. Jean-Luc Chaumeil, *Le Trésor du triangle d'or* (Paris: Lefeuvre, 1979), 104–105.

when the Inquisition thrived) are more in evidence here than elsewhere. Abbé Saunière, child of the region who, it may be said was
so close to the people, could not have remained unaware that the
majority of sorcery rites are only religious rites performed backwards, and all the folklorists, for want of exorcists,[15] have an abundance of backwards prayers in their files as well as stories of old
women walking the path of the Stations of the Cross backwards
while muttering inaudible threats.[16]

We should not forget that Abbé Saunière placed his so-called
Visigothic pillar upside down and his path of the Stations of the Cross
backwards. No doubt he never forgot what united the rustic sorcery of
the Razès with the distinguished magic of the Decadents, the
Symbolists, and other "initiates" of High Paris while the century was
drawing to a close.

Even if he found himself somewhat intimidated by fashionable
Parisian gatherings, Abbé Saunière was not naïve and knew full well
that Jules Bois and his friends were striving to manipulate psychic
forces—sometimes dangerously—not to mention those subtle and invisible forces whose secrets they claimed to hold. Around Claude Debussy,
Stéphane Mallarmé, Maurice Maeterlinck, and Maurice Leblanc
crowded a swarm of hacks and more or less influential muses such as
Georgette Leblanc and the beautiful opera singer Emma Calvé, mistress
of Jules Bois—for the moment, at least. This very stylish high society
had connections with the Theosophical Society, the Rosicrucians, and
the Freemasons (Scottish Rite), and individuals moving within it displayed very bold positions on matters of spirituality. There was a weak-
ness for "heretics," for all those who interpreted the texts of the official
Church in their own way. The works of Rémy de Gourmont and
Huysmans have shown evidence of this. The latest snobbism was to
take part in magic sessions, preferably black ones, and even authentic

---

15. More on this subject can be read in *Traité des Superstitions* by Jean-Baptiste Thiers,
a seventeenth-century ecclesiastic, with an introduction by Jean-Marie Goulemot (Paris:
Éditions du Sycomore, 1984).

16. J. Robin, *Rennes-le-Château, la colline envoûtée*, 144.

black Masses. Wagnerism was newly discovered and dreams were spun from the ambiguous liturgies of Bayreuth. It was *Parsifal* that excited the imagination, especially that of the privileged few who had the chance to go to Bayreuth, for until 1914, by the express will of Cosima Wagner, this strange opera was not allowed to be performed anywhere else. Vincent d'Indy, however, composed a *Fervall,* a sort of French remake of *Parsifal,* and Reyer created a *Sigurd* that displays his tetralogy fully, while Claude Debussy, haunted by the legend of Tristan, obligingly listened to the first drafts of Maeterlinck's *Pelléas et Mélisande.* The Middle Ages was being rediscovered not in the grandiloquent way of the Romantics, but in the more subtle way of the Symbolists, who decoded the most arduous texts and even imposed on Paris architecture the famous "noodle" style, which is only a revised and corrected Neo-Gothicism.

So it was to the fin-de-siècle salons that Émile Hoffet dragged Béranger Saunière. And the little priest from Rennes-le-Château became the star of these soirees that went on interminably. Why? He confusedly wondered what was expected of him, but he did not forget Boudet's revelation: Highly placed people would counsel him to fulfill certain expectations in exchange for which he would receive a fortune. It was not that Béranger Saunière loved money, but he needed it to embellish the church and the entire villge of Rennes-le-Château. When he recalled this, Abbé Saunière listened with his fullest attention, seeking to penetrate further the fine allusions others made in his presence.

In fact, he listened so attentively that the bewitching voice of Emma Calvé penetrated much more deeply than expected. Emma Calvé was one of the greatest sopranos of the day, whose talent, in the words of her contemporaries, was incontestable. She was the darling of the latest salons and was tied by friendship to Claude Debussy, who had her sing some of his melodies, though she was the mistress of Jules Bois. Now, Jules Bois's intimate acquaintances were never innocents when it came to esotericism, hermeticism, and magic. Did Emma Calvé belong to that mysterious brotherhood whose shadow always hovered over Béranger Saunière? Her real surname was Calvat, which she changed for euphonic reasons. She was a distant cousin of Melanie Calvat, the shepherdess of La Salette who was the heroine of those fraudulent appearances of the Virgin[17] that so greatly helped the reactionaries of the mid-nineteenth century.

Béranger Saunière quickly became the lover of Emma Calvé. Had she been lightning struck by the man she called "her little provincial priest"? Was she acting on the orders of Jules Bois to better circumvent and influence Saunière? Both answers are possibly correct and are not contradictory. Subsequently, Emma Calvé visited Rennes-le-Château. It was even claimed that the soprano was able to buy her dream castle in her homeland thanks to the priest's generosity, and that she bore Saunière a child, but there is obviously not a shred of proof to support these claims.

Despite their affair, Emma Calvé did not drive the priest's mission from his mind, and if he did forget, she would have been the first to remind him of it. When the manuscripts had been examined by Abbé Bieil and Emile Hoffer, Saunière presented himself to hear the two experts' conclusions. He was told that three of the manuscripts were of no interest but that the fourth—that mysterious genealogy—was quite exceptional. The two then proposed a deal to Saunière. They would keep the manuscript and in return they would give him certain clues that would allow him to find a lost treasure. The priest accepted. What else could he have done? He felt caught in a trap from which he was unable to extricate himself. Furthermore, he had made his choice. He who wishes the end wishes the means, and his objective remained to embellish and glorify his parish of Rennes-le-Château.

It is definite that the experts he consulted had explained certain passages of the manuscripts and provided him with a course to follow. How can we otherwise understand Saunière's infatuation with lurking in the Louvre Museum toward the end of this stay in Paris? Until that time he had never shown any particular taste for painting. Nevertheless, he often could be found in the gallery housing Nicolas Poussin's painting *The Shepherds of Arcadia*—and this was not the only work he

---

17. During a resounding trial, the staging of these appearances was judicially recognized and Jean-Marie Vianney, the priest of Ars, received the confession of a shepherd who declared that he had seen nothing at all. Sickened by the uproar caused by the sham, the saintly priest of Ars traveled to Grenoble to lodge a complaint with the bishop there. He was politely requested to return home and keep his mouth shut.

sought. He was fascinated by a painting by Teniers and eagerly wished to find an anonymous portrait of Pope Celestin V, who ruled briefly at the end of the eighteenth century. We must wonder why.

Ultimately, not content with merely viewing the paintings, he acquired reproductions. It was *The Shepherds of Arcadia* that seemed to most motivate his research, as if there was something within this painting, perhaps a clue that his initiators had recommended that he examine attentively. He did not know then that on the Arques road not far from his parish there was a tomb almost identical to the one painted by Poussin. It sat before a landscape that was physically the same as the one represented—or imagined—by the seventeenth-century painter. But might he have known that when Nicolas Foucquet, protector and admirer of Poussin, was condemned to life imprisonment, Louis XIV initiated a search for this painting and did not rest until it was part of his private collection?

It could of course be said that Béranger Saunière, whose goal was refurbishing his church as best as he possibly could, was seeking to educate himself in one of the world's best museums, and to draw inspiration there for ordering the works of art that would be the glory of his own monument. At the sight of the horrors with which he favored the Saint Magdalene sanctuary, however, it would seem that this visit to the Louvre had no effect at all on Saunière's aesthetic sensibility.

The village priest's stay in Paris remained decidedly strange from beginning to end because of both the people he surrounded himself with and the activities to which he devoted his time. Henceforth, he had the conviction that all the famous people he knew took him seriously and considered him to be an important man. What could be more comforting?

Béranger Saunière eventually took leave of his hosts. The separation with Emma Calvé was melancholy, but Béranger savored the incomparable happiness to be found in the fact that he, a poor country priest, had won the favors of one of the most visible women in the capital. They did promise to see each other again, and of course Béranger knew that Marie Denarnaud, his faithful and kind servant, was waiting in Rennes. Onward!

Abbé Saunière could regain without regret the solitude of his eagle's nest; he had not been duped. At the price of a few lies he would still need to soothe the anxieties of Monsignor Billard, who would be greatly surprised at the absence of the parchment and already regretted his letter of recommendation. A lusty fellow such as Béranger Saunière did not need any help getting his foot into the stirrup. All the same, to exchange a genealogical tree for the key to a treasure . . .[18]

Whatever the case may be, Béranger Saunière had at last returned to Rennes-le-Château to the great joy of his parishioners, who were beginning to sincerely like him, although they thought him a bit eccentric. Of course Marie Denarnaud also greeted his return with great joy. Did she pepper him with questions about his stay in Paris? Of course—but the priest must have felt a little anxious around the armpits, as they say, when he mentioned the opera singer Emma Calvé. Saunière did not have a completely easy conscience with regard to his parishioners, his bishop, Marie, and himself, for he never forgot that he was a priest and at no time in his life did he deny his priesthood. When it comes to easing their conscience and obtaining possible forgiveness from God, priests behave as all the faithful do: They confess. Who was Abbé Saunière's confessor? It was certainly not Boudet, who was his partner in some shady dealings. Was it his brother, Alfred Saunière? Surely not, for confessions are neither given nor heard between family members. While Alfred Saunière may have kept himself abreast of some things, it was because he was both Béranger's brother and an accomplice in the famous scandals that would later erupt concerning corrupt Masses. What's more, he himself hardly provided a good example of a priest beyond reproach.

There are two clergymen who seem to have received the confidences and, no doubt, the confessions of Saunière. One of these was Abbé Eugéne Grassaud, who was a professor at the Louis de Gonzague Lycée in Perpignan—to which Saunière went frequently, almost in secret—and who became the priest first of Amélie-les-Bains, then of Saint-Paul-de-Fenouillet in the Perpignan diocese, which was close to the Razès. Abbé Grassaud left behind the memory of an enterprising man, both good and erudite, whose library was abundantly furnished

18. J. Robin, *Rennes-le-Château, la colline envoûtée,* 25.

with books and manuscripts of all kinds. He also strove to repair and embellish the churches in his charge. Furthermore,

> . . . the bonds of friendship between Abbé Saunière and Canon Grassaud were never belied, even when the elder was faced with all the rumors that his trial by the bishopric inspired. Saunière was never scared to visit his colleague in Amélie-les-Bains, a courtesy that the canon often returned very willingly whenever he had enough free time. After the death of his friend Saunière, Canon Grassaud did not spare any pains to help Marie Denarnaud through life's difficulties.[19] It was to Eugéne Grassaud that Abbé Saunière gave a gilded silver chalice around 1893.[20]

Where might this chalice have come from? Probably from the cache Saunière found in the Rennes-le-Château church, the famous treasure hidden by Abbé Bigou.

Another priest, who lived much closer, may have been Saunière's confessor, as well as his confidant: Abbé Gélis, priest of Coustaussa, an elderly cleric who was still of sound mind and who would be murdered several years later under very mysterious circumstances. There is a strong possibility that on his return from Paris, Béranger Saunière went to confess to his colleague in Coustaussa. He certainly had a lot to say. The somewhat "Satanic" atmosphere that had enveloped him during his Parisian sojourn was beginning to weigh heavily upon him. On this occasion might Abbé Saunière have entrusted Abbé Gélis with something to hold for safekeeping—some documents, perhaps? In complete good faith, it seems the answer would be yes.

In Rennes-le-Château, Abbé Saunière devoted himself to some very odd activities. Profiting from construction work undertaken by the municipality in the cemetery, he had a wall erected around, which included the famous portal that can still be seen there today. After its

---

19. P. Jarnac, *Histoire du trésor de Rennes-le-Château*, 334–35.

20. "This is a piece with no great commercial value. It is a superb piece, certainly, and is carved and in perfect condition, but it is only gilded metal. At the foot of the chalice a Maltese Cross, formed by four green enamels, can be seen. This chalice dates at most from the eighteenth century." (P. Jarnac, *Histoire du trésor de Rennes-le-Château*, 336).

completion he often locked himself into the walled cemetery at night. But what was he doing there? By all evidence, he was moving tombstones; in fact he was defacing the cemetery's tombs. What did he hope to find? It can be assumed that he undertook this labor as a result of the clues he had been given in Paris in exchange for the genealogy. He worked particularly hard on the tomb of Marie de Négri d'Ables, Lady of Hautpoul and Blanchefort, who died in 1781. The tomb was built from two flagstones, of which the upright one was the work of Abbé Bigou. The lady's epitaph on this stone had been carved with an incredible number of mistakes, which has not failed to prompt some questions. A Latin inscription with some Greek letters can be read on the horizontal stone; it remains incomprehensible.

It is incontestable that Abbé Saunière spent considerable time scratching out the inscriptions that had been carved upon this tomb. He must have had a good reason for this—but he did not know that the carved writing had already been recorded by a conscientious archaeologist; indeed, it was reproduced in 1903 in the bulletin of the very serious Archaeological Society of the Aude. Saunière, therefore, went to a great deal of trouble for nothing, which might be seen as proof that these inscriptions represented something very important—even essential—to him. No doubt these were the very keys that allowed him to direct his nocturnal and quasi-clandestine searches.

The vertical flagstone was inscribed as follows:

CT GIT NOBLe M
ARIE DE NEGRe
DABLES DAME
DHAUPOUL De
BLANCHEFORT
AGEE DE SOIX
ANTE SePT AND
DECEDEE LE
XVII JANVIER
MDCOLXXXI
REQUIES CATIN
PACE

Above this, after the initials *P. S.* and in parentheses was carved PRAECUM. All of this is quite mysterious and lends itself to much analysis. A vain attempt has been made to portray as clumsy or ignorant the seventeenth-century worker who carved this stone—quite a stretch, for even the date is incorrect. When he was attempting to decipher this inscription, Béranger Saunière did not know he would suffer a fatal attack of illness on January 17. Curious, isn't it?

> If one applies to the text formed by the anomalies and connected to a key found within the text itself a decoding method that is well known to cipher experts (the Vugenere Method), and if one doubles this by the "knight's tour," another method requiring a chessboard, a clear text can be obtained that does retain a sibylline aspect: "Shepherdess no temptation that Poussin Teniers hold the key peace 68—by the cross and the horse of God I complete this Daemon guardian at noon. Blue apples."[21]

It cannot be said that this is very comprehensible, but when Béranger managed to "decipher" the inscription it must have been cause for great rejoicing. In fact, it is one of the same messages that he brought to Abbé Bieil and Émile Hoffet and still had at his disposal. All of this proved that the research was pointing in the right direction and that it was urgent, then, to eliminate anything that might put undesirables on the scent of something to which they had no right. Because the mysterious brotherhood had given him the mission to follow his search to its conclusion, Béranger Saunière was ready to do take any measures to eliminate *the others*.

Furthermore, Abbé Saunière held the key to this text. He knew that in order to get to its true meaning, it was necessary to draw a diagonal starting from the first anomaly noted. Now the first anomaly is assuredly the *T* in the place of the *I* in *ci gît* [here lies]. If a diagonal line is drawn from that spot, it will inevitably reach *catin* [trollop], which certainly seems an unpleasant description of the noble woman lying there. Fortunately, Saunière knew that under certain conditions, particularly

---

21. M. Lamy, *Jules Verne, initié et initiateur*, 68.

when it appears where it should not, the *T,* or the Tau in esoteric traditions, is a code that means "treasure" of some kind. He also knew that the word *catin* did not necessarily mean "whore," but could mean "cavity," "cavern," or "uterus." He was thus able to grasp that "the treasure was no longer in the home of the Hautpoul (as there was no longer a *T* in the family's name in the inscription), but had been moved instead into a *catin,* meaning a "cave."[22] This consideration along with the mention of Poussin and the Shepherdess obviously reminded him of Poussin's painting, for after all, a tomb is also a "cavern," especially when it is a *cairn*—that is, a megalithic mound. The most important steps were to determine just what this cairn was and where it was located.

Of course, the other flagstone also held an inscription, albeit in illegible Greek characters and legible Roman characters. Above it were the initials *P. S.* and beneath it Saunière could read *praecum.* In the middle a vertical arrow separated two groups of two words each. On the left were REDDIS and CELLIS. On the right were REGIS followed by ARCIS. The words were quite confusing because they could not be read continuously. The word *reddis* might have a connection with Reddae, meaning Rennes or the Razès; the word *regis* is certainly the genitive of *rex,* meaning "king"; *cellis* is a plural ablative, therefore it is a preposition of place, of *cella,* "cave," or "underground hut"; and the word *arcis* is the genitive of *arx,* "of the citadel."[23] Make of it what you will, but Saunière could have viewed it only as confirmation of what had been whispered to him in Paris: "in Rennes, in a cave of the king's citadel." The treasure of Blanche de Castille is not far from this, or it might be that of the "lost king," the fabled descendant of the Merovingians. This figure was just beginning to make an appearance in the adventures of Arsène Lupin, the character created by Maurice LeBlanc, friend of Jules Bois and brother of Maurice Maeterlinck's companion, Georgette LeBlanc. Béranger Saunière did not greatly comprehend this story of lost Merovingians, but it did not matter. In the cemetery he had made a discovery of great interest.

His quasi-clandestine nocturnal investigations and disruptions earned him the disapproval of the inhabitants of Rennes, however—

---

22. Interpretation made by Jean-Pierre Monteils, *Le Dossier secret de Rennes-le-Château* (Paris: Belfond, 1981), 61.

23. The authenticity of this flagstone is a subject of great controversy.

especially that of the municipal authorities. They admonished the priest, who in turn became angry, yelling, "When someone treads on my turf, I believe I have the right to defend myself!" He eventually came to an accord with the town, which meant he could continue his excavations in the cemetery. But this made the inhabitants of Rennes furious, and they sent a petition to the Aude prefect to alert him to their priest's activities. When they did not receive a response, they sent in a second petition that read: "We are not at all happy about the work being carried out in the cemetery, especially under the present circumstances. The crosses there are removed, as are the tombstones, and none of this alleged work is for repairs.[24] Nothing was done, however, and Saunière continued to pursue his nocturnal and somewhat macabre explorations for a long time.

But these were not the only activities of Saunière to attract attention. For entire days at a time he would pace around the outskirts of the village and hike through the mountains with Marie Denarnaud at his side. To those who asked him what he was looking for, he responded that he was picking pebbles to use in constructing a Lourdes grotto. In fact, he was often seen returning during the evening, bent under the weight of apparently full sacks. Sometimes when his walks took him in the direction of Rennes-les-Bains, he would happen to run into Abbé Boudet, who was involved in archaeological explorations that included recording the position of certain rocks or discovering a rupestrian inscription or an ancient cross buried in the brush.[25] All in all, Saunière's projects kept him constantly busy but did not prevent him from writing to individuals throughout France and the rest of the world.

Then an extremely serious event took place not far from Rennes. The following article can be found in *La Semaine religieuse de Carcassonne,* dated November 5, 1897:

A horrible crime was committed sometime during Sunday night or Monday morning in the Coustaussa parish. Abbé Gelis died as the result of wounds suffered to his head and lay in the presbytery's

---

24. An authentic document presented and published by P. Jarnac, *Histoire du trésor de Rennes-le-Château,* 151–53.

25. In reality it seems that Saunière went hunting. He brought back much game and gave some of it to his parishioners as gifts.

kitchen, bathing in his own blood. . . . There is no lack of conjecture concerning the murderer's possible motive. Mystery still hovers over this sorrowful event, although the public prosecutor and the police are working with a most laudable effort to track down those responsible. Abbé Gelis was a pious priest who reproduced in his every action all the gentleness of nature appropriate to a minister of Jesus Christ.

As mentioned earlier, it seems that Abbé Jean-Antoine-Maurice Gelis, born in 1827, was the confessor and confidant of Abbé Saunière. Indeed, Béranger Saunière was overwhelmed by the news and, along with a large crowd that included the vicar general and many other clergymen, attended the funeral services for his unfortunate colleague.

So just what happened to Abbé Gelis? In the October 3, 1976, issue of *Le Midi libre,* we can read an extract from the 1897 inquest files concerning the circumstances surrounding the unfortunate priest's murder.

The precautions that were taken betray an incredible presence of mind. The kitchen, following such havoc, was put back into perfect order, with no trace of footprints. The murderer was alert enough to avoid three large pools of blood. There were no traces of evidence found outside. On the first floor, in Abbé Gelis' room, two minuscule drops of blood attested to the passage of the assassin, who, without leaving the slightest bloody imprint, forced the lock of a traveling bag that contained various papers and documents belonging to the priest. The murderer opened the bag not to steal items, but to search for something. In fact 683 francs' worth of gold and notes were found in the priest's desk and 106.90 francs were found in his dresser. Stranger still was the fact that the priest's body had been laid out on its back toward the middle of the room, with the head and face in a normal position and the hands folded over the chest. There was but one mute witness to this bloody tragedy, which was committed for no apparent motive. While the priest did not smoke and hated the odor of tobacco, an entire pack of Tzar brand cigarette papers were found floating in the second pool of blood near the window. On one leaf, written in pencil, were the words *Viva Angélina* [Long Live Angelina].

What did Béranger Saunière think of all this? No one will ever know. Did he who was working so hard on decoding messages understand the exact meaning of *Viva Angélina* written on a cigarette paper? Béranger Saunière did smoke, though he should not have because of his heart condition. Perhaps he knew much more about this matter than he cared to say. In any event, no one ever asked him a thing about it. In the days following the discovery of the crime, the authorities arrested the victim's nephew, a good-for-nothing who was always short of cash and had been harassing the aged priest with his incessant demands. It was quickly established, however, that on the night of the murder he was definitely somewhere else. Abbé Gelis's killer—a smoker who was *looking for something* and who *left behind a message*—was never found.

We may wonder for whom this message was intended. This was probably what Béranger Saunière was wondering as he headed back up to Rennes-le-Château during that sad month of November 1897, for Abbé Saunière was not involved in the affair in any way. Unless . . .

In any event, he had, as the expression goes, other fish to fry. His plans were grandiose in nature and he refined them every day on paper, ordering construction here and there and supervising what he could when time allowed. Thanks to his obliging brother, who had many worldly acquaintances due to his collection of mistresses, he did not forget to ask for Masses from the more well-to-do. The donors responded, and Béranger Saunière took advantage of it to begin collecting stamps, for that was his passion, or, as we might say today, his hobby.

This was the time when he began seriously concerning himself with his financial affairs. As the child of a peasant family, he was quite capable of managing his holdings. He opened accounts in banks that were not all regional, which can appear surprising for a modest country priest. Bankers, however, are discreet individuals who are very good at spotting the most attractive clients—that is, those who will be the most profitable. Saunière trusted banks but did not put all his eggs on one basket. It was claimed that he had an account in Austria and even that he went to England twice. All that is known for certain is that his main bank was in Perpignan, which he visited often under strange circumstances.

When he left, he never said where he was going. He would travel down to Couiza, where he caught the train for Carcassonne. And after?

We now know that he often went to Perpignan, where he stayed in the modest Eugéne Castel hotel. Each time that he was absent for several days, though, he wrote letters in advance, mainly addressed to the bishopric, which he would have posted over the following days by Marie Denarnaud. This disconcerting behavior could not help but prompt questions among all who knew him, but his parishioners said nothing. He was a good priest, very understanding, and in addition to all the renovations he had obtained for the church and the village, he devoted much time to those in abject circumstances and did what he could to ease as much as possible the problems of those in need. In other words, he had a very good reputation among his flock, and despite some temporary differences with the mayor on some minor matters, he got on quite well with the elected municipal officials of Rennes-le-Château. All of this was noted when he invited his bishop, Monsignor Billard, to inaugurate his new church.

It was apparent that his time had not been wasted. Frescoes, the Stations of the Cross, the statue of Asmodeus, statues of the saints, stained-glass windows, the new altar, a rebuilt sacristy (with a secret room serving as a storage area), a renovated rostrum, a beautiful wooden confessional—everything was in place. During that memorable day, in the presence of all the inhabitants and clergymen of the region, Abbé Saunière gave a homily praising the merits of charity. The monsignor could only congratulate him for his achievements. We can only wonder what he really thought of the bizarre decorations installed through the pains of the priest of Rennes-le-Château, though we must acknowledge that according to the legend, Monsignor Billard was part of the mysterious brotherhood whose name Saunière never dared speak aloud.

Abbé Saunière had certainly fulfilled his mission in his parish, and he had certainly fulfilled it with regard to other individuals. From this time on he launched himself into sumptuous expenditures that were not all intended to further good works. It was as if the priest of Saint Magdalene Church had suddenly found himself in possession of an immense fortune.

He started by buying the lands that lay to the west of the church, or rather purchased them through Marie Denarnaud, for everything was in her name, though it was he who actually paid. On this newly acquired land he built a neo-Gothic villa, which he would name Bethania in honor of Mary Magdalene. Then he had the walls next to the presbytery extended to the edge of the promontory, where he planned to construct a neo-Gothic tower intended to be his library and office and to be called the Magdala Tower, again in honor of the patron saint of the parish. While awaiting the completion of this construction, he continued to reside in the presbytery—now renovated—in the lone company of his faithful servant.

Yet this was not all. Aside from the construction, the priest saw to it that green spaces were planned and arranged. Between Villa Bethania and the Magdala Tower he set up a veritable park, with pools, beds of rare flowers, shaded allées, greenhouses, an orange grove, and even a small zoo. As he was a practical man, he did not neglect to plant a vegetable garden there as well. It was a veritable paradise: "In this domain, which has cost his servant, a poor hat maker, the bagatelle of three million gold francs, the priest, who had arrived fifteen years earlier without a penny to his name, began to live in very grand style."

Of course, he published postcards portraying his domain—photographs in which he liked to appear and which he sold at a profit. Certainly he received Masses and gifts, but nothing that came close to justifying his luxurious daily life.

> He acquired a rich library and a collection of 1,000,000 stamps, brought in a bookbinder and photographer, and bought extremely expensive furniture and tableware. Everything was made to order and, quite often, revealed a taste for luxury that bordered on extravagance. We saw, for example, a service of crystal glasses; Saunière had them manufactured in such a way that when they were struck lightly in a certain order, the glasses played Ave Maria![26]

The priest of Rennes-le-Château also entertained a great deal. His table was open not only to the few colleagues who cared to make the climb up the plateau the better to denigrate his architectural and decorative fantasies, but also to distinguished guests who normally would

---

26. J.-L. Chaumeil, *Le Trésor du triangle d'or*, 109.

hardly be expected to take the trouble to visit the modest priest of a mountain parish. The local populace was not very familiar with those who visited, but many recalled a very beautiful woman who sang magnificently. This was Emma Calvé, of course. "Gentlemen" had also been seen, no doubt writers such as Maurice Leblanc; and artists and painters such as Dujardin-Baumetz, who was also a representative of the Aude in the Chambre des deputés, a Freemason, and temporarily the undersecretary of state for the fine arts. A handsome foreigner was also noted—Jean Orth—but few knew that in reality he was Jean-Salvator of Hapsburg, cousin of the emperor of the Austro-Hungarian empire. He visited quite often and Saunière treated him with great esteem. The two men sometimes held private discussions that lasted for hours, though by all evidence their relationship was based more on business than on friendship. This, however, did not stop Orth from taking part in the fashionable gatherings Saunière organized in Villa Bethania.

For it was in the villa that he received his guests. Marie Denarnaud, a splendid cook, gave orders to some second-rate servants hired for the occasion and prepared savory feasts that allowed the guests to appreciate great French cuisine, especially that of Occitania. We do not know whether Marie Denarnaud might have been seized by the temptation to add a little rat poison to the soup on those evenings when Emma Calvé was visiting. Marie Denarnaud was a modest spirit, entirely devoted to the man in her life and probably completely dominated by his authority, presence, and generosity. She knew when it was necessary to keep her mouth shut and swallow certain resentments that threatened to compromise a situation that, after all, was not so disagreeable. Marie knew well that the soprano would never take up residence there, but she held against Béranger the gifts he gave the singer. Had she heard talk of the large sums of money that Saunière had rained over Emma Calvé, funds that permitted her to buy the castle of her dreams in the Aveyron and (even nastier gossip) to raise the child she had with the priest of Rennes? People are so wicked!

People, of course, lend only to the rich. Bankers also arrived to visit Béranger Saunière. Was it for the loans he asked them to give him or was it to help his "savings" grow? Nasty tongues offered that he fed ladyfingers to his ducks. Regardless of the truth of this, what is certain is that he overlooked nothing when it came to food and drink, as his account book for November 1 testifies: "one cask of Martinique rum in case ABS no. 1031; 45 liters at 2 francs = 90 francs. 50 liters of rum at 2.35 francs (perfect, almost historic, vintage). 33 liters of Haut Barsac white wine. 33 liters of Malvoisie. 17 liters of golden quinine tonic wine. 55 liters of Banyuls. 12 liters of muscatel."[27] It was definitely good to receive an invitation to Monsieur the abbé's during this "Belle Époque."

> But didn't the flashy luxury of their host—who perhaps eased his conscience by thinking of the precious nard that Christ in Bethany had allowed Mary Magdalene to use in anointing his feet—have the scent of scandal to the bishop of Carcassonne, that poor Monsignor Billard, whose previous largesse had opened the doors to Saunière's kingdom? He displayed great discretion and left our priest to his construction and gatherings. Did he think that Saunière had acquitted himself with his tribute to the glory of heaven by restoring his church—his first concern, let's concede him that much—before launching into profane construction? This is very hard to believe, given that the very "Italian Renaissance" style employed by the priest in this instance through the support of a plethora of artisans hired at his own expense lacks discrimination and, more important, any sense of taste.[28]

How could an Austrian archduke, a famous Parisian opera singer, and other important figures tolerate the *visible* work of Béranger Saunière, a strange and disparate work that we might say was struck by the Angel of the Odd?

But times change. Monsignor Billard grew old, and in the last month of his life he was practically powerless. He was replaced on the seat of Carcassonne by Monsignor de Beauséjour, who did not have a reputation for being very tolerant. Assuredly, Saunière must have thought during his nomination in 1902 that this individual was not part of "our" brotherhood. In truth, he would soon learn this at great cost to himself.

---

27. J.-L. Chaumeil, *Le Trésor du triangle d'or,* 109.

28. J. Robin, *Renne le Château, la colline envoûtée,* 27–28.

The first thing a bishop does when he assumes his position in the diocese is to travel through it and see for himself what is working and what is not. Abbé Saunière's behavior did not seem to comply very much with the evangelical teaching of poverty. Monsignor de Beausejour was certainly accustomed to Episcopal palaces that were infinitely more comfortable than rural presbyteries, but all the same, there are limits— and there is a hierarchy. If a simple country priest assumes a grander lifestyle than a bishop, who knows where it might lead to next?

Monsignor de Beauséjour waited until 1905, however, to offer Abbé Saunière a new parish. Saunière bluntly turned it down on the pretext that he could not leave the parish where his interests held him. The bishop insisted and summoned the priest to hear him. Despite several summons, Saunière hid, each time producing phony medical certificates. Then in 1909, realizing the ill will of his subordinate, the bishop named him priest of Coustouge in the Corbières, and rushed an abbé Marty to replace him in Rennes-le-Château. This was a catastrophe for Saunière. He obviously refused his nomination—which was actually a promotion, for his new parish was more important than his earlier parish. It was then that his real hardships began.

Until this point, everything had gone right for Béranger Saunière. From the role of poor priest he had attained a high degree of ease as well as *moral potential* with both his parishioners and the "strangers" with whom he had an unusual relationship. Was he happy? No one knows. He appeared to enjoy an endless stream of peaceful days in the company of his mistress-servant, and from time to time would spend his days with Emma Calvé, who made sure to treat him appropriately as a transfixed lover, as a Beast enamored of his Belle. Emma Calvé belonged to no one man. Instead, she belonged to her public and to that mysterious brotherhood that pulled the strings. How could she consider Béranger anything but a pawn, though a very sympathetic pawn, to be sure—a pawn with Herculean strength, which women like. But Béranger Saunière was only a *pawn* on a chessboard, and the game masters were absent from the visible stage. So we find the priest of Rennes-le-Château in some difficulty. Neither Emma nor those who were behind her lifted a finger to help him. It was up to him to find his way out of his difficulty. After all, when he was ordained a priest, he swore obedience to his bishop.

Saunière was of another stamp, however. He did not have the temperament of a slave. Furthermore, he knew that he held certain documents and certain *secrets*. The problem was that he did not know how to make use of them. He had a veritable nuclear bomb at his disposal, but he did not know the instructions for using it. As a result of opposing Monsignor de Beauséjour, who wished to empty Rennes-le-Chateau of his presence (no doubt the bishop had his reasons), he stepped outside the law—and as everyone knows, "outside of the Church, there is no salvation." Saunière soon had the sad experience of this, and not one of his so-called friends whom he received at his Villa Bethania at such great expense would make any effort on his behalf. To the contrary, they did all they could to sink him and reduce him to nothing. They no longer needed him now, for he had fulfilled the mission that had been intended for him. He was out of service and out of the game. He was thus abandoned. Only the unconditional devotion of Marie Denarnaud saved him from despair.

Monsignor de Beauséjour, bishop of Carcassonne and legal representative of religious authority, being unable to dislodge him from Rennes-le-Château, sought to attack him through his weaknesses. These did not include Marie Denarnaud. That kind of arrangement was so common in the clergy that no one could decently hold it against him, especially given that the situation had not created any scandal among those around him and that Our Holy Mother Church was not besmirched by it. No, the bishop of Carcassonne attacked him there where he was weakest: He accused him openly of selling Masses and indulgences, the equivalent of what was once called simony, from the name of the famous Simon Magus.

The plan behind the accusation was quite simple: Béranger Saunière had undertaken construction work that cost a great deal of money. Let him say *where* and *how* he acquired such significant sums of money at his disposal. We can see that the attack was not a direct one, but was nevertheless one that could not be ignored. The priest had to account for himself before his hierarchical superior.

As the bishop expected, Saunière did not precisely explain himself. He simply presented rows of numbers that meant nothing, for he was incapable of proving the origin of the funds that he attributed to generous donors, an attribution through which he incriminated himself, making himself guilty of canvassing, not only in the diocese but elsewhere as well, for honorariums for Masses. Béranger Saunière, in the eyes of the Episcopal authority, was if not guilty, then at least greatly compromised. All that Monsignor de Beauséjour requested of him was a justification for his extravagant expenditures.

Of course, he clearly felt that Saunière would never be able to justify them. Saunière then came up with a statement whose rough draft we've had in our hands.[29] For the church construction work alone, he admitted 193,000 gold francs. This was a considerable sum. In that time a French ambassador earned only forty thousand francs a year. But Saunière was cheating; examination of his bookkeeping (which he made sure not to include with his statement) showed that he spent fifteen times that amount,[30] which does not include any of the cost of his civil constructions.[31] The bad faith of the Rennes-le-Château clergyman is more than evident here.

Béranger Saunière was thus found guilty. At first he was temporarily *suspens a divinis;* the bishop simply wished to give him a warning and make him accept his new nomination. But as was his right, Saunière made an appeal to the court of Rome, where this kind of affair could drag on for years. In addition, he claimed he could not move out of the Rennes-le-Château presbytery and the municipality sided with him, claiming that the location worked for Saunière and no one else. Apparently the priest of Saint Magdalene Church was well liked by his parishioners, even by those who did not attend church.

In 1913 Béranger Saunière—by occult means, perhaps?—won his

29. Since Saunière's time, the different statements drafted by him—in particular, the paid (and unpaid) bills—have been gathered and published in part in two important parallel works: *Le Fabuleux Trésor de Rennes-le-Château,* by Jacques Rivière (Nice: Éditions Bélisane, 1983) and *Historie du trésor de Rennes-le-Château* by Pierre Jarnac (self-published). These authors dedicated themselves to remarkable investigations, and the results match, taking into account the quite understandable divergences in interpretation. There is no need to repeat their work, which is notable for both its patience and its precision. The photos published in these two books are documents that speak for themselves.
30. I leave it to Jean-Luc Chaumeil to take responsibility for his contention.
31. Jean-Luc Chaumeil, *Le Trésor du triangle d'or,* 110.

case in the court of Rome. Monsignor de Beauséjour returned to the offensive, however, and demanded the priest's obedience. This time, because war had broken out, the atmosphere had changed completely. Suddenly Béranger Saunière was no longer paying his bills and was obliged to borrow money. Nothing was going right anymore. The wicked tongues chimed in, of course, and the figure of the Austrian archduke resurfaced, at least in conversation. The civil authorities suspected Saunière of indulging in espionage and maintaining relations with the enemy. It is obvious that his relationship with the archduke of Austria (since proved to be an absolute fact) constituted a serious charge against him. Saunière was considered an agent who passed information to the central empires. Of course, nothing about his actions has ever been proved—and nothing will ever be proved, for any idea of espionage is now banished from consideration when it comes to the Saunière affair—but it was said that the Magdala Tower served as an observatory for enemy spies and that some of them hid in the "secret chambers" of Villa Bethania.

Thus we next find Saunière in the defendant's chair. In truth, he defended himself so clumsily that he gave credence to every slanderous word said of him. In 1915 he was *suspens a divinis* once and for all, which meant he no longer had the right to exercise his ministerial duties, to perform Mass in public, or to confer the holy sacrament of the Catholic Church. Rennes-le-Château now had a new priest, though one who did not live there. This in no way prevented the townspeople from attending the services that Saunière held in the chapel he had had built beneath Villa Bethania, for the villa, its gardens, and the Magdala Tower were still private property (belonging to Marie Denarnaud) and no one had the right to evict him. The presbytery, with the official complicity of the municipal authorities, was still legally rented to Béranger Saunière and not to the official priest. It was a curious situation.

Here the various serials written about Saunière go in different directions. Some say that Béranger Saunière and Marie Denarnaud traveled across Occitania in search of money, even selling blessed medals to wounded soldiers being treated in hospitals. Others maintain that the priest and his servant hid out in their domain and avoided leaving it too often. Others show Saunière using every means at his disposal in the attempt to have his position in the church officially restored. All concur to say that Béranger and Marie were hounded more and more by their creditors. Fortunately, if we may say so, the war was going on, and the recovering of debts was not the chief concern of the courts. The ex-priest of Saint Magdalene Church in Rennes-le-Château and his loyal servant made it through the storm relatively unscathed.

Since 1914 every family in France had been gripped with great anxiety, for who did not have a friend or relative at the Front? Who did not include in their immediate entourage at least one person "who died for his country"? In Rennes-les Bains, Abbé Boudet was growing old. The tumult of war did not affect him, but his strength was declining. He resigned his post and retired to Axat, home of his family. In 1915, although the war was still going on, the Germans had been momentarily stopped and no one knew what might happen next. Anxiety still ruled, even in these remote rural regions of the Aude, where the war was known only through newspaper articles and the stories of soldiers on furlough, generally the convalescing wounded. In Axat, which was not far from Rennes-le-Château, Abbé Boudet felt his last hour approaching. He summoned Béranger Saunière, who wasted no time in coming to his colleague's side. What did the two of them discuss then? As might be expected, no one witnessed their conversation. On March 30, 1915, Henri Boudet gently left this earth, apparently at peace with God and himself.

It was at this point that Béranger Saunière's fortunes changed dramatically. He abruptly paid off his most pressing debts and reimbursed his suppliers. He regained his taste for life. Now full of hope, he started making ambitious plans. He wished to furnish Rennes-le-Château with a canal system that would bring clean water into every house. He wished to improve living conditions in the village and to build a large tower on the east side of the town that would balance the Magdala Tower and from which he could preach the good word to all those who wished to listen. Of these there would be many, he had no doubt. He put in his orders and made his down payments.

Just what happened to prompt this turnabout? The simplest explanation for this "resurrection" relates to Abbé Boudet. Perhaps before dying he entrusted Saunière with the great secret that the priest was still lacking. Was this secret an inexhaustible treasure or important documents? Calculations can allow us to make brisk progress here: The fact remains that in 1916 Béranger Saunière became again the man he once was—a man of boundless ambition, ready to perform great feats and build things more beautiful than any of his earlier achievements to ensure that he would be remembered for a long time to come. This would be his revenge against Episcopal authority, for while he had quarrels with the bishopric, he had in no way renounced his faith and continued to hold Mass in his chapel, most often in the presence of the faithful of Rennes, who preferred to forgo the official Mass performed by a priest they did not accept. Until the end, Béranger Saunière remained "priest" of Rennes-le-Château.

The year turned to 1917. The war dragged on. The list of those who had died for their country grew longer every day, and soon on the Rennes-le-Château square a monument was erected that had not been on Abbé Saunière's wish list, a memorial to the dead similar to those erected in all the communes of France. Béranger Saunière was now sixty-five and still in fit condition. His powerful build impressed his visitors. He worked on his plans while waiting for the time to realize them concretely. Nevertheless, on January 17 (recall the date on the tombstone of the marquise d'Hautpoul) an illness took him down while he was crossing the threshold of the Magdala Tower, and he never recovered. He was carried into his room in the presbytery, and while Béranger suffered, Marie Denarnaud anxiously sent someone in search of a doctor.

He had known he was ill for some time, but had always pretended otherwise. Several days went by, and then he asked Marie to bring a priest. It was Abbé Rivière, the priest of Couiza, who made the climb to Rennes. He closeted himself in Saunière's room. The confession, or conversation rather, went on for a long time. When the Couiza priest came down from the village, he was pale and livid. It has even been claimed that he remained laid out for a long time before recovering his peace of mind. What frightful secret might his colleague Abbé Saunière have entrusted to his ears? It is also claimed that at the moment of his death, the priest of Rennes-le-Château had uttered this mysterious name in the presence of Doctor Courrent: Jean XXIII. It was also claimed that he received Extreme Unction only conditionally two days after his death, before being buried in the small cemetery bordering the church he had loved so well.

We will never know the truth. The dead take their secrets with them or entrust them to the confessional. Abbé Rivière never said a word about his last conversation with Abbé Saunière, but after the priest's death on the night of January 22, 1917, tongues were wagging at top speed, if only about his funeral arrangements. Through the efforts of Marie Denarnaud, he was allegedly placed on a throne in the large hall of his villa and clad in rich robes sporting crimson tassels. There was a crush of visitors from all over, coming to pay final homage to this exceptional man through whom scandal had arrived in Rennes-le-Château. It was even said that a barouche brought a beautiful woman whose face was concealed behind a black crepe veil—Emma Calvé, of course![32] Following the somewhat pagan ceremony in which the visitors tore the tassels from the robe of the deceased, the townspeople carried Saunière's coffin into the church, his church, where Abbé Rivière officiated. The priest's tomb was erected against the wall of the sanctuary.

When the will of the deceased was read, it was discovered he owned nothing. All his properties were in the name of Marie Denarnaud. As for his bank accounts, no trace of them has ever been found. Marie Denarnaud, trapped in her grief, never left Villa Bethania. She led a sad existence there, living in the memory of Béranger Saunière without ever revealing any of his secrets. It was often said that she repeatedly told the villagers that they were walking on gold. If so, then why did this old woman die destitute in 1953, in such financial difficulties that she was forced to sell her property to Noel Corbu in return for the right to live there the rest of her life? If there had really been gold coins underfoot, she should have been able to profit from them herself. We have to believe that this was not the case, that this web of invention has been so tenacious that it now passes for historical reality.

---

32. Jean-Louis Fournier has done a remarkable job of transferring this to the screen in his television film on F.R. 3, *L'Or du Diable* [Devil's Gold] (1989), based on two novels by Jean-Michel Thibaux. It is fiction, of course, but is no more absurd than all else that has been said and written *seriously* about Béranger Saunière. I would even go so far as to say it is more honest.

Yet there is the Church of Mary Magdalene in Rennes-le-Château. There are Villa Bethania and the Magdala Tower. There is the fact that Béranger Saunière's shadow is present everywhere. Where is the line between truth and fiction to be found in this absurd though highly instructive story?

There is a Saunière myth, but no myth exists that has not been grafted upon an inner reality, even if it difficult to see that reality through the fog of the imaginary. There was a Saunière mystery, no doubt about it. Who, then, was this uncommon individual?

5

Who Was Abbé Saunière?

On June 1, 1967, the vicar general Georges Boyer published a fairly long article in *La Semaine religieuse de Carcassonne* under the title "Clarification and Warning." It includes this particularly notable line:

> For several years our old Razès has periodically become the theater of disappointing searches, impassioned excavations, and sensational publications. The epicenter of this tidal wave is located, appropriately enough, in Rennes-le-Château, where it extends concentrically over Coumesourde, Rennes-les-Bains, the plateau des Fées (Las Brugos), Blanchefort, and Campagne sur Aude—in short, over this Visigothic center rich in history but even richer today in legends and a wealth of apocryphal documents. It is declared unhesitatingly that a treasure is hidden there in an ancient necropolis and that the bishop of Carcassonne knows of the existence of this necropolis but refuses to disclose its secret. . . . The explanation of the fortune—and the expenditures—of a former priest of Rennes-le-Château, Abbé Saunière, who died in 1917, stretches in a rich gamut of assumptions, from the profits of wartime espionage to the discovery of a Visigothic, Cathar, Templar, or royal treasure.

After all, the hunt for treasure is a healthy, if not profitable, diversion, and the work of the imagination—even that of an unbridled imagination—does not justify some kind of warning in a religious weekly, which, by nature, should be peaceable. The quote continues:

146

Until then, it was permissible to smile. But after that point it has
been no longer possible to hold our silence. After a long inquiry we
now have a whole bundle of proof and presumptions.[1] Because the
reputation of our priests is sacred to us, we wish to have it clearly
heard in the preceding that we will not allow them to be attacked
unjustly and will not allow their names to be used for dubious or
commercial ends . . .

It is easy to see that by its very nature the subject is a delicate one.
Whether we like it or not, Abbé Saunière, devoted priest that he was,
now belongs to history, and history belongs to everyone. The main
objective becomes knowing what any given person is trying to prove. In
a display of total bias, anyone can force the facts and documents to
deviate support to one view over the other, depending on whether the
desire is to whitewash Saunière against certain accusations or to exploit
the personality of this unusual priest to the extent of claiming that he
had sold his soul to the devil. We have to accept that confusion reigns
in this domain and that it can be quite difficult to separate the reality
of the events from the sometimes absurd interpretations that have been
made of them. Given, then, that a Saunière "mystery" really exists, an
attempt must be made if not to solve it, then at least to explain it. To
this end, the first thing to do is to learn, based on reliable documents,
just who Abbé Saunière was before legend took hold of him.

Béranger Saunière was a native of the region. This is a reality that
should not be overlooked. He was born in Montazels, near Couiza, on
April 11, 1852. Astrology's devotees would be able to deduce from
this—why haven't they done so already?—that Saunière was an Aries.
The chief characteristic of this sign is a subconscious desire to ram into
obstacles headfirst, even if the consequences can be quite onerous.
Béranger was the eldest son of an honorable family: His father was then
steward for the marquis de Cazemajou and the manager of the castle's
flour mill—that is, he held an important position, especially in that era.

---

1. The bishopric released a portion of the documents from this inquiry, which were subsequently published and analyzed in Jacques Rivière's work *Le Fabuleux Trésor de
Rennes-le-Château* in 1983, and in Pierre Jarnac's book *Histoire du trésor de Rennes-le-
Château* in 1985. These two books form the essential foundation for any objective study
of the case of Abbé Saunière.

The land in the Couiza Valley is rich and well irrigated. The valley is full of pastureland and orchards. The Cazemajous are related to the oldest families of the region and are cousins of the Négri d'Ables. It was a family devoted to the Christian cause and could count many priests and nuns among its members. Consequently, it can be declared that the Saunière family, although commoners, albeit not run-of-the-mill ones, shared the same conditioning. Two of Joseph Saunière's children became priests: Béranger and his younger brother, Alfred.

We should also examine the era during which Saunière grew up. This was the time of the Second Empire. The noble families of the Occitan region and their "supporters" voted en masse for Louis-Napoleon out of fear of the Republicans and especially the Socialists. Here, individuals were Catholic by tradition, principle, and conviction, and those who shared this view could not place any trust in individuals who, under the influence of Jewish bankers and Freemasons of every stripe, were apt to betray the interests of the Church. Following the disaster of 1870, most of those in Occitania were, of course, anti-Communard,[2] praying for the transformation of the young Republic into a monarchy with, at its head, a man worthy of the rank—in this instance, Henri V, count of Chambord and incontestable heir of the *legitimate* line, for in Montazels people were legitimists who believed in the monarchy of divine right and damned the Orleans pretender to Hell. They could not forgive him for being the descendant of Philippe Égalité, a well-known regicide and grand master of the Freemasons during the years that preceded the Revolution. This is why the accusations made concerning Béranger Saunière's membership in a Masonic order are not only ridiculous, but completely unrealistic as well. We know it is the checkerboard pattern of the floor of the Saint Magdalene Church that has given rise to that opinion, but anyone who is a partisan monarchist in favor of the legitimate line is also a fundamentalist Catholic; it could not be otherwise. When Napoleon III drove the pope from his papal states by means of Italian intermediaries, it was quickly explained that the deed was motivated by an agreement between

---

2. [This refers to the Paris Commune that took control of the capital and established a popular government following the debacle of the Franco-Prussian War. The Commune was bloodily suppressed by the Republican government of A. Thiers. —*Translator*]

the former Badinguet[3] and those diabolical Masons who wished to pervert the world. Napoleon III had shown hypocrisy in this matter, for he was, as we know, personally dependent on the Carbonari. It was to conciliate the French Catholics that he pretended to aid the pope. Fortunately, Pope Pious X soon appeared, and without beating around the bush, he condemned all forms of democracy as counter to the designs of God. There were the producers, the warriors, and those who pray. This is the famous Indo-European tripartition that the Middle Ages raised to a position of honor and which corresponds to the Divine Plan. Of course, it is always possible for someone who starts as a producer to become a member of the sacerdotal class. In fact, this is what Béranger and his brother Alfred did.

This is the ambience in which the young Béranger was raised. All his life he would remain loyal to his monarchist convictions, no matter how reactionary or paternalistic they were. It also goes a long way toward explaining the work he wished to accomplish in Rennes-le-Château: A priest must be the engine of society on both the material and the spiritual plane. Why would Béranger Saunière want to be anything else?

In 1874 Béranger entered the large seminary of Carcassonne, where he pursued the appropriate course of study. After his brother Alfred had been ordained, a year earlier, he was ordained a priest in 1879, which illustrates that he had some difficulty making his way through and that he was clearly not of exceptional intelligence. Yet he managed to attain the goal he had set for himself. He was twenty-seven years old and was named Vicar of Alet, with a salary of nine hundred francs a year as established by the law governing the concordat realized between Church and State.

He showed himself to be a devoted priest and never missed a chance to combine his duties with humanitarian actions, by either seeking to give or having others give money to his neediest parishioners. This was a constant with Abbé Saunière: Although he was accused of amassing a fortune, it must be acknowledged that he always planned on using it for others. This is obviously quite a paternalistic tendency, which conforms completely with the behaviors of the aristocratic class of the time. The

---

3. [This is Napoleon III's given name. —*Translator*]

implications of this system are immediately apparent: They maintain the French populace in a state of dependency upon the Church and those who have concluded an alliance with it—in other words, the monarchists and the right-wing Republican parties who were always ready to rally to the Royalist cause. Saunière's attitude, which he shared with a good number of his colleagues, was obviously a result of his education in the shadow of an aristocratic family.

When the priest had some free time, he liked to stroll through the streets of Alet. He was a man of the country with a large build and seemed to exude strength and health. He loved to go out and "take the air," and was always interested in what he might see on his walks. One of his favorite paths led around the ruins of the old cathedral and the remnants of the monastery. He regretted the bygone splendor of the monument and was sorry that Viollet-le-Duc had decided against restoring this edifice in 1862. Saunière could also often be seen before the tomb of the former bishop of Alet, Nicolas Pavillon, the friend of Vincent de Paul, who also gave charity to the poor and had envisioned—extremely rare in his time—both the participation of women in the spreading of the gospel and the education of the rural populace. Saunière often pondered on the example given by the twenty-ninth bishop of Alet, and when he took responsibility for the parish of Rennes-le-Château, he made every attempt to put into practice his vision. Might he have recalled the ambiguous words of the Occitan troubadour Uc de Saint-Circ—words related to a completely different matter—that claimed that it was through Woman that one attained God? Perhaps his thoughts had turned, even at this early age, to the strange figure of Mary Magdalene. After all, it was she to whom the resurrected Jesus turned when he needed someone to bring the news to his disciples.

Over the course of these "archaeological" promenades, Béranger Saunière met an individual who has received scant notice in the whole Rennes-le-Château affair, though he turned the priest's life upside down. This meeting may have been an essential influence in Saunière's life, or at least justification for a part of the work he accomplished. Why has no one pointed out the importance of these meetings in the life of a man as mysterious as Abbé Saunière? This individual was Henri Dujardin-Beaumetz, a painter whose works have not been passed down to posterity, but who himself had a decisive affect on Saunière's activities. He appeared later as a favored guest at Villa Bethania.

Henri Dujardin-Beaumetz was born in 1852. Though an artist by profession, he could not earn a living from his paintings and so entered politics. He became a general councilor for the Aude, after which, in 1889, he was elected deputy. He took an active role in the Chamber of Deputies and later rose to the position of undersecretary of state of fine arts. Dujardin-Beaumetz was a member of the Radical party and, what is of most important consideration here, a die-hard Freemason. It was a curious friendship that linked these two men. One was a monarchist and legitimist ready to fight for the Right, a sincere believer and priest who was scrupulous of his duties; the other was anticlerical, which is not to say atheist—a man who was ready to fight for the Left, a partisan of laity and *combisme*.[4] And yet neither betrayed the friendship, which lasted until the death of Dujardin-Beaumetz in 1910.

What could these two men have found to talk about? They discussed politics, of course, for neither hid his opinions and neither was close to changing his mind, but they also likely discussed art and archaeology as they strolled together through the ruins of the Alet abbey. Saunière was completely ignorant on this subject. Before the modern era, little thought was given in seminaries to developing the artistic sensibilities of future priests. This is the reason why so many village priests have sold beautiful statues at bargain prices to antique dealers and replaced them with the horrible Saint-Sulpician plaster statues that are the disgrace of many sanctuaries. This is why, before the time that buildings were classified and listed as historic monuments, countless priests murdered their churches, transforming sanctuaries of prayer and beauty into conference halls.[5] Béranger Saunière listened to what the painter had to say, and no doubt to his explanations on the very rich and *very symbolic* ornamentation of

---

4. [This was a radical political position based on the ideas of Emil Combes (1835–1921). —*Translator*]

5. I could cite numerous examples of this deplorable ignorance, particularly that of the very pretty parish church of Tiranges (in Haut-Loire) in which the priest (who meant well) called for the Romanesque columns with their capitals to be removed on the pretext that they made it impossible for him to see who was and was not attending Sunday Mass. The witnesses of this transformation are still conspicuous by their absence.

this venerable and neglected sanctuary that quarrymen continued to devastate with the permission of the administration, despite the protests of Dujardin-Beaumetz. No doubt Saunière pondered the great necessity of giving people concrete examples and images of the Christian doctrine, even if these examples sometimes bore an unsettling aspect. As a Freemason, Dujardin-Beaumetz knew such symbolism and taught the young vicar certain keys. This is not a matter for debate.

But a man such as Béranger Saunière does not remain a vicar forever. On June 16, 1882, the new bishop of Carcassonne, Monsignor Felix Billard, named Saunière priest to serve the parish of Le Clat, in the deanery of Axat. This was a village of some 282 inhabitants, perched on the edge of a plateau that looked out over the magnificent landscape of the Sault region. The parishioners were quite poor and supported themselves by breeding mules. This was hardly a desirable posting, but Saunière behaved appropriately, keeping in mind his desire to improve the fate of the populace and leave behind some architectural traces of his passage there. He remained there for three years in great solitude.

It is said that Saunière had a passion for books, but people have refrained from saying *for what books,* and no one has ever been able to discover just what his library held. Surely it held sacred texts and also books in Greek, Latin, and Hebrew. But Saunière was no intellectual; he was instead a man of action—a builder, not a meditater. While in the village in Axat, he probably suffered patiently, knowing that one day or another he would be given a parish worthy of him.

In 1883 important news made its way to Le Clat: Saunière learned of the death of the count of Chambord, who was also Duke of Bordeaux, the legitimate pretender to the throne of France, who was called Henry V by his followers. It is known that his intransigence, his refusal to accept the tricolored flag, and his obvious disdain for the people alienated a portion of those who would otherwise have accepted his return to the throne. Yet he died in exile in Austria, without an heir. From then on the sole pretender of Capet origin was the count of Paris, an Orleans.

We know that during that same year Royalist committees, which were particularly active and benefited from rather anonymous largesse, erected monuments to the memory of the count of Chambord. One of these monuments still exists in Sainte-Anne d'Auray (in Morbihan), in the addition to the basilica that was erected on during 1883 in honor of the patron saint of the Bretons, and which is a characteristic example of the triumphalist and reactionary art—or rather pseudo-art—of the Catholic Church of the end of the nineteenth century. Other famous—and aesthetically horrific—expressions of this style are Sacre-Coeur in Paris; Notre-Dame de Fouvière in Lyon; the new basilica of Ars-sur-Formans (in Ain); the hideous basilica of Notre-Dame de la Salette (in Isère); and the painful-to-see basilica of La Louvesc (in Ardèche). There is also the basilica of the turncoat who remained nonetheless a devoted extremist, Saint Francis-Regis, the "apostle" of the "repentant" Protestants, and, finally, the zenith denounced by all artists and the very pious Grillot de Givry, the basilica of Notre-Dame of Lourdes. The intransigent and reactionary Christianity of Pious X (since canonized for the needs of the cause) was in the midst of a triumph. Its traces can be found in the Dreyfus Affair and in the machinations of Leo Taxil over the Freemasons, as well in the overly famous "Protocols of the Elders of Zion." This fake document, duly recognized as such today, wreaked havoc in earlier fundamentalist milieus and prompted the first manifestations of an anti-Semitism that would eventually lead to the crematory ovens of Nazism (which some intellectuals who today confuse history and ideology deny ever existed).

What characterizes these monuments and churches is not only bad taste, but also something that could be described as a systematic challenge to beauty. Everything in them is ugly, formless, and grandiose, with just a shadow of the image of a bogeyman deity who inspires respect and thus terror. It should be emphasized that Béranger Saunière was a pure product of this era and this tendency. It was his own culture. Because his artistic sensibility was not very developed, he strove to conciliate his ideological views with the advice he was given. This is why it is difficult to blame him entirely for the bad taste that prevails at Rennes-le-Château. His lack of artistic sensibility left him open to influences that included those that completely contradicted his personal positions.

Whatever the truth may be about his intellectual and artistic speculations, Béranger Saunière dreamed of something grandiose. He visualized himself at the head of a new Lourdes, where countless crowds of the faithful would come to worship not him, but the religion he represented.

Unfortunately, Monsignor Billard did not offer him the means to realize his plans. He was discharged from the parish of Le Clat, but in the form of a promotion was offered Rennes-le-Château. It was the tiniest of promotions: He moved from a parish of 282 inhabitants to one of 298.

Was Monsignor Billard trying to get rid of him? The promotion does indeed seem strange. Ordinarily, when someone serving a parish has performed satisfactorily for a certain period of time, he is offered the responsibility of a more important parish where he can bring his talents to a larger number of people. There are cases, however, where a clergyman who served a parish as vicar or priest is named to another parish because he displeased his superiors in one way or another. Such a move is presented as a promotion but in reality is a punishment for certain failed initiatives. The new parish customarily turns out to be extremely poor or stained by some kind of vice, the nature of which is not always very clear.[6] The hierarchy of the Roman Catholic Church wants its spiritual servants to pursue a course that conforms to that which is expected of a priest. Usually, after an apprenticeship—a trial period in a place that is difficult to manage—the newcomer is given a position that suits his aspirations as well as the common good. But it does not seem that this was the case for Béranger Saunière. He found himself in a new parish equivalent to his first, though perhaps more difficult to administer than his previous

---

6. I have personally witnessed a case of this nature. The example with which I am most familiar is that of Abbé Henri Gillard, whom I rightly consider to be my spiritual father. Given his age, and after having fulfilled his duties as vicar in two parishes, where he displeased both the incumbent titleholder of the parish as well as the bishop of Vannes, on whom he depended, he was named rector of Tréhorenteuc (in Morbihan). What was seemingly a promotion turned out to be only a snare because the parish, numbering no more than one hundred inhabitants, was not only the poorest in the diocese but also the most difficult to administer both temporally and spiritually. It was actually known locally as the "chamber pot of the diocese." No need to say that Abbé Gillard met the challenge and transformed this modest parish into one of the most important centers of spiritual and secular pilgrimage currently existing on the peninsula. But it seems, on reflection, that this promotion was actually a punishment for having shown too much independence and spirit of initiative. For more about this, see my introduction to Abbé Gillard's book *Les Mystères de Brocéliande* (Paris: Ploërmel, 1983), which consists of the republication of several pamphlets that Abbé Gillard published while still alive. Personally assembled by him, the book also includes commentaries by Pierre-Jakez Helias, Yann Brekilien, and Charles Le Quintrec.

charge and without the merit of being more prestigious. This state of affairs brings up the problem of Monsignor Billard, bishop of Carcassonne and hierarchical superior of Abbé Saunière. It should be noted that originally only bishops were considered Christ's true heirs and therefore the only ones eligible to give sacrament. It was only during the later development of the Church that the bishops delegated some of their powers to those "charged with the mission" (the actual meaning of the word *curé* [priest]) to fulfill for rural populaces the apostolic work that they, for lack of time, could not fully realize themselves.

This brought Béranger Saunière to Rennes-le-Château. His first impression must have been one of disappointment: It was a hole lost in the middle of a barren mountain. What could he have hoped for from this parish, which then had a reputation for being difficult and hardly "enriching"? Every parish has its good dioceses and its bad dioceses. The reputation of Rennes-le-Château was long-standing: The populace was poor and few in number. The stingy salary allotted by the state took care of the priest's basic needs, but anything else—the repair of the church and the presbytery, for instance—would have to depend on his own efforts. So work he would, while recovering a legacy left by his predecessor and trying to win the support of the local church council, in charge of administering parish property, and the municipal authorities, who are the local sponsors of a state body controlled by the Ministry of Worship.

The poverty of Rennes-le-Château and the state of dilapidation in which he found the church and presbytery determined Béranger Saunière to act. If something needed to be done, he would do it, even if this "something" was out of the ordinary and marginally legal with respect to the laws of that time. When evaluating Abbé Saunière, it is good to recall the unfavorable situation in which he was plunged on his arrival in Rennes-le-Château. His loud and ill-timed stance on the elections did not help matters. Though forced out, he was protected by Monsignor Billard and recovered his position as priest with the reestablishment of his salary, which, as we saw earlier, was suspended for his "failure to maintain his duty to show detachment." To whom did he owe his rapid reintegration after appearing on the blacklist of the Republican regime: the intervention of his friend the Freemason Dujardin-Beaumetz, who was very much in favor in Paris, or that of

Monsignor Billard, his bishop, who could also have a "long arm" at times? No one knows and no document offers answers to this question.

There are, then, the fierce desire he displayed to restore the church; his odd association with Marie Denarnaud; the incomprehensible indulgence of his bishop; the excavations in the church and the discovery of *something;* the defacing of tombs in the cemetery; his wanderings on the stony plateau; the discussions with Abbé Boudet; the confidences he gave and confessions he made to Abbé Gelis; the metamorphosis of the humble country priest into the great feudal lord; his actual achievements in the village; his definite relationships with people foreign to this region; his repeated journeys (all proved except for his trip to Paris); his astoundingly rich lifestyle; his continuous support for monarchist positions; his unsettling and controversial refurbishment of the church; his exchanges with the archduke of Austria, who was known as Jean Orth (this is indisputable); his quarrel with Monsignor de Beauséjour, who succeeded Monsignor Billard to the Carcassonne seat; the accusations of trafficking in Masses that were lodged against him; his clumsy defense of himself; his refusal to explain the true origin of the funds at his disposal; his temporary disgrace and first rehabilitation in the court of Rome; his definitive ouster as *suspens a divinis;* his relentless desire to stay lodged in Rennes-le-Château; his temporary poverty at the beginning of World War I; his return to strength following the death of Abbé Boudet, complete with the display of more grandiose and onerous plans; and finally his death, which was quite sudden, the mystery that hovers over his last moments (did he receive absolution or not?), and the strange attitude of Marie Denarnaud until 1953. All of this raises a number of problems that lie in areas of significant shadow.

Béranger Saunière was a secretive man who was little inclined to sharing confidences, and he managed to convince Marie Denarnaud to keep quiet about him after he had stepped into the beyond. This she did, thereby respecting the wishes of the deceased, to whom she had been, in one way or another, blindly devoted for her entire life. In the photos taken of him (which he subsequently published as postcards and sold at a profit), Saunière liked to strut. He customarily had these pictures of himself and Marie Denaraud taken in front of Villa Bethania, at the Magdala Tower, or in his convoluted gardens. He had pride in his work and showed the assurance of someone who has nothing to lose, even in matters that could prove harmful to him. In a word, Abbé Béranger Saunière was a secretive and discreet man all his life, and one whose deepest reality is difficult to single out. This is why it is important to meticulously scrutinize the areas in shadow. Paradoxically, they may shed light on the personality of Béranger Saunière and give rise to considerations that are completely different from those in the story that was built up around him forty years after his death.

THE SHADOW OF MONSIGNOR BILLARD

Too much emphasis has been placed on the "complicity" that might have united the bishop of Carcassonne and the priest of Rennes-le-Château. It has even been said that while the bishop named him to this hardly glorious posting, it was because he had charged the priest with a secret mission: to find, if not a treasure, then at least documents of priceless value to the Church that were most likely hidden there, probably by Abbé Bigou before his exile to Spain. This explanation of Monsignor Billard's attitude toward Saunière has the advantage of being logical. But why choose Saunière over someone else? Some people maintain that the bishop was acting on orders—but on whose orders? Did he receive them from his archbishop or from the Vatican itself? Minds that are both ingenious and opaque have suggested that Monsignor Billard was acting in the name of a mysterious brotherhood that supervised the Saunière operation. There is no pressing evidence for this explanation, however. It appears normal for the ecclesiastical hierarchy to take an interest in documents concerning the Church, and even to be ready to place these documents in a secure location (for it is not good to publicize everything). Nevertheless, this hypothesis of collusion is a valid one that no more casts doubt on the honesty, good faith, and Christian zeal of Monsignor Billard than it hurls opprobrium on his subordinate Abbé Saunière. To reward Saunière for having succeeded in his mission, it is conceivable that Monsignor Billard would have let the priest act as he saw fit in the renovation of his church and the building of the original structures he had created in his imagination. Yet to do this, the bishop would have had to shut his eyes to Saunière's financial affairs.

It is true that Monsignor Billard always left Saunière free to accomplish whatever he wanted to undertake. While he may have been shocked at the bizarre ornamentation of the church and its surroundings, he never let it show. It seems that he saw in this decoration only the desire of a priest to present something that would distinguish his from neighboring parishes. That is all. There is nothing intrinsically shocking about the devil at the entranceway, for he is depicted in submission, fulfilling a role he detests: holding up a holy water stoup. There is nothing heterodox in this. Indeed, we may wonder how Monsignor Billard might have been able to reproach Saunière for displaying such an eloquent symbol. Whether it is in good taste is another matter entirely—but perhaps the aesthetics of Monsignor Billard matched those of Abbé Saunière.

The argument that Monsignor Billard entrusted Saunière with his mission on behalf of a mysterious brotherhood is based on the fact that following Billard's replacement as the head of the diocese by Monsignor Beauséjour, circumstances changed and Abbé Saunière found himself in the defendant's seat. It is not far to travel from there to claiming that Monsignor Beauséjour was unaware of his predecessor's dealings. Yet there is nothing that prevented Monsignor Beauséjour from sharing the same outlook as his predecessor. In reality, however, during Billard's final years in his post the atmosphere had became too lax. His successor naturally wanted to take things in hand and restore order to the diocese; he was no doubt deeply shocked at Saunière's overly visible display of what was called his fortune. A priest in a diocese owes obedience to his bishop even if he can, in certain cases, take advantage of rights made available through canonical law.

The attitudes of Monsignor Billard and Monsignor Beauséjour appear perfectly comprehensible. Nothing whatsoever gives any basis to the accusation that Monsignor Billard was involved in some kind of weird game. Furthermore, there is not a shred of evidence that he belonged to some sort of brotherhood that worked in the shadows, and it is dishonest to claim otherwise. While Saunière gave his bishop documents that he had discovered in his church—for it is certain that he found some—in doing so he was only fulfilling his duty as a priest. Likewise, Monsignor Billard, by hiding these documents, was only fulfilling his duty as a prelate. All the rest is mere story.

THE SHADOW OF ABBÉ BOUDET

There were definitely numerous contacts and a relationship based on friendship and mutual respect between Abbé Boudet and Abbé Saunière. No one would dream of denying it. But this friendship has been used as the basis of the claim that Abbé Saunière was personally manipulated by the priest of Rennes-les-Bains, who obviously was a member of the mysterious secret brotherhood and the on-site instigator and overseer of Sauniére's searches and achievements. This story is supposedly supported by two pieces of evidence, one of which is perfectly concrete: The first is Abbé Boudet's fondness for archaeology and linguistics, and the publication of his book on the true Celtic language. The second is an unverified assertion that involves Abbé Boudet's account books. Regarding the first assertion: It is incontestable that Abbé Boudet had a lifelong interest in local history and archaeological explorations. These were his passions, even if his efforts were amateurish in the most pejorative sense of the term. Unfortunately—for him and for everyone else—he wrote and published his appalling book on the true Celtic language, the ineptitude or naïveté of which is so enormous that it has fueled the belief that the work was set down in code, in a "language of the birds," to borrow an expression dear to fans of esotericism.

The second piece of evidence would be serious if it could be verified—the conditional is imperative here. It is said that Abbé Boudet's account books indicate that from 1885 to 1901 the priest of Rennes-les-Bains gave Marie Denarnaud the fabulous sum of 3,679,431 gold francs, which would invalidate any discovery of treasure on Saunière's part as well as demolish accusations that he trafficked in Masses. But what would be the reason for such generosity? What secret mission was this fortune intended to support? It is clear that this assertion would lend credibility to the theory of Saunière's "manipulation" as well as the discreet but effective presence of a mysterious brotherhood behind the figure of Boudet, for it is not imaginable for a single second that such a sum could have come from the personal account of a poor country priest. Assertions like this keep perpetuating the story.

Unfortunately, this bit of information is provided only one time and by one man, Pierre Plantard de Saint-Clair in his preface to one of the reprints of Boudet's *La Vraie Langue celtique*.[7] Now Pierre Plantard de Saint-Clair clearly seems to have been, if not the creator, then certainly the one who inspired the story built up around Saunière since 1956. It is hard to take him at his word, especially given that Boudet's papers still exist at the family home in Axat. No one has yet come forward to verify the authenticity of these rather strange "donations."

All of this calls for thought. Henri Boudet was born in Quillan on November 16, 1837. When the vicar of Quillan noted his keen intelligence, he was sent to the seminary of Carcassonne. There he excelled in his studies and obtained a degree in English. He was ordained a priest and served two parishes before being named to the post at Rennes-les-Bains in 1872. He remained there until 1914, when he retired and moved back to Axat to live with his brother, who was a notary. He led a quiet, simple life and left in his parishioners' memories the picture of a good priest who never neglected duties, although he used his free time (of which there was plenty in a country parish!) for archaeological and linguistic work. He was close to his family and never lost touch with his mother and sister. No scandal sheet ever noted any transgressions or the slightest hint of mystery in his past. Abbé Boudet was "certainly not as poor as some have implied. He was born into a petty bourgeois family. His elder brother, Edmond Boudet,[8] was the notary in Axat (in Aude). In the deeds I have viewed, one of which is still in the possession of Boudet's grand-nephew, it can be seen that Abbé Boudet earned substantial revenues from lands he owned jointly with his sister."[9]

Because Henri Boudet's life appeared too simple and clear cut, however, inventions were called for, sometimes at the price of an incredible dishonesty. This accounts for the testimony (false, of course) given by a certain Abbé Courtauly regarding an edition (false, of course) of *Les Pierres gravées du Languedoc,* a collection attributed (falsely, of course)

---

7. Paris: Éditions Belfond, 1978.

8. It is this brother, Edmond, who was the author of the famous map found at the end of *La Vraie Langue celtique*. Edmond Boudet's signature at the bottom of the map has inspired much commentary on the potential wordplay there: It is alleged that it conceals a message.

9. P. Jarnac, *Histoire du trésor de Rennes-le-Château*, 278. If Pierre Jarnac, who consulted the Boudet archives, had found any reference to the famous "gifts" to Marie Denarnaud, he would not have failed to share his discovery.

to Eugène Stublein, a local scholar from the end of the nineteenth century, who was said (falsely, of course) to be an archaeologist. Courtauly did in fact know Saunière and Boudet in his youth. He was an extremely conscientious priest as well as a very original and tireless seeker. He died in his native village close to Limoux in 1964 at the age of seventy-one. In 1966—that is, two years after his death—his alleged preface graced the false collection of *Pierres gravées de Languedoc* and included some outrageous remarks. Here are a few examples:

In 1908 I spent two months at Saunière's home in Rennes-le-Château. I was barely eighteen. It was a splendid location but extremely drafty. Saunière was remarkable. With his help I completed a small painting in the Rennes's church.[10]

There was a big fuss with Boudet. He left Rennes-les-Bains in May, 1914. He had had some problems with the bishopric. . . .[11] His manuscripts were destroyed before his eyes, his book *Lazarus* was burned.[12]

Abbé Rescanière, diocesian missionary, took over as priest of Rennes-les-Bains in May, 1914. He tried to shed some light on the Boudet-Saunière matter, but one Monday, toward one or two in the morning—it was February 1, 1915—he received two visitors no trace of whom has been found since. That morning he was found dead, still dressed, lying on the floor.[13]

But there is more.

---

10. Courtauly did in fact help Saunière restore the painting of Mary Magdalene beneath the high altar.

11. This is false. Aged and weary, Abbé Boudet was only thinking of retiring.

12. False. Boudet never wrote *Lazarus* and his manuscripts were never destroyed or burned. But in order to make the story exciting, there is a great need to make an allusion to the Holy Inquisition, which, although long vanished, remains unfailingly present in everybody's mind.

13. In reality he died of a heart attack, but this was too prosaic a detail for a sensational story.

Boudet, depressed, was in Axat; he decided to write the bishopric on March 26, 1915, about Rescanière,[14] but when the delegate from the bishopric arrived on Tuesday, March 30, 1915, Abbé Boudet had just died a very painful death. Over the course of the day he had received a visit from two men.

With this excerpt we are definitely in the middle of a mystery novel, or a "whodunit." During the Middle Ages, people would have concluded that these two men, obviously in black, were devils sent by Satan. Here, the preference is to say nothing about them, implying that they belonged to that mysterious brotherhood, or even a rival group that wished to take possession of secrets held by the clergymen. It seems that the author was inspired by the actual murder of Abbé Gelis some twenty years earlier. Why not embroider on the theme and accuse Saunière of it, if need be? Wasn't it true that after Boudet's death Saunière, who had been experiencing financial difficulties, was suddenly solvent and launching new projects? All is contrived as if someone wished to besmirch Saunière and Boudet for the obvious purpose of increasing the aura of mystery hovering over Rennes-le-Château.[15]

What can be salvaged from all of this? The answer is simple: *Nothing.* Abbé Henri Boudet and Abbé Béranger Saunière were two colleagues and neighbors who found agreement on many points, particularly on the very legitimate love they each felt for their native region, a place they wished, each in his own fashion, to praise and make known as widely as possible. Saunière leaned toward the visible monuments and construction that had the power to attract a large crowd of pilgrims. Boudet worked more in silence, preferring to present his praise in the form of a book, which contributed to available information about the Razès. From the documents at our disposal, *nothing* confirms that Abbé Henri Boudet was the inspirer of Abbé Béranger Saunière, whom he is said to have paid for some kind of mission on the command of a string-pulling, ghostly brotherhood in some kind of

---

14. There is no trace of this letter.

15. For the details concerning this manipulation and the role Abbé Courtauly was—unwillingly—made to play in the basest of circumstances, see P. Jarnac, *Histoire du trésor de Rennes-le-Château,* 268–78.

game. To those who tell the story, it is a game in which no one knows who is who or what anyone's deep and true motives are, just as in the Gothic novels of English authors at the end of the eighteenth century. The shadow of Abbé Boudet, while it exists over Saunière and Rennes-le-Château, has nothing unsettling or diabolical about it—too bad for the purposes of fiction, but that is simply how it is.

THE SHADOW OF THE COUNT OF CHAMBORD

Following his "exile" in the small seminary of Narbonne under the circumstances discussed earlier, Abbé Saunière regained possession of the parish of Rennes-le-Château on July 1, 1886, with, if I can put it this way, three thousand gold francs in his pocket, donated to him by the countess of Chambord. She was the widow of the self-styled Henri V, legitimate pretender to the throne of France, who, through his shilly-shallying and his reactionary intransigence had caused the failure of every attempt to restore the Capet-Bourbons. It is probable that this pseudo–Henri V—whose old statue is currently rusting at the bend of the road from Sainte-Anne d'Auray to Brech, in front of the monstrous basilica erected to the glory of the Breton patron saint (what is a Capet-Bourbon doing mixed up in Breton affairs?)—this king without a crown who pompously called himself Count of Chambord and Duke of Bordeaux, was a colorless figure of no breadth. Nevertheless, the count of Chambord, whatever he was really like, represented something for Abbé Saunière, who had been piously and monarchistically raised in a family of bourgeois peasants pledged to the gloomy clericalism of the aristocrats at the end of the nineteenth century.

Gloomy clericalism is the exact term for these circumstances. After the debacle of 1870, for which the usurper Badinguet, alias Napoleon III, was held responsible, it was necessary in the milieus that claimed to represent the French elite to regild the arms of this poor France delivered into the hands of the Reds—and to exact payment for the regicide of Louis XVI and the abandonment of the country to the Freemasons, who protected Napoleon Bonaparte, a worthy heir to the Revolution.[16] The

---

16. Napoleon Bonaparte was not himself a Freemason, but his brother Lucien was. It is known that it was Lucien who "created" the emperor on 18 Brumaire, with the help of all the lodges of France and Navarre and the complicity of the European lodges.

monarchist faction that still hoped to govern France drew its support from a papacy that was more antipopulist and reactionary than any other in history. The pope did all he could to correct the situation of "this Eldest Daughter of the church," who had cowardly betrayed her mission. None of this is offered as a joke; this was the actual social, political, and religious reality of France at the end of the nineteenth century—a France from which the territories of Alsace-Lorraine had been amputated. There had been the ignominious defeat at Sedan. There had been the capitulation of the emperor-usurper (whom the "Royalists" had been happy to support once upon a time). There had been the Commune and the terrible threat it had posed to French society. There had been warnings from Heaven: The Virgin Mary had already warned the French of the dreadful fate awaiting them if they succumbed to the satanic charms of Republicanism, and especially democracy, which were the worst snares of the devil. In 1846, in Salette-Fallavaux, a commune of the Isère department in the Grenoble diocese, the Virgin appeared to two children who were shepherds, Maximin Giraud (who later retracted his story before the priest of Ars, and who ended his life as an alcoholic) and Melanie Calvat, cousin of the soprano Emma Calvé, the so-called mistress of Béranger Saunière. Calvé was the real mistress of a certain number of known esotericists and Satanists, including the famous Jules Bois.

The name Fallavaux means "false valley," or even "vale of lies." Could this be telling? During the course of a later trial in which she was defended by the Freemason lawyer Camille Pelletan, a future cabinet minister and exalted aristocrat named Constance de Lamerlière was "recognized" as the author of these apparitions. There is nothing dubious about this contention. Constance de Lamerlière had indeed acted on the orders of the legitimist and fundamentalist monarchist fringe that was then infiltrating French society and seeking to restore the Ancien Régime. It is said that the ends justify all means, even deceit. A century later, when Pope John XXIII, who was far from being stupid, became aware of the "third secret" of the Salette, which was divulged only after a long period of time, he declared that it was a monument of stupidities.[17]

---

17. [In September 1846 the Virgin Mary was said to have appeared to two children, Maximin Giraud and Melanie Calvat, at La Salette, France. She was said to have given them secret prophecies, including the restoration of the Catholic faith in Protestant countries. —*Translator*]

The aim of the Salette operation was to terrorize the faithful, even if doing so required manipulation and staging.[18] The legitimist, fundamentalist, monarchist fringe thought it worth their while to lay it on a bit thick following the tragic events of the Franco-Prussian War in 1870. Their plan referred back to the Paray-le-Monial (Saône-et-Loire) affair, where on June 16, 1671, two centuries earlier, a nun named Sister Mary Margaret had a vision of Christ coming toward her. His heart was bleeding and he told her that France would be saved from its enemies only by dedicating itself entirely to the Sacred Heart of Jesus. The defeat of the French, the rise of unionization, the first penetrations of Marxist doctrines, and especially the temptation gripping certain Christians to support social democracy[19] would all lead to an extraordinary reaction orchestrated by representatives of the legitimist pretender.

After this, Paray-le-Monial became the very core of a new form of religion, a *nationalist* religion whose refrain can be found in the famous canticle "Save, save France, in the name of the Sacred Heart . . ." Paray-le-Monial was in the provinces, however,[20] and it became necessary to expand this worship of the Sacred Heart (and its legitimate monarchy) into other regions, mainly Paris, for thanks to the slaughter of Adolph Thiers, Providence had permitted the French capital to escape from the odious Commune inspired by the devil, or at least his usual henchmen, the communists and socialists (who read the Gospel according to "Saint" Marx in preference to the other four canonical scriptures). In this instance, it was deemed appropriate to dominate Paris with a monument. Thus was erected Sacré-Coeur, that papier-mâché basilica, like a giant wedding cake on the hill of Montmartre. But who would fund this basilica? Why, the faithful of course, through a skillfully organized

---

18. This in no way prevents la Sallette from currently being a place of frequent pilgrimage, and *from making a profit* (one of the primary virtues of a pilgrimage site). It seems that the more deceits are denounced, the greater the success of such a place.

19. This prompted the birth of the Sillon movement in France, inspired by Marc Sangnier. Not surprisingly, it was condemned by the pope before going on to become the core of the Christian Democrat party.

20. Currently Paray-le-Monial is experiencing increased activity not only because of traditional pilgrimages, but even more because of the concentration there of fundamentalist groups of fairly obscure purpose and members of the "charismatic" movement, whose true objectives and somewhat secretive financing are no clearer.

subscription drive, but Monsignor the count of Chambord, who bestowed 500,000 gold francs on this undertaking while his supporters traveled throughout France, repeating everywhere that "France will be saved from its enemies only by devoting itself entirely to the Sacré-Coeur."

Now in 1885, two years after the death of the count of Chambord, Béranger Saunière returned to Rennes-le-Château with three thousand gold francs that were a gift from the countess of Chambord. It was quite a small gift in comparison to the 500,000 francs donated for the Sacré-Coeur of Paris, *but is very revealing both of Saunière's intentions and of what certain fundamentalist milieus expected of him.* Keeping in mind the proportions, the comparison is worth making. Funding for the Sacré-Coeur would be covered by the sale of postcards for the more modest subscribers and by direct appeal for donations from wealthy individuals and associations. Now what did Béranger Saunière do? "We have here the model used later, but in more modest fashion, by the priest Béranger Saunière to build his various constructions and fund his restorations."[21] It is quite certain that the sincerely fundamentalist and legitimist Saunière remembered all this. He sought to turn Rennes-le-Château into a pilgrimage site and a place of grandeur.

> In Rennes the large bas-relief of the church, placed there in 1897, is of Christ with a Sacred Heart, like the statue placed on Villa Bethania in 1902. The obsession in 1885 had been the freeing of France from the Republic but we saw the outcome of the elections in the Aude: to deliver France through penitence[22] would also be the sense of *his Mission*.[23]

Instead of embroidering esoteric themes about Abbé Saunière, it would be better to place him and his convictions in the very context in which it is possible to explain him: that very distinctive context of the beginning of the Third Republic, with its openly expressed monarchis-

---

21. J. Rivière, *Le Fabuleux Trésor de Rennes-le-Château*, 57.

22. Do not forget that Saunière had had "penitence, penitence" carved beneath the statue of Our Lady of Lourdes placed upon the upside-down "Visigothic" pillar—a testament to the Mission of 1891.

23. J. Rivière, *Le Fabuleux Trésor de Rennes-le-Château*, 57.

tic tendencies and the intolerance of Rome toward the innovations and transformations of traditional society. Without this, Béranger Saunière cannot be explained. This shows how much stronger the shadow of the count of Chambord loomed over Rennes-le-Château.

The problem lies in knowing how Saunière was able to establish contact with the widow of the pretender to the throne of France and, next, how he maintained his close connections with the monarchist and fundamentalist milieus. Here a new shadow emerges, that of his brother, Alfred Saunière.

THE SHADOW OF ALFRED SAUNIÈRE

Béranger's younger brother, Alfred, certainly had a greater gift for learning than he himself did. He became a priest before his elder brother and, what is more, with the Jesuits, who are known for their elitism and insistence on accepting into their order only those with a strong intellect. But while Alfred Saunière may have been blessed with intellectual gifts, he was much less well endowed when it came to those regarding the priesthood. He quickly became the talk of the town for the scandalous liaisons he arrogantly exhibited, which gave rise to the assertion—as Béranger recognized in a letter to his bishop during his trial—that the priest of Rennes-le-Château quite often ended up paying the penalty for the misdeeds of his younger brother.

While Béranger did pay for his brother, however, it was tit for tat, for his brother, it seems, facilitated his labor on many occasions. While Béranger was only a modest country priest, Alfred was a "gentleman," an honorable reverend father with great standing in the high society of that era, a brilliant debater and man of the world who was quite attractive to women. It so happens that during this time (the end of the nineteenth century), though women may not yet have won the right to vote, in intellectual and aristocratic circles especially they still played a deciding role through their counsels as well by the connections they made among members of this worldly society in which they often figured as muses.

Alfred did introduce his brother to a certain Marquise of Bozas. At that time Alfred was, according to the standard expression, her "latest conquest." He had good relationships with those in high society, in an era when sponsorship of good works was regarded positively, as was regularly attending religious services with great pomp and ceremony. Having a lover, selected from among artists, intellectuals in good standing, or even the clergy worthy of frequenting, was also socially acceptable. This represents a certain corruption of society, but the era lent itself to that magnificently. The end of the nineteenth century and the beginning of the twentieth was a time when good bourgeois Catholics would weep hot tears every time a singer bemoaned the misfortunes of young girls condemned to prostitution, but who at the same time relegated their maids to garrets with no heat or running water, of course leaving them exposed to the temptations offered by all kinds of rogues.

Although fully aware that the "good" society of his time was rotten, this did not stop Béranger Saunière from profiting from it and from asking his brother for introductions to environments he would never have dared venture into on his own. It is during this period of Saunière's life that he solicited certain well-off families for donations that could help him restore his modest church and transform his parish into a sanctuary that would draw hundreds of pilgrims. His was not a vision of another Sacré-Coeur. Others could take care of that. For Béranger it was enough to exploit Saint Magdalene, the Mary Magdalene who makes such a brief and mysterious appearance in the Gospels. This is what would attract crowds and fill the vaults. It is certain that the alliance between Béranger and his brother was at play in the background during 1885–1905. Alfred revealed himself to be an excellent "proxy." Later, when Béranger Saunière explained to his bishop about the gifts he had received, he had to keep quiet about some of them. "High" society appreciates discretion.

It can be certain that Alfred Saunière served as intermediary between Béranger and the countess of Chambord. It is infinitely likely that Alfred was also responsible for introducing Béranger to certain scenes that gladly described themselves as esoteric—not necessarily Parisian circles, but ones that nonetheless wielded great influence on the political and religious planes. This would explain the alleged relationship between Béranger and the occultists grouped around Jules Bois and Claude Debussy.

A valuable clue is provided by the duties held by Alfred Saunière in the Chefdebien family of Zagarriga. He was in fact the tutor to this noble family and was forced from his position because of an indiscretion about which nothing is known. Yet Alfred's sojourn with the Chefdebien family clearly appears to have been the cornerstone on which the

Saunière myth was constructed. But who, in fact, is the Chefdebien family? The name is no doubt the Frenchification of a Breton name. It is the translation of Penmad, which is the name of a Breton family exiled to Narbonne in the eighteenth century for unspecified reasons. What we do know for certain is that the head of the family, the marquis of Chefdebien, was in his time a Freemason of high degree.

> The marquis, an honored counselor of the Scottish Directory of Septimania, would have dutifully frequented the Lodges of the Rhine area, when he was in garrison at Strasbourg, and had published in 1770 a *History of Masonry*. But literature, even esoteric, was not the sole domain in which he produced a creative work. With his father, the viscount of Chefdebien of Aigrefeuille, he founded in 1780 a new rite, the original Rite of France, which had its seat in the Philadelphia Lodge of Narbonne. At the famous Masonic convent of Wilhemsbad he defended the theory according to which the Templar Order still existed in secret, its leaders being none other than the famous "Unknown Superiors" who allegedly guide the destiny of Freemasonry. He hoped that these occult directors, keepers of alchemical recipes to which the medieval Templars owed their immense wealth, would agree to forming a relationship with the Masons that would attempt to resurrect the association in the secrecy of the Lodges.[24]

So here it is. It took a long time for the connection to be made between Abbé Béranger Saunière and a "mysterious brotherhood" more or less linked to the Templar Order. Others would remember it later, after Abbé Saunière was dead and buried, which shows that these bits of information cannot be absolutely confirmed. Nevertheless, it remains a fact that standing behind Abbé Saunière are the unsettling shadows of these secret societies, the heirs, more or less, of the Bavarian Illuminati and the Angelic Society, which developed over the eighteenth century in parallel (and in shared understanding) with Freemasonry. These societies picked up considerable steam in the nineteenth century,

---

24. J. Robin, *Rennes-le-Château: la colline envoûtée*, 60–61.

mainly with the Romantics, and had their crowning successes around 1900 with the triumph of the Rose+Cross and the Theosophical Society, not to mention the many sects whose hierophants were such individuals as Jules Bois, Stanislas de Guaita, Claude Debussy, and Maurice Maeterlinck, and whose great idolized priestesses were Annie Besant, Renée Vivien, and Emma Calvé after the models of Velleda and the druidesses of the Île de Sein. These models were revised and corrected by the symbolist and decadent poets as well as by painters such as Gustave Moreau and those of the Vienna school who sought to restore to women their roles as revealer and initiator. The figure of Emma Calvé emerges directly from this vision, but the demiurge was Alfred Saunière through his relationship to the Chefdebien family as well as to other families equally committed to this fin-de-siècle style of hermeticism, occultism, and esotericism.

Alfred Saunière, who no doubt wished to know more than he should of the secrets of those families he frequented, was a hunted and persecuted man all his life. He incurred the wrath of his superiors and was excluded from the Company of Jesus.[25] He was also eventually excluded from the families he had exploited and despoiled for his intellectual and financial benefit and found himself more or less defrocked in Montazels, living in a common-law relationship with a certain Marie-Emilie Salière. He died there in 1905, leaving few behind to mourn his passing. This may perhaps explain the letter Béranger Saunière sent his bishop, Monsignor de Beauséjour, in which he complained of being made to pay for the sins of his brother. "The priest of Rennes-le-Château is expected to atone for the sins of his brother, who died too soon."

That is a bizarre way of putting it: "died too soon." This expression is quite ambiguous. Had Alfred died before he was able to explain his true attitude and motives? Or else should we read it to mean that Béranger was nothing without his brother, Alfred? We cannot answer these questions. The letter contributes little to shedding any light upon the shadow of Alfred Saunière that continues to hover over his brother, the priest of Rennes-le-Château.

---

25. [The Company of Jesus refers to the Jesuit Order. —*Translator*]

THE SHADOW OF EMMA CALVÉ

Of all that has been said about Abbé Saunière, his "liaison" with the great opera singer Emma Calvé is not the smallest of contributions to the construction of a fine love story set against a backdrop of espionage or manipulation. Yet however necessary this relationship may be to the invention of a good story, it is necessary to know whether it might actually have corresponded to Béranger Saunière's real life.

In fact, *there is not a single shred of proof concerning any liaison between Emma Calvé and Béranger Saunière.* The entire assumption is based on that famous trip to Paris he allegedly made following his discovery of the parchments inside a hollow pillar of the altar in the church of Rennes-le-Château. Yet no one is even capable of providing the specific year in which he made this journey. Was it in 1888, 1891, or 1893? The truth is that *there is also a lack of any evidence for Béranger Saunière ever making this trip to Paris.*

Actually, it is not all that absurd that Saunère might have traveled to Paris to have Church authorities examine the documents that resisted his comprehension. It would be logical, that is, if pains had not been taken to add the anecdote about Monsignor Billard commissioning the priest to make the journey, giving him the letter of recommendation addressed to Abbé Bieil, and paying the travel and expertise expenses out of his own pocket. As bishop of Carcassonne, Monsignor Billard would have had access to other means of investigating these parchments—unless, of course, we accept the ridiculous theory that the bishop belonged, either tangentially or directly, to the invisible brotherhood.

Let's assume, however, that out of curiosity, the bishop of Carcassonne authorized his subordinate to show these parchments to some specialists. Why would he send Saunière to the director of the seminary of Saint-Sulpice and his entourage rather than to a paleographic archivist who could translate and transcribe the text and share his observations? Would Monsignor Billard *and Béranger Saunière* have distrusted a paleographic archivist, even one who shared monarchist and Catholic opinions? If this were the case, then we must also assume that the two clergymen already knew, at least generally or broadly, what the manuscripts contained. It can be seen that by following this line of reason we will inevitably be forced to accept the existence of a secret society that did not want certain documents to go astray or end up in the hands of those who were not members of the brotherhood.

Let's assume a certain naïveté on the part of Monsignor Billard and Abbé Saunière. Let's assume that this journey actually took place and was paid for through Saunière's agreement to return with *three* parchments instead of four. It seems that there would be some traces of this journey, whether at the bishopric of Carcassonne, in Sauniére's personal papers, or in the works of the celebrities introduced to Saunière. Yet there is no such trace.

Some, of course, will raise the objection that the bishopric of Carcassonne is under no obligation to present all the files from this dossier, that Saunière had no need to mention his journey in his records (even though he kept excellent records of everything he did), and that because the people he met in Paris were naturally inclined to secrecy, it is normal that they should leave no trace of this trip. *All of this is handy reasoning when someone wants to make up a portion of a story.*

The sole elements that lend credence to Saunière's trip to Paris and his encounters there with the group of intellectuals who gravitated around Jules Bois are certain novels by Maurice Leblanc and Jules Verne's *Clovis Dardentor.* No one has ever claimed, however, that Béranger Saunière met Maurice Leblanc or Georgette Leblanc and Maurice Maeterlinck. *Pelléas et Mélisande* is certainly a "Merovingian" drama. It is certainly a symbolist work that is extremely rich symbolically and even strongly initiatory. But it is going a bit far to consider this major work to have been inspired by the Saunière affair, even if Béranger is viewed as Pelléas (the Fisher King from the Grail Romances), Jules Bois is seen as Golaud (the cuckold), and Emma Calvé is cast as Mélisande, a role that she nevertheless would have interpreted brilliantly. Maeterlinck and Debussy, whose work was thoroughly permeated by this fin-de-siècle hermeticism, gave *Pelléas et Mélisande* the full power of their genius. But did they really need the unfortunate Saunière to reach this point?

Clearly, novels such as *L'Aiguille creuse* [The Hollow Needle] and *L'Île aux trente cercueils* [The Isle of Thirty Coffins] by Maurice Leblanc have plots that can appear unsettling when we know the story built up around Abbé Saunière. *L'Aiguille creuse* involves the treasure of the kings of France that is supposedly hidden somewhere near Fécamp in a cliff that can be found only by completing an entire initiatory journey full of pitfalls. *L'Île aux trente cercueils* goes even further, involving the Secret of Secrets, a sort of philosopher's stone (or kind of Grail) of Bohemian kings that can bestow power and glory and which greatly interests an adventurer who claims to be of royal blood. Fortunately, Arsène Lupin, a gentleman thief but also a good and gallant Frenchman, appears on the scene to reestablish order to a certain degree and see that the guilty get their just desserts. All of Arsène Lupin's adventures revolve around this same theme, which, if you think about it, is no less than that of the quest for the Holy Grail in all its shapes and forms, including the variation of *sangreal,* or "royal blood." The literary, artistic, and esoteric circles frequented by Maurice Leblanc had a passion for Wagner and were particularly obsessed with *Parzifal.* This is no secret to anyone.

The correspondences between the Renne-le-Château affair and Jules Verne's novel *Clovis Dardentor* are much more intriguing. The so-called North African country described by Verne is a camouflaged Razès, and the name of its capital, Bugarach, is significant. We know that Verne was a member of a more or less secret "brotherhood" similar to the Rose+Cross and the Masons, but not even those who have created the story of Abbé Saunière claim that he met Jules Verne during his stay in Paris. In reality, Jules Verne had no need of Béranger Saunière to be familiar with the Razès and Rennes-le-Château. He had already visited the area *and, while there, was made aware of certain local traditions concerning a lost treasure.* This fact indicates that Abbé Saunière had no need to go to Paris to learn that astounding claims were made about a very ancient hoard hidden somewhere in a cave or even a tomb near Rennes-le-Château. It was even Punchinello's secret.

Neither Maurice Leblanc nor Jules Verne needed to rely on Béranger Saunière to construct his fictional intrigues. To the contrary, it has been the far more recent creators of the Saunière story who have had to rifle through not only the basement level of Rennes-le-Château but also the novels of Maurice Leblanc and Jules Verne to lend weight—and letters of nobility—to their fictional narrative. After all, why couldn't it be assumed that Abbé Saunière read—and appreciated in every sense of the word—Jules Verne's *Clovis Dardentor?* This may in fact have been where he discovered the famous "key" that allowed him to find, if not the treasure, then *something*. It is hard to see what useful purpose was met by introducing into the story Émile Hoffet, Abbé Bieil, Jules Bois, Claude Debussy, or, least of all, Emma Calvé. It can be definitively stated that the beautiful soprano was never recognized in Rennes-le-Château during those times when Béranger Saunière was treating his guests in a lordly manner. There were more than enough beautiful wives of notaries and doctors in the region around Dujardin-Beaumetz.

Emma Calvé's shadow over Saunière's head is definitely nothing more than an airy phantom that the slightest wind could dissipate and destroy.

THE SHADOW OF JEAN ORTH

There was one fairly mysterious figure lurking around Abbé Sauniére. He had been labeled the Foreigner but called himself Guillaume. There is no doubt that this was John-Salvator of Hapsburg, son of Leopold II, imperial prince of Austria, royal prince of Bohemia and Hungary, and grand duke of Tuscany. Proof of this is provided by police documents, for as Pierre Jarnac notes, the abbé, who was a fundamentalist monarchist from the time of his arrival in Rennes-le-Château, had become the pet hate of Doctor Espezel of Espéranza, who was a fervent Republican, Freemason, and anticleric. He never missed an opportunity to denounce any of the priest's activities that appeared bizarre to him. It so happened that the presence of the Foreigner excited Doctor Espezel's curiosity, which led to a police inquiry. Their investigation quickly revealed his true identity, which they transmitted to the Deuxième Bureau,[26] as was called for in such cases. These visits occurred in 1888, 1889, and 1890. But never again after that time.

In fact, because of his profound disagreement with Emperor Franz-Joseph, John-Salvator of Hapsburg eventually renounced his titles and even his Austrian nationality. He had become a simple citizen by the name of Jean Orth, borrowed from the name of one of his castles. In 1890 he set off on a long journey from which he never returned (though

---

26. [This was the name of the intelligence service of that era in France. —*Translator*]

this does not mean that he lost his life). It is certain that Orth came to Rennes-le-Château for three years in succession and spent time with Abbé Saunière. The archduke's shadow is thus perfectly real.

Of course, the authorities very politely asked Jean Orth to explain the reasons for his sojourn. They had a right to know just what a representative of one of the most illustrious Europeans families—even one who had renounced his title—was doing in one of the most underprivileged regions of the Aude department.

> He claimed that while traveling from Italy and Spain, chance had led him to Couiza. There he took the wrong road, which fortuitously led him to Rennes, where he had been introduced to Abbé Saunière. He was traveling incognito, he told them, in search of a refuge for himself and his family.[27]

His answer held up and he was allowed to come and go as he pleased.

We can question, however, the famous stroke of luck that brought the archduke to Saunière's presbytery, just as we might question how the countess of Chambord—an Austrian, in fact!—knew of this modest parish priest and sent him three thousand gold francs for his good works. Chance does not explain everything; it is obvious that if the fallen archduke came to Rennes-le-Château, he had a valid reason for doing so.

But raising these questions is not the same as answering them. The mysterious shadow cast by Jean Orth keenly excited people's imagination, at first because the locals had trouble understanding what business a lordly gentleman had in their town. By 1914, when the war broke out, a fairly long time had elapsed since the archduke had disappeared,[28] yet the memory he had left behind had not faded. Tongues began to wag about the odd relationship that brought together the priest and an Austrian (thus enemy) prince. From such a place it was only a small step to accusing Saunière of being a spy in the pay of the

---

27. P. Jarnac, *Histoire du trésor de Rennes-le-Château*, 355.

28. One tradition, which has nothing to do with Rennes-le-Château, claims that Jean Orth took advantage of a shipwreck to disappear and build a new life under another name in America. Why not? For more on this subject, see Maurice Paléologue, *Le Destin mystérieux d'un archiduc: Jean Orth* (Paris, 1959).

Central Empire. It can hardly be doubted that Doctor Espezel was among those who howled this charge the loudest. It was said that the Magdala Tower had been built to support artillery. But what would this artillery fire upon? It was rumored that Saunière had received enormous sums of money for selling information to the Kaiser and the Austrian emperor, which would explain his expenditures. Yet no one wondered just what the priest might have been spying on in this remote region with no military value. Some suggested that Saunière provided a safe house where German or Austrian spies could find shelter, passing as artists—painters, in particular. Clearly the sumptuous feasts of Villa Bethania had not been forgotten!

So it was the shadow of Jean Orth that was responsible for the charges of espionage so readily hurled against Abbé Saunière. It must be admitted that with all his more or less clandestine travels, Béranger exposed himself to his critics and excited imaginations. When he took the train to Couiza, he did so simply to go on to Carcassonne, and from there to Perpignan. But while we know on reliable authority that at least one of his banks, the Veuve Auriol et ses fils, was in Perpignan, it is just as easy to believe that he used his visits there to go farther. Perpignan was an important transit center that would have allowed him access to any destination he chose. In fact, thanks to documents published by the archivist René Descadeillas, we know that Saunière visited affluent and charitable individuals in the regions of Narbonne and Béziers to solicit donations. Nothing about this is mysterious, however, although according to certain testimonies, it appears he may have visited London twice.[29] Now, while these accusations of espionage may now be laughable, during World War I they gave rise to harsh criticism, which must have contributed to the disgrace that struck the priest of the Saint Magdalene Church of Rennes-le-Château when he was tried by his bishop for canonical infractions. Béranger Saunière's behavior,

---

29. This detail comes from a confidence of Marie Denarnaud. P. Jarnac's *Histoire du trésor de Rennes-le-Château* (page 356) gives a detailed list of the periods of time when Saunière could not fulfill his duties to the parish, which of course suggests that he was absent. The list shows many such examples until 1909. Jarnac takes pains to note, however, that those periods during which he did not perform services (baptisms, marriages, funerals) were not necessarily times of absence; though if he was away, it could only have been during these times.

which many found incomprehensible, would easily have caused him problems, but did so especially during wartime.[30]

In any case, the relationship between Jean Orth and Abbé Saunière was a business relationship, according to all the evidence. The archduke's visits corresponded to the years when Saunière was making his first discoveries. No doubt he sold some objects to Jean Orth. *But if this was the case, might they not have been objects connected to Austria?* Of course, nothing is known about these objects. Were they jewels? There was talk of a crown—could it have been a royal or imperial crown that once belonged to the Hapsburgs? Why not? The objects Saunière found in his church were those hidden in the church by Abbé Bigou before he went into exile—surely objects belonging to the Hautpoul family. It is known, however, that there was a connection between the Hautpouls and Austria. Perhaps the objects were important documents that the Austrian family needed to take back into their possession. No one knows for sure, which means that everything is imaginable. People have even gone so far as to speak of a precious cup that might be the Holy Grail! It is true that no one ever saw what Béranger Saunière found, and he refrained from ever speaking about it to anyone, except, of course, to those to whom he could sell the results of his searches. Jean Orth was one of this number.

He could serve to explain the origins of Abbé Saunière's fortune. The shadow of the archduke is quite heavy indeed.

---

30. I should point out some information that Pierre Jarnac provides in a footnote on page 362 that comes from an article in *Midi libre* (February 13, 1973). A certain Monsieur Espeut, who had consulted Saunière's personal papers around 1930, said with regard to the charges of spying that he was authorized to make two revelations.

The first: Baron von Kron, head of the German Secret Service, lived in Barcelona during the war. The Deuxième Bureau wondered, after the war, if Abbé Saunière's domain might not have been an ideal relay station between Germany and Spain for enemy agents. But of course nothing was proved. The second certainly touches upon a state secret: At that time, the mother superior of a convent close to Rennes-le-Château was a German nun. She was the kaiser's own sister . . .

Pierre Jarnac was even more specific, saying that "this monastery was that of Prouilles." All of this speaks volumes about the Saunière mystery and the difficulties he encountered at the beginning of World War I.

THE SHADOW OF THE DEFILEMENTS

When Bérenger Saunière began the transformation of his church, he made discoveries perhaps by chance, although information seems to suggest that Saunière had long known what he was searching for. Yet this is not a serious concern; after all, if objects were prudently hidden by Abbé Bigou during the Revolution, it was his duty to remove them from their hiding places. The real question is whether Saunière had the right to sell these objects for personal profit. Yet here, too, he can be forgiven, for he restored the church and he constructed buildings not only for his personal use but also as a retirement home for aged priests (which, of course, he himself would one day be). When accused of embezzlement by his bishop, he openly displayed his charitable intentions, but we know that there are gaps in his accounting: There was a huge imbalance between the enormous sums he spent and the rather minor receipts he agreed to acknowledge.

A much more serious matter, however, is the shadow of the defilements he was responsible for in the parish cemetery. Here there is proof, if only in the petitions sent to the Aude prefect, that Bérenger Saunière spent many nights turning the cemetery upside down and *defiling tombs,* not to mention scratching out inscriptions on the flagstones of the marquise d'Hautpoul's tomb. Not merely a matter of legends or ill-wishing gossip, these actions were quite real. This obviously raises certain problems, not so much from the perspective of morals (Saunière's were rather elastic), but from a consideration of the exact object of his search and his choice of specific tombs. In a word, Saunière *knew* what he was looking for—and he wanted to find it, no matter what it cost.

The prevailing sentiment today among those who are trying to objectively view Saunière's clandestine activities is that he discovered the sepulchers of the ancient lords of Rennes inside the church, and that as a result of selling these finds, or some of them at least, he made his fortune. It is also believed that he gave to several people—one of whom was Marie Denarnaud—some of the jewels he unearthed. But it is also thought that he did not dare sell—or was unable to sell—what he had discovered in the cemetery. This assertion, however, calls for some consideration.

The obsessive nature of Saunière's excavation of the marquise d'Hautpoul's tomb and the tactless act of erasing its inscriptions are much too flagrant to be aspects of a single episode. To the contrary, it seems that this tomb might be at the very heart of the mystery—indeed, if we pay strict attention to it, it will allow all the elements of the puzzle to fall together.

The Hautpouls, as the lords of Rennes, were clearly in possession of all the ancient documents relating to the region, and they certainly would have inherited the documents of those families that married into theirs. As the one who was responsible for the burial of objects and documents, Abbé Bigou was the family's confidant. The Hautpoul hoard is incontestably at the very heart of all Saunière's discoveries and is consequently the source of everything imaginable about the objects or alleged documents that Saunière would have sold, exchanged, or even kept for unknown purposes, even if simply as a secret bargaining tool that could guarantee him immunity or the assurance of being left alone in peace.

The vandalism of the tomb of Marquise d'Hautpoul, Marie de Négri d'Ables, could have even greater significance than previously thought. It is certainly connected to the donation of the countess of Chambord. I am surprised that no one discusses this connection, for it is quite evident and plays an essential role in the whole affair of Saunière.

In fact, "this singular donation to the priest of a remote village from the Upper Aude Valley is greatly disconcerting," remarks Jacques Rivière, who offers three explanations for it. The first explanation consists of a request Saunière personally made of the pretender's widow at a difficult time—to wit, the elections of 1885, when the monarchists lost their majority. The second is that the donation was a sign of the countess's gratitude to Saunière for his loud and brazen display of his legitimist opinions. In both cases the intervention of Alfred Saunière would have been key, for, as we know, he had extensive contacts inside the aristocracy.

It is the third explanation that deserves our extra attention. We know that the countess of Chambord was Austrian and had little love in her heart for the French, whom she deemed frivolous, fickle, and disloyal to the great values of the past. But she:

. . . was not unaware that the parish of Rennes-le-Château was an ancient Hautpoul fiefdom, and the Hautpouls were no strangers to her. In fact, in 1834 an Hautpoul-Felines was tutor to her husband, the young Henry V. The marquis Armand d'Hautpoul had turned down all recompense for this teaching post and testified on several occasions of his esteem for the duke of Bourdeaux. Notably, he traveled through all of Germany with him and visited him again in London in 1843.[31]

So these are the pieces of the puzzle collected from the Hautpouls. What confidences might Armand d'Hautpoul have shared with the pretender? Could it be that something of great importance to the legitimate French monarchy was located in Rennes-le-Château? This provides a much better explanation for the donation to Saunière than does the gratitude of an Austrian countess who despised the French. Might the donation have been for the purpose of helping him find something? In this case the defilement of the tomb of the marquise d'Hautpoul would simply be the execution of a mission entrusted to the priest of Rennes-le-Château by the royal family, rather than an act of vandalism. This explanation also has the merit of accounting for the visits by Jean Orth, the fallen archduke, and the negotiations he would necessarily have held with Saunière.

It is an attractive hypothesis, one that is not at all absurd and allows us to better understand Béranger Saunière's bizarre behavior, especially given that he never relinquished his legitimist opinions. Thus, without needing to go so far as imagining that what Saunière discovered was the will of Blanche de Castille, we can still consider that what he found might have been essential documents concerning the French monarchy, its origins, and its authentic legitimacy. It may be recalled that Blanche de Castille displayed a relentless desire to dispossess Trencavel of the Razès and did everything she could to place at the earldom's head men whom she could trust, while still demonstrating great indulgence toward the title holder who had been stripped of his rights. There is indeed a mystery in the Razès—one that indubitably touches on a state secret, but there is no need to invent false Merovingian genealogies in order to present a convincing case of its existence.

Could the shadow of the defilements performed by Abbé Saunière in the Rennes-le-Château cemetery merely cover an imperative for discretion concerning a matter of great importance?

---

31. J. Rivière, *Le Fabuleux Trésor de Rennes-le-Château*, 47.

THE SHADOW OF THE TRAFFICKING OF MASSES

We should remember that during the entire period in which Monsignor Billard was bishop of Carcassonne, he never asked Abbé Saunière to account for his receipts and expenditures. When Monsignor de Beauséjour took over, the priest's lifestyle appeared excessive to him in relation to the obvious poverty of his parish, which numbered no more than two hundred inhabitants. A certain amount of oversight of Saunière was initially exercised discreetly, followed by the suggestion to give him a promotion that would take him away from Rennes. It is logical to think that this removal of Saunière was necessitated by the bishop's desire to save his priest from becoming compromised by shady financial deals and to keep such a scandal from tainting the other clergy in the diocese.

At this time France was no longer under the concordat regime; the Combes laws of 1905 had instituted the separation of church and state. Priests, whether of a parish or simple vicars, were no longer civil servants and were no longer paid any salary by the state. It was up to them to figure out how to make a living by appealing to the faithful, who, according to the logic of this system, were the priests' "customers" for everything concerning spiritual life. It is necessary to use terms of commerce here, for no one is obliged *to buy* Masses, baptisms, church marriages, and burials. The Catholic Church became merely another private enterprise, though with one slight advantage that would eventually turn out to be quite positive: All buildings of worship and presbyterial residences were taken over by the government, in this instance the municipal governments (and by the state when historic monuments were involved, in keeping with its role as guardian of the national patrimony).

It was thus the responsibility of the faithful to pay their priests with honorariums for every Mass and other sacerdotal services. This was a triumph of economic liberalism exalting free enterprise. Before the Combes laws went into effect, priests who did enjoy a salary could still receive gifts. This gifting was indeed necessary because church upkeep was expensive and municipal authorities often required a bit of persuasion before opening their purse strings for this purpose. Before 1905, then, priests still appealed to the generosity of their congregations, but after 1905 this appeal became a vital necessity. Hence, there existed ecclesiastical rules whose broad lines still remain in effect. Services such as baptisms, marriages, and funerals are subject to a certain set price, first in each diocese, then on a national level to avoid any abuse or unfair pricing. Masses that are requested for various purposes are paid according to the principle that all labor should be salaried. The officiating priest is thereby transformed into simply another worker or employee. Again, though, to avoid any unfair practices the bishops of all dioceses have specifically ordered that priests refer to the proper authority of their dioceses every time they receive honorariums for saying Masses.

In fact, there is little demand for Masses in some parishes, while in others, mainly pilgrimage sites, there is an almost limitless number of requests. In the interests of fairness and equality (Republican ideals have infiltrated into the Church), it is a matter of concern that every priest have enough income to live in dignity and fulfill his priesthood. What could be more normal? In this way a high demand for Masses at one parish will be redistributed by the bishopric to those with little demand, whether in the same diocese or in others that are less privileged. This is not *trafficking in Masses* but rather is redistribution to all priests of special Masses demanded and bought for specific purposes by the faithful. It guarantees every priest, whether active or retired, *at least one Mass daily and the honorarium that goes with it.* A *minimum living wage* is thus provided to every member of the clergy. No one should find anything abnormal in what is essentially a perfectly honest and balanced system. In addition, priests have never been forbidden to accept gifts either for their personal use or to do *good works,* as the time-honored expression would have it. These involve giving assistance to the more indigent members of the congregation, including covering the costs incurred by worship. Here, too, all is consistent and perfectly fair. If abuses do occur in specific instances, they are considered infractions of canon law.

These principles are still valid today[32] and it would be good if certain "simplistic" anticlerical critics took this into consideration before

---

32. It should be specified that today, as a general rule, the requests for Masses for the dead are no longer subject to fixed fees. The individuals requesting them pay what they feel is right according to their means.

attacking the "wealth of priests."[33] While there are sometimes scandalous exceptions, they only prove the general rule: The French clergy overall live quite modestly while fulfilling their priestly duties in often difficult conditions.[34]

Having said that, it is now high time we addressed Monsignor de Beauséjour's accusation that Abbé Béranger Saunière trafficked in Masses. It has been asserted that the bishop of Carcassonne would have said—the conditional is always mandatory in such cases—that this accusation was merely a pretext. It was primarily because Saunière refused to leave Rennes-le-Château that Monsignor de Beauséjour instituted canonical proceedings in 1909.

The issue is a complex one:

Two essential points emerge from examination of the ledger of receipts. First, the abbé intentionally doubled the actual revenues from the collection boxes installed in the church as well as the salaries of the family welcomed to Rennes.[35] In reality, this false accounting masks the trafficking in Masses he had been perpetrating

33. I can personally testify to a number of cases that should inspire pity in this regard. During the 1950s, I spent quite a bit of time in the presbyteries of Brittany, where I could come and go as I pleased. I saw priests who, despite living in deplorable conditions, had lost none of their faith and fulfilled their priestly duties in complete honesty. I have a particularly moving memory of the rector of Iffs (in Ille-et-Vilaine), a parish famous for the magnificent stained-glass windows of its church, who lived in complete want. I also remember the rector of Nostang (in Morbihan) who lived in a kind of dank and unhealthy basement with no comforts whatsoever. He wore the sad smile of those who know that life on earth is but a transitory moment in an incomprehensible eternity. I would like to take a moment here to pay homage to these modest and *good* priests. And I have not yet mentioned the rector of Tréhorenteuc, who lived on hot sweetened water and stale bread because he put all his money toward the restoration and decoration of his church. Where is the author who will dare write a nonpolemical book on the wretched conditions in which much of the French clergy live at this beginning of a new millennium.

34. I want to take advantage of this to tell those who accuse me of anticlericalism to consider the arguments I have put forth. I am not at all "knee-jerk" anticlergy and I am familiar enough with the issue to avoid getting hung up on appearances and to direct discussion to the most essential considerations.

35. This refers to the Denarnaud family, which speaks volumes about the exact nature of the relationship between Béranger Saunière and Marie Denarnaud.

since 1896 . . .[36] Saunière always declared that he had never enriched himself with the honorariums he received for Masses. He acknowledged in 1911 the reality of these requests for Masses[37] but claimed in his defense that he collected these honorariums to redistribute them among a certain number of priests whom he named[38] but who, in 1910, were deceased or unknown to the bishopric.[39]

There is obviously fraud here, but does it concern trafficking in Masses? And precisely what does it mean to traffick in Masses?

No doubt it would be more fitting to speak of Saunière's actions as "beating the bushes." The specific purpose of his many trips was to "fish" for Masses. What arguments did he rely upon? No doubt those that emphasized the distinctive worship offered to Mary Magdalene in Rennes-le-Château, given that she was the patron saint of the parish. Béranger also wrote many letters in which he repeated the same requests, which allowed him to put together a collection of stamps from various countries. While the priest of the Church of Mary Magdalene was condemned for having engaged in "trafficking" around 1905, we should not overlook that the system had been in place ever since his arrival in Rennes-le-Château or that he was aided in "beating the bushes" by his brother, Alfred.

Nothing is known of the understanding they shared concerning what should be called "beating the bushes" for donations, but whatever the arrangements were, it cannot be denied that it was quite effective. Each played their roles to perfection. Saunière spared no effort in writing to numerous religious communities and countless well-off and charitable souls. To those he knew to be poor he sent letters fishing for old stamps, ancient post cards, pious images, and so forth.

---

36. I leave to the author of these lines the responsibility of his judgment, which I personally contest most energetically.

37. Through small advertisements (mainly in *Les Veillées des Chumnières*) and personal visits he solicited specific Masses from the rich and pious, especially those with monarchist tendencies. This is a proven fact; he was creating propaganda for his parish.

38. In doing this he substituted himself for his bishop, a transgression of canonical law.

39. J. Rivière, *Le Fabuleux Trésor de Rennes-le-Château*, 135.

*A bird's-eye view of Rennes-le-Château. In the upper central portion
of the photo, the Magdala Tower and, immediately
to its right, Villa Bethania can be seen.*

Abbé Béranger Saunière

Marie Denarnaud

*The Visigothic pillar inside of which Saunière discovered
the mysterious parchments*

The holy water stoup held up by the devil Asmodeus
at the entrance of the church

The Magdala Tower

The Shepherds of Arcadia, *by Nicolas Poussin*

The tomb near Arques that is said to have been
modeled after Poussin's painting

To those he knew to be rich he wrote letters soliciting aid for rebuilding "a ruined church" and for constructing "a retirement home for aged and disabled priests." He in fact relied very little on the classifieds, preferring to personally prospect for his clientele through correspondence or repeated mailings that would not be sent in vain.[40]

The problem raised by the bishopric was the fear that the priest of Rennes-le-Château was simply depositing in the bank the honorariums for these Masses and was never celebrating them. Indeed, if he had been forced to celebrate all the Masses for which he had received honorariums, he would have been doing nothing else both night and day. But he divvied up this money, as we know, among other priests whom he knew, even those outside of the diocese. In addition, it is always a possibility that Saunière's benefactors gave him more than the normal price for the celebration of a Mass. There is not a great deal of support for the accusation that he was trafficking in Masses. Because the bishopric sought to bend Abbé Saunière to its will, the prosecuter of the Officiality[41] lodged three complaints against him. The first was that he trafficked in honorariums for Masses and had done so for many years, especially after 1896. The second was that he had used these honorariums, at least partially, to realize his restoration and construction work in Rennes-le-Château. The third and final charge was that he disobeyed his bishop, who had forbidden him to "beat the bush" for Mass honorariums.

In fact, based on his account books, it clearly seems that Abbé Saunière collected some fifteen hundred to two thousand gold francs a year. This in no way begins to explain the expenditures he made or the construction he undertook. Ultimately, this accusation was dropped by the bishopric because it could not be proved beyond the shadow of a doubt. It must be admitted that with his clumsy attempts at defending himself and especially with his refusal to reveal the origin of the funds

---

40. P. Jarnac, *Histoire du trésor de Rennes-le-Château*, 338. Numerous facsimiles of Saunière's notebooks can be found in this text, including the lists of those to whom he wrote and those who responded. This allows a better idea of the incredible amount of correspondence he put together during his life.

41. [Eccesiastical court. —*Translator*]

he had received, Abbé Saunière only aggravated his case in the eyes of the Officiality responsible for conducting the trial. This is the explanation for his removal from his post at the parish of Rennes-le-Château by a rather roundabout method, namely the *suspens a divinis* against which he appealed to Rome. His removal was followed by a period of flux, one that was as ambiguous as his own position. He still lived in Rennes-le-Château—in fact, still at the presbytery—while no longer officially holding the post of parish priest and being forbidden to celebrate Mass and services *in public,* which gave him full latitude to say Mass in his *private* chapel at Villa Bethania. The local residents continued to attend these Masses, for they were quite fond of their priest and always remained faithful to him.[42]

It is hard to know what Beranger Saunière thought of all this in his soul and conscience, but it is quite certain that he did not consider himself guilty of embezzlement when he used the donations he received for the construction of Villa Bethania and the Magdala Tower, which were intended to function later as a retirement home. In fact, even if Saunière appeared to live a luxurious lifestyle (which public rumor no doubt

---

42. Canon law is fairly complex when it comes to the attribution of parishes to priests. It can vary in each diocese and even in each ecclesiastical province with regard to certain cases. Accordingly, in the current ecclesiastical province of Brittany, which includes the dioceses of Rennes (as well as Dol and Saint-Malo), Saint-Brieuc (and Tréguier), Quimper (and Léon), and Vannes, the officiant of an ordinary parish, called the *rector* (in Breton it is *person*), cannot be transferred without his consent, which is not the case for the holder of a deanery, the deacon/priest. But in the ecclesiastical province of Narbonne, of which Carcassonne is a dependency, this distinction does not exist. Saunière could be moved from the parish of Rennes without his consent. This is why, at a certain point in the trial, Saunière, playing on the subtleties of canon law, resigned his post as priest of Rennes-le-Château. The bishop did not fall into the trap and refused to accept this resignation. If he had accepted it, he would have implicitly recognized that Saunière was tenured for life in that position. The least that can be said is that Monsignor de Beauséjour could not do very much of anything against Saunière and that the charge of "trafficking in Masses" was a makeshift attempt to force the recalcitrant priest to decamp from his parish. There is always a large gap between the apparent strictness of canonical law, with its corollary obedience to the bishop, and concrete reality. The priest from the lay clergy retains some of his autonomy, which is not the case for the regular clergy, in which every monk is closely subordinated to higher authority and compelled to strictly observe the Rule. In any event, the case of Béranger Saunière must have given nightmares to Monsignor de Beauséjour.

exaggerated to a considerable extent), he never lost sight of the fact that he was there to fulfill a mission—a mysterious one, perhaps—from which others would profit.

It would seem, then, that the shadow cast by Saunière's trafficking in Masses is quite a thin one.

THE SHADOW OF ABBÉ GELIS

No one talks about the matter of Abbé Gelis. Apparently most place it outside of the events concerning Béranger Saunière, but further examination shows that it cannot be merely an epiphenomenon. The priest of Coustaussa knew Abbé Saunière quite well; it could not be otherwise, for they both were part of the same deanery.[43] Of course, it is impossible to know if Abbé Gelis was Abbé Saunière's confessor, but we do know for certain that Abbé Saunière spent time with Gelis and that the priest of Coustaussa was aware of some of his colleague's "affairs." It is therefore impossible to consider the priest's mysterious murder without introducing it into the framework of the Saunière story, even if we are left with only conjecture.

Regarding Gelis, it is first necessary to recall the facts. On November 1, 1897, the abbé Jean-Antoine-Maurice Gelis, priest of Coustaussa, seventy-one years of age, was discovered murdered in the kitchen of his presbytery. His killer was never found and the motives for the crime remain unknown. Near the victim, who did not smoke and who was repulsed by the odor of tobacco, an entire packet of cigarette papers was found. An inscription on one of the papers read: "Viva Angélina." This might be the promising start of a good detective novel.

All that is known of the tragedy for certain is that earlier that evening Abbé Gelis, who by nature was very suspicious and lived cloistered behind locked doors, had received a late-night visitor. Because the

---

43. As a general rule, the priests of the same deanery (since the time of the Concordat, the deanery has most often corresponded to a civil canton) are expected to meet on a regular basis. These meetings generally took place over a meal at the homes of various priests, each of whom hosted by turns depending upon a priest's activities and other circumstances. During these fraternal agapes, priests exchanged news and discussed the religious life of the deanery.

entrance door had not been locked again, it can be assumed that he received a visitor he knew well and that his murderer would be none other than this visitor. But who could it have been? No one in the village had the slightest information to give the gendarmes, but the crime was assumed to have been committed by someone the priest knew.

It was determined that theft was not the motive: All of Abbé Gelis's savings were found intact. His nephew, who was held for several days, would certainly not have wasted an opportunity to pocket whatever turned up, for he was chronically short of cash and was constantly badgering his uncle for assistance. But on the night of the murder he was somewhere else, which removed from the list the heinous crime of a murder for money.

The police report mentioned another very important piece of information. "The body had been arranged in the center of the room on its back, head and face in a normal position, hands folded over the chest, like a figure on the lid of a tomb." This suggests that the murderer was not a run-of-the-mill criminal. He took pains after the act to place his victim in a dignified, even *religious* posture, as if he was expressing the respect that he may have held for the person he had just murdered. Strange.

There was no theft. Unless . . . According to the police report, the assassin went upstairs to the abbé's room (as if he were familiar with the premises). There, while taking infinite precautions to leave no trace of his passage, he "forced the lock of a travel satchel that contained various papers and documents belonging to the priest." This next point is essential: "[T]he murderer opened the satchel *in search of something.*" Of course there is not a single clue to help identify just what the murderer was looking for, but it must certainly be admitted that what he was looking for must have been *extremely important* in order for him to be able to commit such a cold-blooded crime and then display such calm and confidence in his search.

Finally, there is the inscription on the cigarette paper: "Viva Angélina." What was the meaning of this message and to whom was it addressed? Altogether these are the elements of a mystery that no one has been able to solve and, as we may imagine, which creates a particularly dreadful shadow hovering over the Saunière affair.

Under such dreadful circumstances, it is normal to ask questions. Because the "elimination" of Abbé Gelis, a priest beyond reproach whose life had been without incident and whose vocation was dedicated to doing good around him, is not *normal*. It surely conceals something.

> Was Gelis the keeper of a secret or documents whose possession provided justification for this crime? Did anyone benefit from his disappearance from the scene? The inquest revealed that his murderer knew the abbé and the premises. The crime appears to have been premeditated, though the motive was not money, but the recovery of documents. What might these documents have held? The murderer was, however, respectful of his victim's body and laid him out like the recumbent figures in Christian sepulchers . . .[44]

People are free to embroider as they wish on this diverse array of facts. Coustaussa is only a mile and a half as the crow flies from Rennes-le-Château. During the time when Gelis was priest of Coustaussa, the priest of the parish of Rennes-le-Château was Béranger Saunière, who devoted his time to strange pursuits, He discovered buried objects and documents, defiled the sepulchers of the parish cemetery, and established relationships with people whose beliefs were foreign to his religion. This adds up to quite a number oddities. Perhaps the message "Viva Angélina" left behind by the murderer was some sort of rallying cry. But to what? Could the shadow of the mysterious "brotherhood" that has so often been connected to Abbé Saunière also have been hovering over Abbé Gelis? "The mystery remains intact," says Jacques Rivière, who adds this somewhat perfidious remark: "We cannot help but note that following this event, Abbé Saunière's behavior seemed different. It was at this point that he devoted himself to his municipal construction through the investment of significant sums of money."[45]

It seems there are two pieces of information that add up: First, Abbé Gelis was the keeper of certain secrets (which the rifling of his satchel appears to prove). Second, an unknown person wished to take them for himself (and succeeded), warning through his message that it was better to

---

44. J. Rivière, *Le Fabuleux Trésor de Rennes-le-Château*, 145–46.

45. Ibid., 146.

obey, under pain of death, the mysterious brotherhood in the Razès. Having received the message, Abbé Saunière no longer excavated the tombs but devoted himself to his municipal construction, which he claimed was charitable in nature. Or, in another scenario, the assassin was seeking to take possession of the final piece of a puzzle that could lead him to a complete and full understanding of its secret. In this case, although there is nothing whatsoever to support such an illogical declaration, the murderer might be Béranger Saunière himself. Is raising such a possibility an insult to the memory of this priest? Similar questions have been asked before. The ambiguity of Saunière's attitude is such that an outright categorical rejection of this monstrous accusation is impossible. Béranger Saunière might have been, then, not only a prevaricator, an embezzler (why not a swindler?), and a trafficker in both stolen objects and Masses that were never performed, but also a murderer capable of doing anything to achieve his ends—that is, the mission he was fixed upon or *that someone had entrusted to him*. What is so deplorable in this story is that we find it impossible to wash Saunière completely clean of the accusation.

There was a consequence to the Gelis affair that did not appear immediately but instead hounded Saunière all his life. From precise testimonies we know that someone was blackmailing him: the tutor Jamet, who was also the town clerk. It has been proved that Béranger paid him in money and jewelry to keep silent. But to keep silent about what? About the finds the priest made in the Church of Saint Magdalene? About the priest's defilement of tombs in the church's cemetery? Or about something else entirely? Although Jamet has been recognized as being perfectly odious (to the extent that his descendants changed their name), he does cast a fairly legitimate shadow over the generally reassuring image of Saunière as a well-built, strapping man who was nonetheless incapable of hurting a fly.[46] Yet there is nothing more deceptive than appearances. What were the truths behind the tutor's blackmail of Abbé Saunière to the tune of a substantial sum? Let he who is without doubt cast the first stone.

---

46. Personally, from the bottom of my heart and soul, as people are apt to say in such circumstances, although it might seem that the murder of Abbé Gelis could have benefited the priest of Rennes-le-Château, I absolutely refuse to believe that Béranger Saunière was capable of such a criminal and monstrous deed. In spite of his faults, Saunière was *good,* and demonstrated that quality on numerous occasions. This is my personal conviction, but I am unable to support it with any proof.

It is true that while no one can clear Béranger Saunière of the accusation of murdering his colleague Abbé Gelis for extremely obscure reasons having to do with the "treasure" of Rennes, neither can anyone prove he committed this abominable act. Whatever the case may be, the shadow of Abbé Gelis hangs quite heavily over the Saunière affair.

THE SHADOW OF MARIE DENARNAUD

According to contemporary opinion, Béranger Saunière is inseparable from Marie Denarnaud, who forms with him, in the imagination, a handsome couple that tugs at the heartstrings of people everywhere. Just think about it: Saunière gave her everything he owned! He must have been in love with his sweet Marie. As for her, what devotion! What faithfulness to his memory! What constancy in her refusal to divulge the secrets of a man to whom she had devoted her life! She must have been in love with Béranger.

It is true that the shadow of Marie Denarnaud is entwined with that of the priest of Rennes-le-Château. In fact, the priest himself did all he could to bring this about, even going so far as to have himself photographed in the company of his "servant" in the gardens of Villa Bethania and then publishing the photos as postcards. But at the risk of disappointing those who have been nostalgically imagining a relationship similar to that of Tristan and Iseult, the relationship between Marie Denarnaud and Béranger Saunière may not have been all that it seemed. True enough, loans are made only to the rich, and it appears that Saunière had a reputation for "hot-bloodedness." Without a doubt, however, his brother, Alfred, was "hot-blooded," even though he was a priest and, what's more, a member of the very honorable Company of Jesus, or Jesuit Order. Should his bad reputation extend to the Jesuits as a whole?

Béranger Saunière complained so often about paying for the sins and transgressions of his brother that little scrutiny was given to his relationship with Marie Denarnaud. When all is said and done, in fact, there is strictly no proof of an amorous liaison between Marie Denarnaud and the priest of the Church of Mary Magdalene. No one has ever been able to put forth a definitive claim that Marie was the mistress, companion, or, if you prefer, concubine of Béranger Saunière.

It must be admitted, though, that there are strong grounds for presuming that the two did have a relationship of this kind. A country priest who hires a fairly young servant—who was also pretty, according to testimonies—is only laying himself wide open to suspicions. A twenty-four-year-old female servant in the presbytery will cause tongues to wag, that is for sure,[47] especially given that Saunière was a resident of Occitania, where there is a great willingness to tell stories about priests who sleep with their servants. Occitan folktales are full of stories of this sort, some even bordering on the scatological and impertinent.[48] In Occitania people say a priest is still a man and has the right to act just like other men. No harm is seen in this. Their main concern is that their priest "not make everything too black and white" with regard to others who "sin" and that he be morally flexible toward the women from whom he receives confession. And this being the case, why not find some mutual understanding? In Rennes-le-Château no one ever complained about the parish priest's ambiguous situation, and when Saunière was hauled up before the bishop's tribunal, he was never faulted for living with Denarnaud. There are some things that the bishopric has to ignore, however real they are. In Saunière's case, doubts about his relationship persisted, which was all the more reason that it was never addressed. Let Saunière sin; it's his business, provided he doesn't cause a scandal.[49] But unlike his unfortunate brother, Alfred the Jesuit, Saunière never caused a scandal in this area.

The story of how Marie Denarnaud, who came to offer her services to Abbé Saunière (whether or not she was sent by Abbé Bigou) and

---

47. Normally a female servant in a presbytery must be of canonical age—that is to say, forty-five to fifty years minimum. This rule is not based on moral or theological reasoning; it is simply very realistic, for a woman of canonical age is not at great risk of giving birth. This circumvents any possible scandal as well as the practical consequences concerning the raising and educating of a child.

48. For more on this subject, see the excellent books published in Carcassonne from 1984 to 1987 by GARAE (Groupe audois de recherché et d'animation ethnographique), *Les Contes licencieux de l'Aquitaine* and *L'Anneau magique*, works we owe to Agen native and folklorist Antonin Perbosc, a contemporary of Saunière.

49. Recall the scene in Molière's *Tartuffe* when the worthy representative of the Party of Devotees, meaning the Brotherhood of the Holy Sacrament (Saint Vincent de Paul, Abbé Ollier, and Nicolas Pavillon), gave a brilliant sermon on the theme "sinning without causing a scandal is not sinning."

immediately fell in love with the "great man," is beautiful and moving—but it is utterly false. At the beginning of his stay in Rennes-le-Château, Saunière moved in with a charitable parishioner. When the initial renovation and repair work was completed, he lived in the presbytery in what must be described as rather precarious conditions relative to comfort. It was not until 1892 that he invited the Denarnaud family, whom he knew well, to Rennes-le-Château, for this family would help him crown his works with success.

The Denarnaud family, natives of Espéranza, consisted of four people: the mother, the father, a daughter, and a son. The son and father were both skilled artisans. The daughter, whom they named Marie, was born in 1868 in Espéranza. She was twenty-four years old when she arrived in Rennes-le-Château to help her mother "maintain" the presbytery. Saunière in fact moved the Denarnaud family into the presbytery. He would speak of it as a family of "hospitality," meaning they lodged with him in return for a rent that in this instance consisted of repair and renovation work. Later father and son left to work in the factory in Espéranza. Marie's mother soon followed them, effectively leaving Marie alone with Béranger. Seen from this angle, the story is less novelistic and less romantic. Of course, there is nothing to say that a liaison did not exist between the priest and Marie, even during the time when her family lived at the presbytery. Yet there is no proof of such a relationship, not a single clue. What's more, in the receipts and written proof that Saunière gave the bishopric at the time of his trial, he made sure to note the salaries he claimed to be giving Marie Denarnaud and her mother.

Whether or not she was his mistress, Marie Denarnaud remained with the priest and acted as his confidante until his death. She held a boundless admiration for Abbé Saunière, and seemed ready to kill herself for him if he demanded it. Her devotion to the priest even after his death is impressive. She never betrayed a single secret he had confided to her,[50] respecting the law of silence to the end, satisfying herself now and then only by saying that the inhabitants of Rennes-le-Château walked on gold and knew nothing about it. Perhaps, though, these were

---

50. The only time she betrayed the priest's confidence was when she revealed a hiding place to the new owner of the home, Noel Corbu. It was empty, however. No doubt Saunière had cleared it without telling his servant.

words of derision. Marie Denarnaud died poor and impoverished. In order to survive, she was forced to sell her house in return for a life annuity and spend her old age with the family of the new owner, whom she had made her sole legatee.

She was a strange individual, this big-hearted servant who was entirely devoted to the man in her life, happy to remain in his shadow and perpetuate his memory, and discovered to be the incumbent owner of everything the priest had bought and constructed. Of course, this would have been quite an extravagant situation for her if she had not been the priest's mistress. In her receipt of the priest's fortune, there is material to excite the most stubborn imaginations; certainly no effort has been spared to create a beautiful love story out of what after all might have been only a perfect understanding between two individuals who no doubt shared esteem and affection for each other as well as an uncommon love.

Marie Denarnaud's shadow is particularly moving, especially when it lingers over the tomb of Abbé Saunière.

There are many shadows, some murky, others so pellucid that they evaporate in the air's movement. There are some, though, that remain opaque and more resistant to the storms that should carry them off. Who was Abbé Béranger Saunière? It would be a very clever individual who could give us that answer. No doubt the man was neither wholly good nor wholly evil. He was a priest convinced of his mission during a time when it was difficult to be a priest and have political convictions that matched religious convictions. Was he a megalomaniac? Surely he was, but for the worthy cause of leaving behind something that would remind others that *he had lived while doing good*. He was certainly not a Rosicrucian or a Freemason, as has been said too often by those who fantasize about the bizarre decoration of his church. Was he manipulated? He had neither the mentality to be used nor the character to stand for it. Why, then, is there so much mystery around this man? Why, especially in the forty years following his death, has there been so much noise about his alleged activities? Why was Béranger Saunière, a modest country priest, changed into a hero of a legend?

Despite himself and because of circumstances, Saunière embodied a myth, and in order to be seen, myths, like gods, must incarnate in theophanies that give fuel to the dreams of those who are desperately seeking the truth.

6

One Train Can
Hide Another

In January 1956 three articles on Rennes-le-Château, with photos of Villa Bethania, the Magdala Tower, and of course the church, appeared in the very serious journal *La Dépêche du Midi*. The title of one of these articles was a complete item in itself: "With one blow of his pickax to a pillar of the high altar, Abbé Saunière brought to light the treasure of Blanche de Castille."

The die was cast. In the weeks and months that followed, other publications, both regional and national, made certain to publish their own articles on the mysterious case of a millionaire priest. There was enough here to restore life to this lost corner of the Aude, which usually slumbered at the wind's pleasure without inspiring anyone even to take a few days of vacation in its healthful environment, free from pollution, let alone to visit in search of treasure.

It is curious to observe that while he was alive, not a single journalist found it worthwhile to write the tiniest column about Abbé Saunière's discoveries or bizarre construction. Also interesting is that from the time of the priest's death in 1917 to the appearance of the articles in 1956, no one besides Marie Denarnaud and the parishioners who retained a poignant memory of him had mentioned the priest who had discovered a treasure. It would take thirty-nine years for tongues to loosen and pens to start scratching. There is food for thought here, especially given that the Saunière affair ultimately went far beyond its original framework, spreading throughout Europe by way of newspaper articles, so-called documentary films, television broadcasts, and finally books with large print runs.

Odd, you say? But you don't know just how odd it is. . . . This is the common reply that has applied perfectly to the Saunière affair (and an *affair* it is) ever since that memorable January in 1956, thirty-nine years after the death of Béranger Saunière and three years after the death of Marie Denarnaud. Of course, everyone interprets the facts to his or her own liking, and there are those who took the bait and added a great deal more to the story. Some have proclaimed their skepticism for all to hear, earning the snubs of the true believers. Then there are both the indifferent, who have simply kept score, and those who work in the shadows. These last had already been working for a long time in secret. We might ask why they waited until 1956 to emerge, or pretend to emerge, for since that year the shadows that hover over Rennes-le-Château have grown singularly thicker.

In addition to the newspaper articles concerning Abbé Saunière's work with a pickax, the year 1956 witnessed three events that may have gone largely unnoticed by the general public, but which eventually took on great importance in the affair. First, the strange *Book of Constitutions* was published in Geneva by Éditions des Commanderies de Genève, an entirely unknown publishing house. Next, there was the deposit at the Bibliothèque Nationale in Paris of a study on the Merovingians by a certain Henri Lobineau (who turned out to be totally nonexistent), along with genealogies that threatened to overturn all current knowledge on those remote times. Last, at the prefecture of Haute-Savoie, located in Annemasse, and as defined by the Law of 1901, there was the founding or "declaration" of the Association of the Priory of Sion. Those who declared were Pierre Bonhomme, Pierre Defagot, Jean Delaval, three unknowns, and Pierre Plantard, whose name was familiar to those steeped in esotericism and the serial novel.

These three events merit some clarification. The *Book of Constitutions* concerns the Priory of Sion, asserting that this order, whose original seat was the Abbey of Our Lady of Mount Sion, was founded in 1099 in Jerusalem by Godefroy de Bouillon. In the disorienting flood of information delivered by this text we can eventually grasp that this Order of Sion was somehow taking up the torch from another interrupted order with Gnostic tendencies, and that it shortly thereafter became the occult group that directed the Templars. After separating from the Templar Order during the famous split that took place beneath the elm of Gisors,[1] the Order of Sion survived in secret, century after century, surreptitiously acting in the world's affairs and presiding over the destinies of a number of annexed or subordinate brotherhoods. Its list of grand masters included such prestigious names as Nicolas Flamel, Leonardo da Vinci, Isaac Newton, Charles Nodier, Victor Hugo, Claude Debussy, and Jean Cocteau. It was this Order of Sion that presented itself in Annemasse, in legal compliance with the rules of the French Republic, as the Priory of Sion, more or less under the leadership of Pierre Plantard de Saint Clair, who let it be known to any who wished to listen that he was the last descendant of the legitimate Merovingian line.

We should note that according to the *Book of Constitutions,* the Order of Sion had assumed the mission of safeguarding the Merovingian blood that flowed in the veins of Godefroy de Bouillon until such time as an authentic descendant of the authentic line could remount the throne of France. In this way they would drive off in the same opprobrium not only the Republicans and the Bonapartists, but also the Capets, the Bourbons, and the Orleans as usurpers of a throne that did not belong to them.

Was it the Priory of Sion that across the centuries whispered their punishment to Godefroy's descendants, the dukes of Lorraine? Was it the Priory of Sion that armed the Fronde against Louis XIV? Was it the Priory of Sion that inspired Nicolas Poussin's painting *The Shepherds of Arcadia,* and entrusted to him the dangerous secret he confided to Nicolas Foucquet? Finally, was it the Priory of Sion that supported the efforts of the Company of the Holy Sacrament?[2]

---

1. See my book *The Templar Treasure in Gisors* (Rochester, Vt.: Inner Traditions, 2003).

2. J. Robin, *Rennes-le-Château: la colline envoûtée*, 80. The author devotes his efforts to a subtle demystification of the Priory of Sion, whose existence is dubious, to say the least.

Jean Robin poses these questions with great clarity, yet obviously without giving them any credence, but this does not change the fact that the appearance of these pieces of information on the Priory of Sion at the moment the Rennes-le-Château affair was unleashed is somewhat unsettling.

The documents deposited at the Bibliothèque Nationale under the false name of Henri Lobineau are in complete agreement with these pieces of information. They amount to a veritable *re-reading* of Merovingian history that peremptorily brings the Razès into the mix for the first time. It is in the Razès, they contend, where the last descendant of the legitimate lineage of the Merovingians sought refuge. As proof, they include genealogies that at first look like the result of enthusiastic research. Unfortunately, they quickly reveal themselves to be false. The author (or authors) of this hoax was content to slightly modify existing—and trustworthy—genealogies by adding a name here and subtracting one there. She or he could not have been more casually dishonest about historical matters.[3] As they were presented, however, these genealogies have had a great effect on the fans of the sensational and on those who are always seeking to rewrite history in a way that suits them. The Lobineau "documents," although exposed and demystified on several occasions, have had offspring.

There is no need to speak further about falsifications that are of interest only to those who launched them into the public arena. There is no need to expand more on the ghostly Priory of Sion, that mysterious "brotherhood" that hounded Saunière's every step, at least in the story that has been built around him. It is worth knowing, though, that the *Book of Constitutions,* the Lobineau "documents," and the "official" birth of the Priory of Sion form part of an overall scheme intended to emphasize the Rennes-le-Château affair and the very distinctive adventure of Béranger Saunière. Three individuals have been the promoters of this conspiracy: One was Noel Corbu, heir of Marie Denarnaud and owner of the buildings constructed by Abbé Saunière; and the other two were authentic aristocrats, the count Pierre Plantard de Saint Clair, who calls himself a hermeticist, and the marquis Philippe de Cherisey, a writer and

---

3. For more on this subject, see Richard Bordes, *Les Mérovingiens à Rennes-le-Château* (Rennes-le-Château: Éditions Schrauben, 1984).

actor whose hour of glory was caught by the antenna of France Culture when he played the Gregoire of Roland Dubillard's *Amédée*. Once Noel Corbu had vanished due to a car accident, the "conspiracy" found an ally—or rather, performer—in the very talented writer Gerard de Sede, who in 1967 published a vast epic, *L'Or de Rennes* [The Gold of Rennes], which spread word of the Saunière affair throughout the world, though, as we might expect, revised and corrected for the public at large.

We will have to take a few steps back in time to discover the genesis of this skillful machination—for that is what it was—that has earned an unprecedented success. At the end of World War II, Marie Denarnaud, who still lived in Rennes-le-Château and enjoyed a modest lifestyle in memory of Abbé Saunière, was beginning to experience hard times. She was getting old: She moved around with difficulty and did not always have a very clear grasp of reality. After the Liberation it was necessary to exchange old bank notes, for many were counterfeits made by the Germans during the Occupation. The inhabitants of Rennes-le-Château then saw "Mademoiselle Marie," as she was respectfully known, burning a pile of bank notes instead of going in to exchange them. Was she afraid of something? Some questioned her rather indiscreetly, but what was done was done and Marie Denarnaud was even more hard up than before.

At this point Noel Corbu entered the scene. He was an industrialist who had opened several small companies and had even published a detective novel. During the Occupation he had experienced some ongoing difficulties regarding his attitude. Corbu knew the Razès quite well and had visited it often. He had heard of Abbé Saunière and asked all he met to tell him all they knew about the priest and his story. Perhaps the topic interested him as a potential subject for a new novel, though it seems that the idea of a hidden treasure strongly appealed to his imagination, which was naturally drawn toward adventure.

Wishing to leave the region of Perpignan, where there were too many uncomfortable memories connected to his black market dealings, Noel Corbu moved himself, his wife, and two children to Bugarach in 1944. There he made friends with the village grade school teacher, and it was probably he who first spoke of Béranger Saunière. In 1945 the Corbu family made an excursion to Rennes-le-Château and it was then that Corbu made the acquaintance of Marie Denarnaud, who showed him some souvenirs of "that poor Monsieur the abbé." Corbu returned several times to

Rennes-le-Château, and a warm fellow feeling developed between the old servant and the Corbu family. Very sincerely, without revealing in any way his ulterior motives, Noel Corbu proposed to buy Marie's property. In exchange the Corbu family committed to taking care of the old woman. This deal was sealed before a notary on July 22, 1946. Noel Corbu and his wife became the sole legatees of Marie Denarnaud, who disinherited her entire family on this same occasion, as the notarized document attests.

Marie Denarnaud continued to live on her property and the Corbu family left for Morocco. Following some poor business dealings, however, Corbu was forced to return to France. And where could he go there if not to Rennes-le-Château? It became necessary for him to rebuild the family fortune that his Moroccan business affairs had so reduced. The intelligent and tenacious Noel Corbu knew how to turn everything to a profit. It was probably on his return to France in 1950, then, that he hit upon the idea of exploiting in one way or another the Saunière affair. Marie Denarnaud trusted only him and his wife. She had even promised one day to give him a "secret" that had been entrusted to her by "that poor Monsieur the abbé." Corbu waited patiently and scrupulously respected the commitments he had made to Marie. It does seem that the Corbu family had a real affection for the old woman, and she clearly returned it. In 1953, however, Marie died at the age of eighty-five without having passed her "secret" to her heir. She was buried in the little cemetery next to the tomb of the man to whom she had devoted not only her youth but her entire life as well.

Noel Corbu was now owner of everything that had belonged to Saunière and Marie Denarnaud. His innate business sense gave him the idea to transform Villa Bethania into a restaurant and hotel, which did not prevent him from searching wherever he could for documents that might put him on the trail of Béranger Saunière's famous "secret." The plan to transform the Rennes property offered two advantages: A restaurant and hotel would bring in revenue and the propagation of the story of the old Rennes priest through his clientele could bring in elements that might guide his search. The villa was ready for business by the last months of 1953.[4] Yet the few clients who frequented the restaurant

---

4. P. Jarnac, *Histoire du trésor de Rennes-le-Château*, 296.

brought in no information that Noel Corbu did not already know. He knew then that it would be necessary to look farther afield: If the information was not coming in, he would have to supply it. He discerned that in this way, even if he was unable to discover the secret, he would at least profit from an influx of tourists who were fans of unsolved mysteries.

There was certainly no shortage of such people in the region. Montségur was not so far away, and even at that time visitors gathered on the pog where the Cathar castle sat—travelers not only from France but from other countries as well, all obsessed by the story of the fabulous treasure of the Cathars, which might even be the Grail. Why not channel toward Rennes-le-Château those who had ventured to Montségur? It would be enough to spread as best as possible—discreetly, of course, for secrets are always more exciting—the story of the priest who discovered a treasure in his church. But the narrative had to conform to the model that had already been well established at Montségur. The Saunière affair would not have any credibility with the public unless it was tacked on to actual events in local history.

Noel Corbu put himself in charge of this task. As his detective novel demonstrated, he had a certain talent for narration. Thus the owner of the Restaurant de la Tour (the name he had given his establishment) made a tape recording of a short summary of the story to give to his guests to spice up their stay and, more important, to excite their imagination enough that they would return and bring their friends.

This summary was crafted very skillfully: Corbu began by pointing out that "during the entire duration of his Church trial, Abbé Saunière had started no new construction." This was an important point to make, for the story of a priest at odds with his bishop plays well in a region whose heretical past is beyond question. Once the Church had made the rupture official (free at last!), the interdicted priest

> . . . reworked his plans to include construction of the road from Couiza to Rennes-le-Château at his own expense, for he intended to buy an automobile; conveyance of water to all the inhabitants; construction of a chapel in the cemetery; construction of a rampart around the whole of Rennes; construction of a tower 180 feet tall with a circular staircase and library within so that all who entered

the town could be seen; the addition of a winter garden and another story to the existing tower.

We have to admire the genius of Noel Corbu. To entice his clients, he focused on Abbé Saunière's altruistic attitude (which was perfectly real, don't forget) and the grandiose nature of his projects. But how could a humble country priest undertake at his own expense construction projects whose costs were estimated at eight million gold francs, or two billion francs in 1954 France? "[O]n January 5, 1917, in the middle of the war, he accepted the estimate and signed the order for all of the construction." This obviously implies that Abbé Saunière had discovered an immense treasure, or at least knew where this treasure was located. If Béranger Saunière had realized his plans, however, they would not even be worth talking about. It is an interrupted work, especially one halted under certain circumstances, that speaks more to the imagination: "But twelve days after signing, the priest fell ill, and on January 22 he died." Here we have fate, but also a mystery. Who can know if Saunière died of natural causes? Isn't there something unsettling about the manner of his death? This is finally what Corbu allowed his clients to assume.

While it is good, however, to allow mystery to linger, it is necessary to lift a corner of the veil: If Béranger Saunière could order such extensive construction, it was because he knew where to find "the old treasure of the Capets, hidden in the thirteenth century." We can see that the treasure did not yet involve the Visigoths or Merovingians. Pierre Plantard de Saint-Clair had not yet come this way, and to mention the Cathar treasure would offer unfair competition with Montségur. No, Noel Corbu appealed instead to local legends: "The origin of the treasure? The explanation comes from the archives of Carcassonne. Blanche de Castille, mother of Saint Louis and regent of the kingdom of France during the Crusades of her son, deemed Paris to be too unsafe to hold the royal treasure because the barons and the commoners were in revolt against royal authority." There are some gaps in Noel Corbu's history education concerning difficulties that Blanche de Castille, widow of Louis VIII, actually experienced during her son's minority. She was faced with the rebellion of the nobles of the kingdom, led by Thibaud de Champagne, Pierre Mauclerc, and Raymond VII of Toulouse, with Trencavel right behind. There was a crusade, of course, but it was the one against the Albigensians.[5] But in his defense, all of this did take place in the thirteenth century.

This is the point where history suddenly picks up speed. Blanche de Castille

> . . . therefore had the treasure transported from Paris to Rennes [Rennes-le-Château, of course], then undertook to put down the rebellion. She succeeded and died shortly afterward. Saint Louis returned from the Crusade, then left again for the Holy Land and died in Tunis. His son, Philip the Bold, must have known the location of the treasure because he showed much interest in Reddae . . . But the knowledge was lost after him and Philip the Fair was obliged to counterfeit money, for the treasure of France had disappeared. We have to assume that he did not know its hiding place.

A treasure was lost because it was too carefully hidden by the great-grandmother of poor Philip the Fair, who was thus obliged to resort to expedient measures, as history shows, due to a lack of money! But let's keep moving—and don't waste time trying to verify this at the Carcassonne archives. If there had been documents, no doubt Philip the Fair got hold of them and then made sure they disappeared after he found the treasure.

This lack of documentation in no way prevented Noel Corbu from declaring seriously, "Based on the archives, which provide the list of the treasure, it consisted of 18.5 million pieces of gold, some 180 tons in weight, as well as numerous jewels and religious objects." The mention of the jewels and religious objects is important; it established as fact that Saunière found some such treasures in his church. It is essential that a connection be made between the fantastic story of Blanche de Castille and the more modest but more recent legend of Béranger Saunière. Noel Corbu then determines the total treasure to have been

---

5. See Jean Markale, *Le Chêne de la sagesse: un roi nommé Saint Louis* (Paris: Hermé, 1985).

worth four billion francs (at their 1954 valuation). We understand that some people's dreams are bigger than others.

Now, while Noel Corbu was trying to attract as many visitors as possible to Rennes-le-Château by spouting his fairy tale, another figure was lurking in Rennes-les-Bains, where he bought some land and studied the hot springs, particularly that of Magdalene and the one known as the Queen's Baths. He prospected the heights that hemmed in the valley, asked questions of everyone, and seemed quite intrigued by the two tombs of Fleury in the cemetery. The name of this man was Pierre Plantard. He presented himself as an archaeologist, but in certain milieus he was known as a hermeticist. He was often seen in the company of the young Marquis de Cherisey, who had more or less broken with his family because of his desire to be an actor and was trying as best he could to earn his living from small productions. Pierre Plantard was in Rennes-les-Bains by himself, however. All that anyone knew of him was that his bed-stand reading was a book that was almost impossible to find, *La Vraie Langue celtique et le cromlech de Rennes-les-Bains,* written by Abbé Henri Boudet, priest of that area when Saunière was officiating in Rennes-le-Château.

Nowhere is it said that Pierre Plantard and Noel Corbu ever met. But it is impossible to presume that Pierre Plantard never made the climb to Rennes-le-Château and never heard the short recorded speech that was handed out to guests at the Restaurant de la Tour. There is no doubt the two men were made to get along, and while they may never have actually met, we must admit that there is an extraordinary conjunction between the "histories" each of them launched later.

At this time, though, Noel Corbu managed his restaurant and patiently continued his searches, for he firmly believed in the treasure's existence and was convinced that Saunière held the key. He determined that all that was necessary to have access to the fabulous hoard of Blanche de Castille was to rediscover this key. As time passed, word of mouth did its work. An increasing number of visitors were discreetly lurking in Rennes-le-Château. This made its way to the ears of a few journalists who were looking for stories. The result was the three articles in *La Depêche du Midi* in January 1956. The machinery had been put into motion, and it could not be stopped.

It should be emphasized that Noel Corbu never abandoned his

searches on the church's grounds. During that same year, 1956, he appropriately obtained an excavation authorization and he and some enthusiastic seekers undertook the sounding of the church's basement. They found some remains and a human skull "bearing a slot on top"— unquestionably a ritual wound similar to those found on the remains in Carolingian and Merovingian cemeteries. It is possible that the purpose of the wound was to prevent the deceased from reincarnating, according to certain Germanic beliefs. But another motive is also plausible: During ancient times and among so-called barbarians, it was customary to place a perforated skull near treasure that had been buried.[6] Could this skull in the basement indicate that treasure had been buried near there? Noel Corbu certainly thought so, which was why he continued his excavations, only this time in the cemetery. It was wasted effort, however, for nothing was found. After this, no doubt because he discovered some information in the documents of Saunière still in his possession, he led his crew into the park between the Magdala Tower and Villa Bethania to begin digging. There a significant surprise awaited them:

An intensive excavation was begun within an area that was about four square yards. The soil was fill that had been brought there from somewhere else. At a depth of close to five feet our workers unearthed a skull and some remains. Because such discoveries are not rare in the subsoil of Rennes, they gave this no attention and continued their task. Great was their surprise an hour later to see N. Corbu's dogs sniffing these macabre remains, turning them over with their paws, and licking them. In astonishment the men looked more closely. The skull they had exhumed still had pieces of skin and hair adhering to it, along with the remains of a mustache. There were fragments of clothing and linen scattered at the bottom

---

6. This involves a magic ritual intended to repel defilers. Evidence of this tradition can be found in an early medieval Welsh tale that forms part of the Second Branch of the *Mabinogian*. It concerns the head of the hero Bran the Blessed, which had been buried in the White Hill of London. It is said that as long as the head remains there, England will never be invaded. We should also recall that Golgatha is the "Place of the Skull" and that the Capitol of Rome is the spot where the head of a man named Tolus (Caput Toli) was buried.

of the hole. Other remains were also contained therein . . . Struck by a sudden chill, they left the work site and abandoned the area.[7]

Of course, Noel Corbu alerted the police. The mayor ordered a more intensive excavation, during which they found the remains of three young men, twenty-five to thirty-five years of age. Their deaths were relatively recent and their clothing was surely of military issue. An inquest was called and it was learned that members of the Spanish resistance [the Maquis] had stayed in Villa Bethania during the war. Yet the identities of these three unfortunate souls, clearly the victims of a settling of old scores, were never discovered. All that could be done was to rebury them, in the cemetery this time, and after this the case files were closed.

This little incident would certainly add spice to the story. Just how many secrets did Rennes-le-Château hold? "Rennes became famous. Never were there so many visitors and so much curiosity. To the great delight of all visitors the residents obligingly recounted every step of the operation. In affairs of this kind, the macabre element is the crucial factor."[8] There were those who had not forgotten the fabulous treasure and who haunted not only Rennes but also the archives of Limoux and Carcassonne. Noel Corbu wrote a book about the Rennes-le-Château treasure and Saunière that was never published (the manuscript is now lost). As may well be expected, a horde of wild excavators, in complete ignorance and boorishness, dug holes everywhere. In fact, this happened so often (sometimes with the help of dynamite) that the municipality enacted a decree in 1965 prohibiting any excavation on communal property.

There were of course legitimate and duly authorized seekers who ran some search operations with no results. In 1962 Robert Charroux, then host of a well-known television show called *Treasure Hunters,* came in person to see about the story. This is what he offered during an interview with Jean-Luc Chaumeil.

We went several times to Rennes-le-Château, club members and myself, with our detectors. We got readings from two tombs, one

---

7. René Descadeillas, *Mythologie du trésor de Rennes* (Carcassonne: Savary reprint, 1988), 56.

8. R. Descadeillas, *Mythologie du trésor de Rennes,* 57.

of which was Béranger Saunière's. We did not want to defile it,[9] but no doubt there is something to be discovered there. Whatever it is, it does not appear to be lead, which produces very little radiation. The other tomb is even more interesting.[10]

We began some excavations, but took great precautions because the local people were closely watching us. We attacked a given point that was determined by heading from the Corbu property toward area X, but we did not find what we were looking for . . . [11] Today, I suspect Corbu, who was completely charming, of having put us on a false scent, or at least on a secondary trail that undoubtedly was not the best one. He knew better than anyone the history of Saunière and the famous treasure. He had dedicated his life to its discovery. If he truly wished to collaborate with us and the detectors we had at our disposal, I believe we would perhaps have ended up with something.[12] Corbu must have found something by himself: no doubt a part of the whole that Marie Denarnaud, servant and mistress of Saunière, had hidden in a safe place. Saunière himself must have had several hiding places. The priest was a cunning man.[13] He would not have put all his eggs in the same basket. I am certain that Corbu found one of these treasures.[14] I repeat, Rennes-le-Château should be taken seriously . . . [15]

---

9. But others had no such scruples about taking on this task.

10. Robert Charroux purposefully refrained from saying exactly which one.

11. It remains to be seen what Robert Charroux was truly looking for apart from something sensational he could show off in his productions. While certainly an excellent treasure hunter, Charroux exaggerated a great deal when it came to history, archaeology, and even esotericism.

12. The conceit of Charroux is obvious here.

13. It seems that despite appearances (tall and powerfully corpulent), Abbé Saunière had no audacity and even less cunning. The way he defended himself at his trial demonstrates his clumsiness—unless he was playing at being a fool.

14. It is unlikely that Corbu found anything considering the difficulties he encountered later. He wasn't "rolling in money," as they say, and his departure from Rennes resembles pure and simple retreat.

15. Interview by Jean-Luc Chaumeil from his book *Du premier au dernier Templier* (Paris: Henri Veyrier, 1985), 232–33.

So many vain attempts! Nevertheless, the story of Abbé Saunière, whether true or false, would spread and enthuse the crowds. Television got into the act and a crew showed up in Rennes-le-Château to film episodes in the life of the "millionaire priest." It was definitely a memorable period in the life of this remote village.

> Nothing could have brought more excitement to the good folks of Rennes, a number of whom were used as extras in the films. Corbu played the starring role, dressed as priest of 1900, wearing bands and a Roman hat.[16] From the seriousness with which he played his character, the unction that permeated him through and through, the condescension and benevolence that marked his every word and attitude, it is easy to sense that he had long played this role in his mind before putting on the habit. It was Saunière, but a refined, restrained, eloquent Saunière stripped of his athletic appearance, his cheer, and his somewhat vulgar joviality. Yet there was no one other than Corbu who could better repeat the words and gestures that legend attributed to the priest. Viewers could see Saunière slaving away on his research, joyful at his discovery; in his role as patron distributing money to those who had helped him; and as an adviser to these good folks who painfully carried their pails of water until they could soon enjoy the benefit of a potable water system. The picture was complete. All that was missing was the treasure![17]

Ah yes, it was the treasure that was missing but it was not for want of looking. Noel Corbu assuredly did not find it, though his search activities caused him to neglect the management of his hotel and restaurant. Madame Corbu, who was responsible for cooking and supplies, was getting tired of little profit for a lot of wasted time. Noel Corbu, however, never lacked for ingenuity and found a more profitable occupation. In an outbuilding he installed a workshop for the manufacture

---

16. Noel Corbu can be seen as Abbé Saunière in two photos published by René Descadeillas at the end of *Mythologie du trésor de Rennes*.

17. R. Descadeillas, *Mythologie du trésor de Rennes*, 65.

of lampshades and fans. Ultimately ravaged by fire, it ran until 1965. That year Corbu decided to move to Fanjeaux on the old road that goes from Carcassonne to Mirepoix. He left the region, selling the Restaurant de la Tour to Monsieur Henri Bouthon. Thus a page was turned in the history of Rennes-le-Château, but what Noel Corbu had written on it was far from being erased. After leaving Rennes-le-Château, Noel Corbu was involved in some bad business dealings. In 1968 he died in an automobile accident, but the business that had earned him nothing was definitively launched. Unfortunately, it was others who profited from it.

In 1967 a book by Gérard de Sède, *L'Or de Rennes: ou la vie inso-lite de Béranger Saunière, curé de Rennes-le-Château,* appeared in book-stores.[18] It was a smash hit, and this time Abbé Saunière, the modest priest of a no less modest village in the Razès, became a hero not only of local history but of the whole of Europe as well. What is more signif-icant, both for history and for Saunière the individual, is the bizarre role the priest was made to play. He would have been the first to be surprised at the dimensions certain episodes of his life were made to assume.

The subject of this book is both simple and complex: Abbé Saunière, priest of a small parish, discovered a secret, long jealously and piously preserved, concerning the survival of a legitimate heir to the Merovingian king Dagobert II (transformed into Saint Dagobert by popular acclaim). This king was assassinated by the Carolingians (at the time it was rather the forces of Pippin), but earlier he had hidden immense treasures in Rennes-le-Château for the purpose of reconquering the Aquitaine, a task he failed to accomplish and left to his descendants. How did Abbé Saunière discover the secret? That is a mystery. But "someone" let him know that he was authorized to draw from this royal treasure on condi-tion that he keep it secret. This very mysterious and discreet "someone" is obviously anonymous, but we are given to understand that his identity involves a duly mandated representative of the Priory of Sion, a very

---

18. *L'Or de Rennes: ou la vie insolite de Béranger Saunière, curé de Rennes-le-Château* (Paris: Julliard, 1967). The book was republished several times, mainly in the mass mar-ket collection of "J'ai Lu," under the new title *Le Trésor maudit de Rennes-le-Château.* Then in 1977 an edition with a great deal of new material was published by Plon under a third title, *Signé Rose+Croix.*

ancient order parallel to the Templar Order,[19] which was clandestinely survived by it. Instead of respecting his commitments, however, the priest lived beyond his means, which led to a warning from this mysterious "someone." Saunière made a bargain with this individual and was thus given permission to leave clues and landmarks so that others who came after him could have access to the treasure and use it to restore the legitimate Merovingian dynasty. Saunière then died, dreaming of founding a new religion of which he would be the leader.

What should we think about all of this? Mainly, we might acknowledge that Gérard de Sède has a lot of talent. But what can we say about the sources he gives and the documents he so obligingly reproduces? The sources are unverifiable, and when they can be verified, we see that they are based on documents that were falsified earlier. The documents themselves—photographs of stones and manuscripts—are obviously fakes that while not attributable to Gérard de Sède, are attributable to those who inspired him. Such is the case for the so-called parchments of Abbé Saunière, miraculously transferred from England, where they had been sleeping, it appears, in a bank, and of which copies were sent to several people, one of whom is the current owner of Villa Bethania in Rennes-le-Château.

We know that Béranger Saunière found parchments in the pillar that had held up the former altar—all the testimonies agree on this fact—but nothing remains of these documents anywhere, not in a public library or an archival cache. If they do still exist, let's hope someone has the good grace to reveal them.

Some have maintained that reproductions of these exist. This would be welcome news, but we would still have to interrogate the marquis Philippe de Cherisey, talented artist and friend of Pierre Plantard de Saint-Clair.

On visiting Rennes-le-Château in 1961, I learned that following Abbé Saunière's death the town hall had burned down (along with

---

19. Gérard de Sède had already published a book in 1962 on the Templars of Gisors, which enjoyed resounding success. It was in this book that the name Pierre Plantard was cited for the first time, which shows that the relationship between Plantard and the writer is quite old.

its archives), so I took advantage of the situation to invent a story that the mayor had made a copy of the parchments discovered by the priest. Then, at the suggestion of Francis Blanche,[20] I set about creating an encoded copy based on certain passages from the Gospels, after which I deciphered what I had just personally encoded. Finally, through a circuitous route I made sure the fruit of my labor found its way to Gérard de Sède. The results surpassed my wildest dreams.[21]

Cherisey completed his confessions to Jean-Luc Chaumeil, someone who was always quite close to the Saunière affair, by saying: "I fabricated the parchments, whose ancient text I took, *en onciale,* to the Bibliothèque Nationale, based on the work of Dom Cabrol."[22] Philippe de Cherisey, who boasted of knowing the *true* secret of Rennes-le-Château,[23] took this hoax as it deserves to be taken—that is, as a good farce. But upon whom was he intending to play this farce?

There are still more elements to this farce: Other documents presented in good faith in *L'Or de Rennes,* some of which involve the reproduction of carved stone, are more than suspect. The famous stele of the marquise d'Hautpoul is of guaranteed authenticity, but what

---

20. Cherisey met Francis Blanche during a film shoot in Belgium, and the two men became friends. The brilliant Francis Blanche, accomplice of the equally brilliant Pierre Dac, had a well-known taste for derision and mystification. Who could forget the radio program *Signé Furax?* Who has forgotten the "gag" of these two colleagues, who *created a psychiatric clinic for loco weeds?* Someone had to do it! During the course of conversation Cherisey told Francis Blanche what he knew of the Rennes-le-Château affair, particularly about the parchments found by Saunière. Francis Blanche then asked him to manufacture false documents and send them to him to be used in *Signé Furax.* Cherisey conscientiously performed this work—but instead of entrusting the parchments to Francis Blanche through the intermediary of the director, Pierre Arnaud de Chassipoulet, he made sure they discreetly found their way into the hands of Gérard de Sède. At least this is what Philippe de Cherisey says.

21. Philippe de Cherisey, *L'Énigme de Rennes,* typed brochure, 1978. See J. Robin, *Rennes-le-Château, la colline envoûtée.*

22. J.-L. Chaumeil, *Le Trésor du triangle d'or,* 80.

23. Most important is to know whether Cherisey was acting on his own or in the name of Pierre Plantard de Saint-Clair.

about the others? These stones were supposedly cited from a booklet entitled *Pierre gravées de Languedoc* and attributed to Eugène Stublein, a local scholar from the end of the nineteenth century, who happily signed his works "Stublein of the Corbières." But Eugène Stublein would have been greatly surprised to see his name on this rare booklet, which can be consulted only at the Bibliothèque Nationale, for he never concerned himself with archaeology. In fact, he was an amateur astronomer who spent his life looking only at the stars. He never made any study of the "carved stones of the Languedoc." The booklet is a blatant fake, in which, moreover, the unfortunate abbé Courtauly is also introduced—though he too had nothing to do with it.

The farce ultimately took a strange turn. René Descadeillas led a thorough inquiry into the matter and offers that apparently the name Abbé Courtauly had been mixed up with the story of "the carved stones of the Languedoc" and the Saunière affair because he had known the priest in his youth. Yet "[h]ow could this good and old priest have been led to lending his name to such aberrant fictions? What strange chain of circumstances could have been behind it?" René Descadeillas found the answer to these questions, but simply uncovering the pot of gold does not necessarily mean inalienable possession.

> During the final years of his life, while taking the waters at Rennes-les-Bains, Abbé Courtauly frequently encountered a strange individual who had taken to lurking in the neighborhood at the end of the 1950s. This man was a resident of Paris who had no connections or known relatives in the area. Hard to define, he was colorless, secretive, and wily with a gift for language. Those who had contact with him said he was hard to pin down. Because he was not following any regular medical treatments, his presence there raised questions, for he would visit even in winter. People indulged in endless conjecture on his interest in natural and archaeological curiosities, for he was no intellectual. His strange manner intrigued people: He often went out and walked the land, asking about the origins of different properties and setting his cap for those that were overgrown or abandoned and of no interest to anyone. . . . His comings and goings and the questions he posed to all and sundry could not remain long with-

out giving rise to rumor. He was regarded as a maniac and some perhaps laughed at him without realizing that the man was employing every strategy *to build a case in which banal events and trivial facts took on unexpected proportions.* Considerations of little importance, hastily delivered estimations, and *vague* phrases acquired much more definition when placed in the mouths of respectable people who were esteemed for their sagacity but perhaps weakened by age. He had no fear of attributing declarations to those whom he recorded on tape. On recordings, as we all know, it is permissible for anyone to tell any story he likes. Thus he credited Abbé Courtauly with extravagant remarks that did not concur with the priest's life or character. On this point those who knew and dealt with the priest are quite definite.[24]

René Descadeillas did not feel it necessary to name the person whom he had described with such precision, but he noted that the famous carved stones of the Languedoc are mentioned only in a small, multiple-author work that had been placed in the Bibliothèque Nationale of Paris (again!) in 1964. It was entitled *Généalogie des rois mérovingienss et origine des diverses familles françaises et étrangères de souche mérovingieene, d'après l'abbé Pichon, le docteur Hervé et les parchemins de l'abbé Saunière de Rennes-le-Château (Aude).* The avowed author of this odd booklet was Henri Lobineau, who resided at 22, place du Mollard, Geneva. It just so happens, however, that there is no 22, place du Mollard, and that no one, in either France or Switzerland, knows who Henri Lobineau is. These Lobineau papers are also fakes. But who has profited from them?

René Descadeillas is this person: He realized through the play of matching information that the strange visitor in Rennes-les-Bains was the author of the Lobineau papers. This man offered that he was a descendant of Dagobert II.[25]

Before going on, it would probably be a good idea to cite an extract from the book by Gérard de Sède himself, *Aujourd'hui les Nobles:*

---

24. R. Descadeillas, *Mythologie du trésor de Rennes,* 76.

25. Ibid.

The record of Baron Barclay de Lautour is bettered by far by this individual, who flooded the Bibliothèque Nationale with genealogical brochures written under pseudonyms suggesting that he, as a descendant of the Merovingian king Dagobert II, is a much more legitimate pretender to the French throne than the Carolingians, Capets, Valois, Bourbons, and Orleans put together.[26]

Did Gérard de Sède finally realize that he had been literally played for a fool by Pierre Plantard de Saint-Clair? For this is the name of the mysterious man in Rennes-les-Bains whom René Descadeillas described.[27]

But we are only at the beginning of the farce. The placement of the sham booklet *Généalogie des rois mérovingienss et origine des diverses familles françaises et étrangères de souche mérovingieene, d'après l'abbé Pichon, le docteur Hervé et les parchemins de l'abbé Saunière de Rennes-le-Château (Aude)* in the Bibliothèque Nationale was followed by the unexpected discoveries of new documents, each revealed to be just as false as the previous ones. These multi-authored works were still being sent from time to time to the Bibliothèque National, which was clearly running the risk of becoming the municipal dump of Rennes-le-Château if those running this game from the shadows continued to flood the copyright office. In order for one of these works—say, "Dossiers secrets d'Henri Lobineau: a Monseigneur le comte de Rhedae, duc de Razès, le légitime descendant de Clovis I, roi des Francs, sérénissime rejeton ardent de roi saint Dagobert II, son humble serviteur present ce receuil . . . etc."—to be a legally copyrighted, someone must sign a deposit slip and provide an address. But in these instances if the address even exists, no one there has ever heard of the sender. Perhaps the person in the case of this particular booklet is once again the mysterious individual in Rennes-les-Bains. We would have to think so. After all, how well known is it that *rejeton ardent* [hearty offshoot] is simply a translation into modern French of Plantard (plant-ard)?

Meanwhile, no one was asking the inhabitants of Rennes-le-

---

26. *Aujourd'hui les Nobles* (Paris: Éditions Alain Moreau, 1975).
27. Philippe de Cherisey claims it was Count Henri de Lenoncourt, alias Henri Lobineau.

Château their opinion of all of this deception. They simply suffered in silence except for a few outbreaks of complaining.

> It is madness. . . . For fifteen years they have been coming from all over: Montpellier, Toulouse, Bordeaux, Paris, Nancy. There are even foreigners, Germans especially. Sometimes they walk around with a pendulum in hand or some apparatus slung over their shoulder and an ordinance map in their pocket, they indulge in mysterious operations that we are all too familiar with here. As long as this is all they do, everything is fine and we are happy to welcome them. But some of these people are real vandals. They dig and tunnel, break and destroy anything and everything wherever they want, and the cost is high. In Rennes people are generally happy to welcome visitors, even those who have come to hunt for the famous treasure. Residents are fairly relaxed about this; no one is about to discover the trove tomorrow. These people are welcomed—yet no one is at all prepared to see them demolish everything. Some will not give up; they would run right over you if they thought it was necessary. So you see, people have begun to feel they have had enough of these kinds of tourists.

These grievances appeared in a Toulouse newspaper quite some time ago, but they allow us to begin to see why there is no longer a hotel in Rennes-le-Château.

If there was not an entirely authentic component, a piece of undeniable reality behind the Saunière affair, the whole crazy story could be treated with the scorn it deserves. But truth compels us to declare that among the brouhaha and permanent inebriation there exists something real. The inhabitants of Rennes-le-Château are fully aware of this and it is perhaps for this reason that they sometimes reach the limit of tolerance when people come from all over to overwhelm their village. If the Saunière affair profits anyone, it is certainly not the townsfolk.

But, then, who does profit from all this commotion? Never has the expression "One train can hide another" been so appropriate. Who is manipulating this intoxication? Who is pulling the strings of the marionettes onstage? The Priory of Sion?

Recently a small magazine has published a text by Pierre Bahier, a fan of the Priory. The article attempts to serve as intermediary between the curious public and the researchers. In a gripping fable of humor and wisdom, he sums up the situation with just the right choice of words. At the time of the Crusades, ten Knights Templar returned to France with documents seized from the Temple of Jerusalem. The text (quoted here in its entirety) addresses the question of who these knights might have been. Does anyone know their names?

No question is insoluble for the readers of *Facettes*. So here is (based on Jules Moschefol) the list of these ten knights to whom we owe the founding of the Order of Sion

1. Dupanloup of Sion (Haut-Savoie), *Dupanlupus ortus in vico Seduini, in Sabodiae.* The use of the word *vicus,* "town," proves that it is Sion (Haute-Savoie) rather than Sion (Valais), an Episcopal city described in the documents of that era as *civitas.* The adventures of Dupanloup provided the subject of a famous Templar marching song that has since been adopted by the French army.

2. Goupil of Gatinais, *Vulpes Gastinense pagi.* Vulpes should be translated as Goupil and not Renard [fox], which was still quite an uncommon name during that era.

3. Moschefol of Orleans, *Turpis insanus Genabensis, vel Aureliaensis, civis.* The interest of this mention will not escape the experts, for it clearly identifies Caesar's Genabum with Orleans.

4. Ar Pen of Brittany, *Caput Letaviensis.* The name Letavia designates Brittany in several hagiographic legends. We think there is good reason to translate Caput as Ar Pen rather than as "head." Formidable in combat, his German Templar comrades nicknamed him Kaput-Caput.

5. Dupont of Avignon

6. Rouget of Lille

7. Tartarin of Tarascon-sur-Ariege *(sic).*

8. Chapuzot of Tremblay-le-Vicomte (Eure-et-Loir)

9. Fanfan, known as The Tulip, a bastard child of unknown parentage.

10. Pandard of Rennes-le-Château (Aude). This last, a simple Templar of the second class, whereas all the others were petty officers or cor-

porals, was never promoted. His superiors considered him a mental lightweight *(levis insanus)* from all the hard knocks he took—which he survived without a scratch *(nitidi testiculi).* The Marechal Lefebvre—1755–1820—loved to use this expression translated literally. One day his comrades sent him out in search of the key to the drill grounds *(martis campi clavis).* He never returned to the campground. Sometime later it was noticed that the documents, whose seizure he had participated in, had disappeared and with them a parchment known as The Big Word on the Last Judgment *(Ultimi Judicii grandibus litteris),* an overpowering text that contained the exact date and precise time of the Second Coming.

Here is what happened next: The Templar Pandard, weary of his companion's jokes, fled Palestine and returned to Rennes-le-Château, where he became a sacristan. There he wed the servant of the presbytery, who had numerous children by either him or the priest—the scholars of the Carcassonne Society of the Sciences and Arts still debate this question. He thought to sell to the corner grocer the parchments he brought back from Jerusalem, but the village tutor *(Vici puerorum Magister),* having seen the documents and thinking they might be of interest to future generations, advised him to hide them instead beneath the high altar of the parish church, which he did.

In 1887 the documents were rediscovered by the priest Béranger Saunière when construction work began in the church. When the priest traveled to Paris to get an expert opinion of them, he by chance met Jules Doinel, archivist of Loiret, who bought the documents from him. (It is absolutely false to maintain, as some ill-intentioned individuals have, that this meeting took place in One-Two-Two, the famous pleasure establishment on the rue de Provence, whose threshold the two parties in question never crossed, as might well be expected.) Today, these documents as well as those discovered since in Carcassonne by the same Doinel, who took advantage of a job opening to have himself transferred there in 1899, are deposited in the archives of the Order of Sion, which is preparing their complete publication in a French translation by la Pensée Universelle.

Until it appears sometime in the future, readers may look to: Jules Doinel, *Mémoires d'un archiviste départmental* (posthumous work), Carcassonne, 1905; Laguillamette et Croquebol, *Paris by Night sous la présidence de Sadi-Carnot*, Paris, 1950; Pierre Pandard, *Ma Famille et l'Ordre de Sion*, Annemasse, 1957; Bernard de Sade, *La Dernière Charge des Templiers*, Toulouse, 1984; Jean Mabize, *Les Templiers précurseurs de la Waffen S.S.*, Paris, 1986.

—BASED ON JULES MOSCHEFOL,
PRIOR OF SAINT-SAMSON (ORDER OF SION).[28]

There is nothing incongruous about this text, or fable rather, and its humor is perhaps more corrosive than simply irreverent. Readers will recognize who is concealed behind the Templar Pandard and who is being needled in the "bibliography."[29] Most important, this fable, in contrast to so-called serious works, places the Saunière affair back in its exact context—that is to say, between a problematic and phantomlike Priory of Sion and a perfectly real individual, Jules Doinel, who was departmental archivist of the Aude after he performed the same function for Loiret. Doinel was a notorious Freemason, but most notably was the founder of a bizarre Gnostic sect that perfectly fit the tone of the era around 1900, which was halfway between spirituality and the blackest kind of Satanism.

---

28. *Facettes*, no. 187 (May 1988), 26–27. [Most of this firmly tongue-in-cheek article is composed of puns and wordplay that are often untranslatable. For example, the expression "key to the drill grounds" combines two common French expressions, *la clef du champs* (at full liberty) and *champs du manoeuvres* (parade or drill ground). The knights' names also involve wordplay: Dupont, d'Avignon (the bridge of Avignon, as in the popular song); Rouget de Lille relates to Rouget de Lisle, the French soldier who wrote "La Marseillaise," the French national anthem; Tartarin de Tarascon is the name of a work by Alphonse Daudet, and so on. We can also see the names of principal players in the Rennes-le-Château affair slightly altered in the story of the documents. —*Translator*]

29. It will be noted that the only intact name in this bibliography is that of Doinel. This is not without reason, for Jules Doinel probably knew a great deal about the Saunière affair. Among others, attention is directed to Jean Mabize (Jean Mabire, in reality), whose inclusion is explained by his research on the German army and its relationship with secret societies. Do not forget that according to the German version of the Grail legend (by Wolfram von Eschenbach), the Grail is guarded by a troop of Templars who are closer in appearance to the German S.S. than to Christian knights charged with the protection of pilgrims traveling to the Holy Land.

Jules Doinel was present in Béranger Saunière's life, but discreetly and always in the background. If we need to find an explanation for the Masonic symbols in the church of Rennes-le-Château, it is partly to Doinel and partly to Dujardin-Beaumetz that we should look. Béranger Saunière did not have any kind of well-defined artistic sensibility. It is certain that he asked advice from certain individuals. It so happened that Dujardin-Beaumetz was a painter and a Freemason, and Jules Doinel was a Freemason archivist and Gnostic who specialized in hermetic symbolism.

Jules Doinel was also rather an odd duck. Did he have contact with Béranger Saunière at the time the priest made his first finds in the church? Perhaps. Did he have some effect on the behavior of the priest of Rennes-le-Château? Perhaps. Jules Doinel was aware of many of the little "secrets" shared by the various sects and so-called philosophical societies that were swarming over the surface of the earth at that time. He had held a post in Orleans and concerned himself specifically with the Priory of Saint-Samson, which the so-called adepts of the Priory of Sion designated as having been their fallback point when the order was forced to leave Palestine. There is a reason why the *Facettes* article, in principal a humorous one, refers to a Jules Moschefol (which means "mad fly"), who was called the Prior of Saint Samson of Orleans. However real the Order of Sion may have been, it was hiding something, and Doinel was shrewd enough to catch sight of it.

In fact, this singular conservator from the Loiret archives (one who certainly knew the most about the archives relating to Saint Samson) ended his career in Carcassonne, where he was practically assured a connection with the no-less-singular local scholar Abbé Boudet. Now the unfortunate Doinel, who had restored the Ecclesial Gnosis in 1889 under the patriarchal name of Valentine II, seemed predisposed to serve as an instrument of highly suspect influences. In fact, he soon recanted Gnosis before the bishop of Orleans and, under the pseudonym of Jean Kotska, published books that were in the spirit, it might be said, of Leo Taxil.[30]

---

30. J. Robin, *Rennes-le-Château, la colline envoûtée*, 87. Leo Taxil was a journalist and ex-Freemason who wrote anti-Semitic pamphlets and turned against the Masons by publishing a series of invented documents.

Doinel subsequently fell back into his Gnostic errors and published some rather stupefying books in which phrases such as the following could be found. "The count of Saint-Germain was one of the most powerful demon missionaries of Satan." This quote emphasizes what a murky and unsettling presence Jean Doinel was, and how he could allow himself be manipulated by this side or that.

While "one train can definitely hide another" in the Rennes-le-Château affair, we no longer know who is hiding whom or who is manipulating whom. Manipulation necessarily took place, even if we do not believe in the actual existence of certain "philosophical brotherhoods." These groups have had the good sense to remain in the shadows, assume borrowed names, or even infiltrate existing groups that are perfectly orthodox. This is why the Priory of Sion appears to be a red herring. It is intended to hide something, to divert attention, which is very clear with respect to the Saunière affair. It is good to carefully read the abridged version of the facts that the famous Lobineau papers give us:

> One day in February 1892, the young abbé Hoffet received a strange visitor, Abbé Saunière, priest of Rennes-le-Château since 1885, who had come to see him in order to ask this young and knowledgeable linguist to translate some mysterious parchments that had been found in the pillars of the Visigothic high altar of his church. These documents bore the royal seal of Blanche de Castille and revealed the secret of Rhedea with the lineage of Dagobert II, as Abbé Pichon had managed to establish between 1805 and 1814, according to documents discovered after the Revolution.[31] Abbé Hoffet, conscious of the importance of these acts, kept a copy but did not give Saunière the exact truth. The prudent priest of Renne-le-Château consulted other linguists to whom he gave only fragments of documents.

---

31. During the time of the First Empire, Napoleon gave Abbé Pichon the responsibility of classifying, consulting, and possibly selecting the various archives and documents he had been able to seize from the Vatican. The figure of Abbé Pichon was naturally considerably enlarged in the esteem of occultists and other amateurs of the nineteenth century and became almost a myth. He was alleged to have had access to the most dreadful secrets of the papacy.

It is obvious that there was never any question of the lineage of Dagobert II before the so-called Priory of Sion decided to publish information on the subject or disperse this information through individuals acting as buffers. This immediately exuded an odor of fabrication *a posteriori,* for Béranger Saunière never made a single reference to the Merovingian era. Yet the cleverness shown here consists of the close connection between the real folk tradition about the Reine Blanche— the White Queen who would be, for now, the one from Castille, a local legend of Rennes-les-Bains and not Rennes-le-Château (which Pierre Plantard, the inspirer or author of the Priory, knew perfectly well from his long stay at the "Bains de la Reine")—and the completely new discovery of the existence of a direct line descended from Clovis. Poor Abbé Saunière, who was no complete innocent, had never believed as naively as he believed that he had placed his hands on the hoard gathered by his predecessor, Abbé Bigou.

We should note the lack of historically correct information about the members of this famous Priory of Sion. In 1882 Émile Hoffet was merely a simple student of theology. He was not an abbot, and what's more, if he had been a priest, he would have been called Father, for he was a member of the religious congregation known as the Oblates of Mary. The writer or writers of the Lobineau papers would have been able to learn from any clergyman the customs of the Catholic Church and should have been able to make certain that dates coincided.

But these are mere trifles. The most important was yet to come.

> During this time, Abbé Hoffet reestablished, thanks to this valuable information, a complete genealogy of the descendants of Dagobert II, the king Ursus whose ancestors were kings in Arcadia. It so happens that the kings of Arcadia came from Bethany, near the Mount of Olives, from the tribe of Benjamin.

If we understand this correctly, the Priory of Sion, although the guardian of secret traditions, had to wait for Saunière's discovery to learn that descendants of the Merovingians still lived. Without Abbé Saunière, there would be no Lobineau papers and Priory of Sion. But at this point a new legend was grafted onto the first one: the legend of King Ursus, whose ancestors were kings in Arcadia. This obviously brings to mind Nicolas Poussin's *The Shepherds of Arcadia* and the strange tomb located on the road to Arques.[32] We might even connect Arques to Arcadia—against all good reason, for the name Arques comes from the Latin *arces,* which is a plural noun meaning "citadels"—for with a little bit of hocus-pocus it is easy to construe the names Arques and Arcadia to have come from the Indo-European word that gave us the Breton *arz,* which can be found in the name Arthur and which means "bear." So here we have King Ursus and his ancestors, who were kings of the land of bears—that is, Arcadia. The bear has great symbolic importance as the animal that sleeps in the winter and reawakens in the summer. Follow where I am going here: The descendant of the Bear will soon rule over a new Arcadia. Happiness is promised for tomorrow. And all of this is, of course, inscribed in the heavens; we have only to look up to see the Big Dipper[33] and Arcturus. It is truly regrettable that no one thought of citing the British king Arthur in the pseudo-mythological morass; he would have clinched the deal. Perhaps, though, the members of the Priory of Sion did not know Celtic mythology or even the stories of the Round Table.

But let's move on. After having declared that Dagobert II has descendants, there really should be an explanation as to why history never mentions them. But then again, let's not allow that to stop us.

> Here is the motive for denying the existence of Dagobert II.[34] No, not entirely, for before his assassination by the family of the Pepins, who had coveted the kingdom for several generations, Dagobert II saw to it that a large treasure was hidden in Rhedea, the land of his second wife, mother to his son Sigebert IV. The existence of this treasure was an important motive for his murder. Neither Queen Blanche nor King Louis IX dared touch this sacred hoard, even in the year 1251, because legend threatened the destruction of those, whether king or pope, who appropriated it without any right.

---

32. [Since the time of this book's initial publication, this tomb has been destroyed. The current landowner became weary of chasing trespassers off his property and decided to remove it as the object that attracted this unwanted attention. —*Translator*]

33. [Called the Big Bear in French. —*Translator*]

34. History has never denied the existence of Dagobert II, only that of his descendants.

But the story gets better. We learn that Blanche, although a model Christian, was superstitious—she was frightened of the Merovingian curse and for this reason would not lay a finger on the treasure amassed through the pains of Dagobert II. It should be said that the story's detail about the tribe of Benjamin lost in Arcadia and then rediscovered in the Merovingian family will not put some people's minds at ease. Could the first kings of France have had Jewish ancestors? It happens that at the time Saunière discovered the famous parchments, there was no "commissariat for the Jewish Question," as was the case during World War II. If there had been, Saunière would have been suspected not of spying for the Austrians but of betraying France for the benefit of an alleged Jewish plutocracy. Even so, during Saunière's time anti-Semitism was on the rise and his discovery occurred shortly before the Dreyfus Affair. It is easy to see why Saunière would not have wanted to reveal his secret. . . . What was important, though, was to have these documents suggest the theme of the Lost King.

For hope remained.

In the great century, says one of the parchments, the offspring will regain the heritage of the great Ursus. This is the legend in which the Gospel is used to curse in the parchments the malefactor who dares to steal a part of this treasure. One parchment also retraces the history of an epoch about which we have known almost nothing. Abbé Saunière was summoned to the papal court in Rome[35] but refused to explain himself. He was accordingly suspended from office[36] and died in mysterious circumstances on 22 January 1917. His servant and heiress Marie Denarnaud, who died in January 1953, ended her life in seclusion.[37] Without Abbé Hoffet, no one would have known the strange history of a family whose origins are lost in the mists of time. Henri Lobineau, genealogist, March 1954.[38]

---

35. He was summoned before the official Church court—the bishop's tribunal—and that is all. He subsequently appealed his sentence to the pope, but he was never summoned to Rome.

36. He was *suspens a divinis,* which is quite different.

37. This is false, but because she was already old, she almost never left the premises.

38. *Papiers Lobineau,* 14.

First we might note the language employed in these excerpts by the so-called genealogist. In order to understand their meaning, some phrases have to be read twice; it is as if the text has been clumsily translated from German. We can also note that the text does not really acknowledge Saunière for having brought these documents to light. Instead, all the merit is awarded to Abbé Hoffet. But all this simply reveals again that the Priory knows nothing of history and is totally reliant upon fortuitous discoveries. None of this is at all serious—it is surprising that sensible people could put faith in such twaddle. All the more aggravating is that when an inquiry on Émile Hoffet was launched among those who knew and worked with him, it was learned that "he had never taken an interest in the Merovingians and that it was impossible for someone to have consulted with him in 1892, for that was the year he completed his study of rhetoric and solemnly put on the habit as a novice in Holland."[39]

They have made their case.

The Saunière affair is not resolved by giving prominence to the imposter Lobineau, to the pseudo-order called the Priory of Sion, or to any others who may lurk in the shadow of that "brotherhood." Nor does this eliminate the possibility of a mysterious "treasure"—whatever it might be—buried somewhere in the Razès. The enigma of the cursed gold is a reality we must accept or otherwise risk getting bogged down in the swamps of confusion.

---

39. R. Descadeillas, *Mythologie du trésor de Rennes,* 84.

Part 3

THE MYSTERY OF THE CURSED TREASURE

7

Treasure Island

There is not a single region in the world that does not have its own buried treasure tradition. It is one of humanity's most tenacious myths, probably connected to the myth of the Golden Age of Eden, that Paradise Lost slumbering in the depths of every individual. Having been hounded out of Paradise, that marvelous Orchard whose fruits are ripe year-round, we humans believe this place is hidden just out of sight behind a screen of mist or under our feet within the earth. For we feel that the earth is our Mother who produces fruit, provides the water without which life could not exist, gives a haven to the dead, and serves as our "reverse world," which is reached only after much crawling through a darkness that ends in the sudden blaze of light from caverns glimmering with gold and precious stones. All folktales and mythological epics mention caves. Depth psychology has related all these imaginary yearnings to the unconscious desire to return to the womb, but this explanation, while perfectly logical, does not concern how we live life. How we live is fueled by beliefs and not certitudes.

The Razès, like everywhere else, does not lack for legends about buried treasure. It could even be said that they are more plentiful here, for the region's very nature lends itself as much to this kind of fantasy as it does to maintaining the permanence of human relics. It is a borderland of tortured contours; steep-sided, isolated valleys; and ground that is riddled with more or less undiscovered caverns. As everyone knows, all that is needed is a map and, more important, knowledge of how to read it, to find the Treasure. Alas! Few people succeed, for treasure is not only very skillfully hidden and inaccessible, but it is also guarded by beings more or less like fairies or demons that forbid access to anyone who does not carry the famous Golden Bough. In other words, every time we speak of treasure, we immediately speak of a guard at its threshold who must be repelled, pacified, or eliminated if anyone wishes to reach the secret chamber that holds the hoard. The structure of such myths is almost identical everywhere and broadly corresponds to that of the quest for the Grail or even with that of the shamanic journey.

There is no need to travel far from Rennes-le-Château to discovers if not a treasure, then a traditional treasure legend peddled for centuries by the voice (and ways) of the folk, which is the best method for preserving ancestral memory. We need only travel northeast of the village as far as the ruins of Blanchefort Castle. This is the site of a story much like those we hear on long winter evenings, a tale that was recorded in 1832 by a certain Labouisse-Rochefort, an enthusiast of travel and legends.

> We were quite close to the remnants of that fortress of Blanchefort where the devil has long guarded a treasure. The local people are positively convinced that it consists of nineteen and a half million in gold, whether bullion, objects, tokens, or coins.[1]

It can be seen that the legend of cursed gold in Rennes-le-Château does not date from Abbé Saunière. The notion of gold guarded by the devil forms a theme that is particularly widespread in popular memory. It corresponds with the ambivalent nature of all that is secret, obscure, and buried in the subconscious before it takes material form on earth. Desire is inspired by fear, and vice versa.

But this state exists permanently, and could even be called a latent state. It requires a specific circumstance to cause the event to manifest. Here is the story:

> One day, when the devil had some free time (this was before the Revolution) and it was a beautiful sunny day, he started to spread his nineteen and a half million over the mountainside. A young

---

1. Labouisse-Rochefort, *Voyage à Rennes-les-Bains* (Paris, 1832), 149.

shepherdess of the neighborhood who had arisen early that morning saw this huge pile of beautifully gleaming coins and reacted to the sight with a mixture of alarm and surprise and turned back to call her mother, father, aunt, and uncle to the scene. All came running to see it, but the devil is very quick—everything had disappeared before they got there.

A contemporary observer might conclude that what the young shepherdess saw was only the sun's reflection on the white stones of Blanchefort or even that she was neurotic and had only projected her own desire, and there the matter would rest. But once upon a time people did not think this way:

The big news swept through the village, inciting curiosity and much bustle and excitement. Several townsfolk got together to discuss the matter and decided to consult a magician. This they did and told him all about the marvelous discovery. The magician was not stupid; first he specified that he be given half of the treasure once they had taken it, but before that he would need four or five hundred francs to pay for the preparations for his voyage.

The reaction of the magician is also a classic one. Someone who performs magic, or a priest, must always be given something if one wishes the rite to be crowned with success. The magician takes upon himself only the *secret* risks of the mission. It is up to others to bear the material risks.

The money was counted and the townsfolk set off to the magician's. He forewarned them that he would be battling the devil and when he called, someone would have to step up and help him. Everyone swore to keep up their courage and then made their way to the site where the gold was seen. The magician put on a show, speaking invocations and threats while tracing circles and strange figures in the air. All at once a loud noise was heard. The townsfolk took fright and fled at great speed, pursued by stones and firecrackers. In vain the magician cried: Help! Help! Without a glance at the combat they left him yelling there. Finally, a long time later, he reappeared, sad, gasping for breath, and covered with dust. He complained to those who had abandoned him: He had knocked the devil down and was on top of him, and if they had come running at his call, they would have had the victory—and the treasure. He reproached them for their cowardice and, grumbling and mumbling, left for Limoux after having retained the deposit made for his services.

We can immediately hear the ironic tone the story takes here. After all, if the magician only pretended there had been a battle, it would be a very convenient way to earn some money to the detriment of some credulous villagers. In a land such as the Occitan region that has been eaten away by rationalism or by what is called "scientism," this is how the anticlerical—and anti-magician—tendency would be expressed.

In other religions, there might be a slight variation in the ending to this tale. For example, a Breton story from the Auray region recounts a story of treasure buried beneath a menhir that is guarded by the devil. Some villagers decide to take the hoard for their own but make certain to ensure the cooperation of a priest in their endeavor. The plan calls for the villagers to dig while he "reads from his book"; but no one else is allowed to say a word or answer during this task. Of course, the devil assumes different guises and comes to engage them in talk, but they say nothing until at the end one of the villagers cannot restrain himself. At this point a burst of flame erupts from the place where they have been digging. The priest then tells them, "If you had followed my advice, this treasure would be yours. But you could not manage to avoid the temptation to speak. Now, no one will ever be able to get this treasure."[2] The conclusion is much more orthodox here, but it remains quite similar to the Blanchefort tradition.

In any event, the treasure escapes possession by common mortals no matter what strategies are employed to take it. An esoteric journal openly declares in an article entitled "The Fabulous Treasure of Abbé Saunière": "This treasure, whatever its true origin, has been recuperated by secret societies who keep jealous watch over its hiding place. Like many other treasures that are unknown, it must serve to finance

---

2. Jean Markale, *Contes populaires de toutes les Bretagnes* (Rennes: Ouest-France, 1977), 294.

the secret designs of the mysterious masters of the world who direct our steps while we are none the wiser."[3] And who would be the supreme master of these "masters of the universe" if not the devil himself? The devil is convenient because he symbolizes all that is obscure.

We would be wrong to take this warning lightly, even if this story about "secret societies" is laughable to us, for this "cursed treasure" does exist. It even appeared openly in the year 1665, during the reign of the Sun King, who took a keen interest in the Razès following the imprisonment of Foucquet and initiated some mysterious excavations in the region. Here again the event is conveyed by oral folk tradition: One spring day an old shepherd of Rennes was returning with his flock when he noticed a lamb was missing. He followed the example of the good shepherd in the Gospel and returned to the location where he had spent the day. Once there, he indeed heard bleating.

> Drawing closer, he saw that the animal had fallen into a pit. The shepherd climbed down into the hole, but just as he caught hold of the animal, it took fright and burrowed into a narrow tunnel that went deep into the ground. Pursuing the lamb into the dark, where he could make his way forward only by stooping over, he was suddenly dumbfounded when he collided with something. What a marvel! His fingers felt the edges of coins. Groping further he realized with terror that he was also touching human remains. As if pursued by a thousand ghosts, the unfortunate shepherd hastily retraced his path back to the pit, but not until he had first filled his hood with pieces of money. Once back on the surface of the earth, his chief concern was to return as quickly as possible to Rennes with his discovery. He was dazzled by so much gold—he had never seen any before in his life. It was not Providence, however, that put this fortune into his hands. It was his ill luck that news of his discovery ran throughout the village until the rumor quickly made its way to the lord of Rennes, probably Henri d'Hautpoul, who saw to it that the unfortunate shepherd was seized and questioned in order to make him confess exactly where he had found the gold in his possession. But the ill treatment he received at the hands of the torturers prevailed

---

3. *Nostradamus,* no. 51.

over the peasant's advanced age and he succumbed to their mis-treatment. Furious at the ill-trained brutes' heavy-handedness, the lord of Rennes had his clumsy torturers executed.[4]

What we have here is a perfect example of a myth within a histor-ical context. All the ingredients are here: the chance discovery, the underground location, the gold coins, the human remains that inspire fear, and, finally, punishment because someone has made off with part of a treasure that belongs only to higher powers (in this instance, the lord of Rennes), who are the sole guardians of these "infernal abodes." Even though it is possible to date the events in this tale and give the name of the shepherd (Ignace Paris) and that of the lord (Hautpoul), this in no way implies that the adventure really took place. Through this example, however, we can see that the terrain was prepared for the more or less clandestine excavations of Abbé Saunière.

It seems that Saunière knew this story; the strongest proof is that he had it carved on the pediment of his confessional. In fact, we can see there the scene in which the shepherd, with his back bent, is pursuing his lamb through the underground tunnel. It seems that this theme is something that spoke directly to his heart. Of course, it could also be seen as a clue, one of those "keys" that some observers strive so doggedly to find in every minor detail of the Church of Mary Magdalene in Rennes-le-Château.

In the years that followed Abbé Saunière's death, the villagers were convinced, without bitterness or even envy, that the priest and "Mademoiselle Marie" had discovered an underground tunnel that led from the church to the castle. According to popular belief, it was in this underground corridor that Saunière and Marie discovered gold coins, precious jewels, and even a crown. This is what was said. But oral folk tradition is alive and ceaselessly adapts old myths, making them more contemporary within a specific framework.

This has long been the case in the Razès, where both local and regional public opinion, whether or not influenced by the clergy (sole keepers of knowledge), has always concealed places of refuge for fugitives of all kinds as well as for their secrets and their most precious possessions.

---

4. Quoted by P. Jarnac, who believes in the reality of the facts and makes it the starting point of a legend (*Histoire du trésor de Rennes-le-Château*, 108).

It is from this perspective that we understand the large Jewish presence in the Razès. Jews settled there long ago to escape persecution. While it is true that a significant portion of the Aude populace is Jewish, there has never been reason to believe, outside certain authors' imaginations, that they are the descendants of the lost tribe of Israel. There is a firm belief in the region that the Razès likewise provided asylum for Alaric's Visigoths, who were hounded out of Italy; indeed, a similar belief is shared throughout the entire Corbières region and even Carcassonne. This has in turn inspired another belief: that treasure brought by Alaric is to be found there, still hidden in an inaccessible location. There is incontestable historical support for the presence of the Visigoths in the region and the lasting influence they exerted on it, but when myth closely matches history, it provides an open door for all kinds of speculation, including some assertions concerning the treasure of the Temple of Jerusalem.

This tradition is in fact based on verifiable events. We know that in the year 70 C.E. Titus, son of Emperor Vespasian, "pacified" Palestine—or in other words, he sacked it. In the process he took the holy city of Jerusalem and pillaged its temple. This is a memorable date for all Jews, who since that time have never ceased meeting and praying at the Wailing Wall, the sole remnant of the temple attributed to Solomon. The Romans, who could display great tolerance toward religions other than their own, were nonetheless merciless to those who resisted them. The destruction of the Temple of Jerusalem had become a necessity to ensure their presence in the Middle East. Of course, the sacred objects found in the temple—in particular, the huge chandelier made of solid gold—were brought back to Rome, where they figured prominently in the imperial treasury, along with the spoils wrested from all the other peoples subjugated by Roman authority.

The empire's decline was accompanied by the growing menace of the Goths. It was Alaric, the leader of the Visigoths, who seized Rome in 410 and pillaged the city. All the imperial treasure, including the booty from Jerusalem, thus made its way into his hands. Following Alaric's death, his brother-in-law, now leader of the Visigoths, and his people left Italy and settled in southern Gaul. It is thought that Alaric's successors settled in Toulouse. Naturally, they did not forget to bring with them the immense riches they had stolen from Rome. At the time of Clovis,

Alaric II was ruling peacefully over a large Visigoth empire. But in seeking to ensure his hegemony and claiming to be the true successor of the Roman emperors, Clovis could not tolerate the Visigoth presence and invaded Aquitaine. It was at this time that Alaric II made haste to find safe storage for his fabled war treasure.[5]

---

5. One of my former students, Gérard Lupin, who is currently engaged in intensive research on the mountain of Alaric, sent me some information that has the possibility of overturning official notions concerning the struggle of the Visigoths and Franks and the famous treaure of Alaric. A native of Corbières, Gérard Lupin first mentioned a popular saying that he had heard personally: "Between Alaric and Alaricou is the treasure of three kings." The Alaricou is a detached part of the mountain of Alet. Here is what Gérard Lupin has to say about this subject. "This saying alludes to Kings Solomon, Caesar, and Alaric, whose combined treasures would have been hidden in the mountain of Alaric during the era of the Visigoth Septimania. The fabulous treasure would therefore have come from Rome by way of Calabria to be hidden on this mountainous island in the Languedoc plain. There is nothing surprising about this because this mountain, formed of limestone, is a veritable Swiss cheese, liberally seeded with caves, some better explored than others, that neighbor the shafts of abandoned Roman mines. To advance this contention local people rely on the words of the Greek historian Procope, who wrote in the sixth century that the battle between Alaric II and Clovis did not take place in Vouillé, but 'between Carcassonne and Narbonne.' This is where where Alaric would have been buried—in the mountain that bears his name, along with his treasure and his elephants." Gérard Lupin stresses the fact that the placement of Vouillé is based only on the words of Gregory de Tours, who is equally as unreliable as the Byzantine Procope, which means that Procope is just as credible as Gregory de Tours. He goes on to say, "New elements have come to the aid of the Languedoc legend and the words of Procope, by which I mean that work on the highway connecting the two seas has allowed a number of Visigoth sepulchers to be unearthed near the town of Capendu. These were so numerous that work on the highway had to be halted for several months. A good number of these sepulchers do not correspond to customary Visigoth burial rituals, and several skeletons have been found in the same hole, which suggests that such a great battle had taken place there and burial was made in such great haste that the rituals were somewhat neglected." It is not absurd, then, to place the battle of Vouillé here. There are plenty of examples of other false placements. We know now that the true Gregovie is not at the official site on the plateau of Merdogne, but at the Roman hill fort of Côtes, just above Clermont-Ferrand. As for Alesia, it is totally impossible that it was at Alise-Sainte-Reine in Burgundy. The location of Alesia can be found only in the land of the Sequani, meaning the Jura, in Alaise or at Salins-les-Bains. We should not forget that official history is quite often based solely on gratuitous declarations or unique testimonies (however, *testis unus testis nullus!*) that have been arbitrarily retained because it pleased certain individuals, generally local businessmen, who could turn it to their advantage. The same can be said of pilgrimage sites that allegedly hold the relics of this or that saint.

But as to the place where the Visigoth king concealed his treasures, the versions diverge considerably. In one of these variations, the burial place is Carcassonne. This, in fact, is what can be deduced from a passage of Procope (*De Bello Gothico,* I, 2) that mentions the arrival of the Franks in Carcassonne: "having heard that they held the imperial riches the old Alaric had carried away when he captured the city of Rome. Among these riches, it was said, were a good number of Solomon's furnishings, said to be adorned with jewel work, and something beautiful to behold. The Romans had once brought these furnishings out of Jerusalem." We may note that the chandelier is not mentioned at all and that the description involves only a part of the treasure.

This bit of information gave birth to numerous hypotheses. According to some, another part of the treasure was secreted in the mountains and divided among several hiding places. According to others, it is in what is still called the mountain of Alaric. For some, the remnants of Solomon's treasure are housed on the sides of the peak of Bugarach. And, of course, the citadel of Reddae also figures into the equation. In any event, Alaric's treasure, whose existence there is no reason to doubt, has experienced quite a few moves in these unstable times. Alaric II was defeated and killed at Vouillé in 507. The riches that were still in Toulouse fell into the hands of Clovis, but everything that had been moved earlier escaped his grasp. Theodoric then came along to transport the treasure to Ravenna, but it was subsequently returned, taken to Spain, then hidden again in Carcassonne or in the Corbières—and what better hiding place, at least according to the legend, than the fortress of Reddae?

This was the version of the story that was popularized during the nineteenth century. It is based on fairly specific traditions: the famous German smelters brought into the Razès by the Templars during the twelfth century and the searches made during Colbert's time. In addition, a fair number of fortuitous discoveries have been made over the centuries, modest finds to be sure, but enough to suggest that a much larger deposit still lies hidden underground somewhere in the region. When he arrived in Rennes-le-Château, Béranger Saunière could no more ignore the legend of Solomon's treasure than could anybody else in the area.

Complications arise, however, when a parallel is drawn between the incontestable Visigoth presence in the region and the equally incontestable presence of the Templars. Whatever the motives behind the Templars' decision to settle in Bézu (surveillance of the road to Saint-Jacques of Compostella, a safe haven near the frontier, military reasons?), the region's inhabitants have always believed the knights came to this remote area to find a safe place to store treasure, and folk tradition still echoes this belief today. We should not forget that the Templars of Bézu were dependents not of the kingdom of France, but of Roussillon and thus, indirectly, of Aragon, whereas those Templars in Campagne-sur-Aude answered to France. This complex situation has given rise to strange speculations. According to tradition, the Templars of Bézu

> . . . concealed part of their monetary reserves, which were not safe in Roussillon, in very secret caches. They also stored in such places the monetary reserves entrusted to them by the great families of the "Majorcan" part of Roussillon, who, incidentally, would not recover their deposits, including perhaps the property of the king of Majorca. Their presence in the valley of Bézu encouraged the belief that they were hiding treasure here and in the immediate surroundings. In reality, a large portion had been entrusted to the Templars of Campagne-sur-Aude, who would have hidden it in an underground cache located beneath the church and the area around the church. What has contributed to giving credence to this tradition is that Campagne is a small medieval town that is curious for all the vestiges of the past it contains and for the presence of underground tunnels beneath it, some traces of which still remain. What also substantiates the tradition is that strange discoveries have been made on the Lauzet Plateau and in the Bézu Valley.[6]

Under these conditions, we can see why so many treasure hunters throughout history have come to this region, where it is relatively easy to create "caches." In light of this, the moving of the Templar tradition to the village of Rennes-le-Château is self-evident: Popular opinion

---

6. Abbé Mazières, *Les Templiers du Bézu* (Rennes-le-Château: Édition Schrauben), 24.

maintains that the caches were divided over the entire region. All the data are combined and the treasure of the Temple of Jerusalem makes its way back to the surface.

In fact, the Knights of the Temple, who were first established in Jerusalem and charged with the security of pilgrims making their way to the Holy Land (this was the original and *admitted* purpose of the order at its creation), enjoyed long periods of contact with the Middle East. It is even claimed that they saw eye to eye with certain Muslim sects. In any event, they had a profound knowledge of the Holy Land. From this it is not far to imagining that they had recovered documents from the site of Solomon's Temple. Given that they had done this, why wouldn't they have discovered Christian documents as well concerning the life of Jesus, the Crucifixion, and the Resurrection? This question has been raised many times, and the strange behavior of the Templars, who spat on the Cross while denying the Crucified One, is not the least of the arguments used both to condemn them and to cast them as the keepers of dreadful secrets. Thus, along with the Templars' reputation for possessing immense wealth (though in reality it seems they may only have owned lands), it was realistic to assume that they also owned documents, manuscripts mainly, that were even more valuable than gold or material goods.[7]

All of this cannot help but add to the mystery of the "treasure" that could be discovered in the Razès, and it had a great influence on the story built around Abbé Saunière after 1956. To render the figure of Saunière more alluring, it was necessary to make him, if not a member, then at least the involuntary servant of a secret society. Now, what could be more secret than the Order of the Temple, officially disbanded by Pope Clement V, but that some claim has survived clandestinely! This fact has inevitably prompted much speculation around the ghost-like Priory of Sion, which, according to the Lobineau papers and other "secret dossiers"—highly suspect documents—would have been the invisible higher power that manipulated the Knights Templar and survived their fall. It is certain that Béranger Saunière never accorded any faith to what has been said about the Templars. He had better things to do, for he was aware of the secret deposit hidden by Abbé Bigou dur-

---

7. See my book *The Templar Treasure at Gisors* (Rochester, Vt.: Inner Traditions, 2002).

ing the Revolution. There was thus no need for him to have recourse to either the Templars or the Visigoths. If he did discover documents (parchments), as we believe, his find was fortuitous. He was not looking for them, at least at the start of his excavations.

These documents are obviously Abbé Bigou's perfectly real "treasure"—or, rather, the Hautpoul family treasure, of which Bigou was merely made the depositor, placing it in safekeeping when the situation had become untenable.

The Bigou treasure does not conflict at all with the Visigoth treasure (thus Solomon's treasure) or with the Templar treasure (also from Jerusalem). The Hautpoul family was heir to all the great families that succeeded one another in the Razès. They were thus keepers not only of objects passed down for generations, but also of archives of various documents, some of which should be of great significance, especially given that the Hautpouls of the eighteenth century seemed to have a connection with secret societies. The story only waxes and embellishes more as it compiles the list of the possible treasures hidden in the Razès. What a windfall for those who developed the tale of Abbé Saunière! It would be difficult to find richer material in which history and myth are so closely combined that it is impossible tell one from the other.

There are other hypotheses that remain unverifiable but conform to the essential outline already noted in the traditions mentioned above. There is the old story of the cursed gold of Delphi: During the third century B.C.E., the survivors of a Gallic expedition to the Balkans headed by a certain Brennus returned to Gaul with the booty gained from the pillage of Delphi. Historically, this expedition to Delphi is a reality, but it came to naught, and the Gauls and Brennus were scattered. Some moved on into Asia Minor, where they settled and founded the kingdom of the Galatians. Of course, myth has come to history's aid, and the epic of Delphi, passed on in fragmentary fashion by Greek and Roman authors, has become a veritable mythological tale. The "treasure" of Delphi cannot be left out, however. The Gauls, who had the habit of sacralizing their booty by plunging it into a lake, would have thus entrusted the gold from Delphi to a certain lake that some Toulousian traditions place to the west of the city (others say it is in an underground lake beneath Saint-Sernin). When the Romans invaded, it is said that they took the treasure. Because this was sacred gold, however—thus cursed gold—it was bad luck for the consul who appropriated it. Some of this gold had of course been saved by the Gauls and hidden elsewhere. What better place for such a hiding place than the Razès, home of the Redones? This gold still lies somewhere in the region but it is dangerous to touch; for touching it is the equivalent of committing a sacrilege. This treasure has been combined with the fictions of the Lobineau papers concerning the royal treasure placed in safekeeping by Dagobert II, the hoard that Blanche de Castille did not dare touch. We can see, then, where the story of the Merovingian treasure had its origins. It is not a folk tradition but instead the recuperation of another tradition that has been diverted to the benefit of a dubious ideology.

There is also the royal treasure that Blanche de Castille allegedly concealed in the Razès during a time of difficulty with the high lords of the realm, when the Albigensian Crusade was in full swing. This matches the true folk tradition of the presence of a White Queen [Reine Blanche] at Rennes-les-Bains, though no one knows which white queen precisely. It is likely related to a fairy, the souvenir of ancient fertility goddesses who procured riches for their hierophants, not to mention their lovers. This is an entirely mythological theme and it was the name of Blanche de Castille that prompted the hatching of the legend. But we should bear in mind the interest in the Razès displayed by the mother of Saint Louis and her relentless striving to wrest the region from the unfortunate Trencavel. Here again, myth and history get along well.

Of course, there is still the treasure of the Cathars. This tradition is closely combined with that of the Templars, as it is known that the two parties concluded an objective alliance. The Templars often protected the Cathars, gathering them together and hiding them and also managing their properties. But the Cathar treasure also involves documents on the Cathar doctrine, rather than a material hoard. The assembly of this sacred treasure at the time of Montségur's fall could very well have been effected in the region of Rennes-le-Château, in particular on the slopes of Bugarach, for Bugarach has mystical and geographical connections with the pog of Montségur. The Razès was a Cathar country and even formed a diocese of the Cathar's pseudo-church. There would be nothing unusual about the prefects profiting from the rallying of the Razès's inhabitants, nobles in front, to entrust to them this important heritage. This holds up historically. In addition, the concealment of a "treasure" of documents belonging to the Cathars of Montségur has been historically proved. We know that the four escapees from Montségur entrusted with this mission went into the Razès. But did they stay there? It is not likely. Of course, this does not mean it is of no avail to search at Bugarach or in isolated ravines for the last traces of the Cathars of Occitania.

Finally, there is the Grail. This, however, is a recent tradition and not part of the older folklore of the region. It is an intellectual creation from the end of the nineteenth century, born in literary, artistic, and "hermetic" circles that were frequented, some stubbornly maintain, by Béranger Saunière during his alleged visit to Paris. In full Wagnerian tradition, haunted by the grandiose and mysterious image of the "Holy" Grail, the fin-de-siècle intellectuals tried on several occasions to determine the location of the Castle of the Grail. We may recall that they recognized it in Montségur, though at the same time others recognized it in Glastonbury.[8] If anyone speaks of the Grail in the Razès, it is primarily from the influence of what took place at Montségur, which is not so far from there, remember.

All these traditions refer back to one basic outline: the quest for the lost object that, once found by those worthy of possessing it, will restore harmony to the world and happiness to humanity. It is a quest for perfection diverted into a quest for material objects and, finally, into a simple search for wealth. The main consideration is the goal that one proposes to seek.

Now, this hunt for treasure presumes an *initiation,* for chance discoveries do not count, and discoverers "by chance" never profit from their find. Further, as a rule they find only a disabled portion of what allegedly exists. Such was the case with Béranger Saunière, who owed his initial discoveries somewhat to chance. *He was missing something.* It was probably this "something" that he then searched for ceaselessly. Of course, nothing can be found without the *key* that allows the seeker to open the secret door, which is on the inside or, according to the expression

---

8. For more on this, see my book *Montségur and the Mystery of the Cathars* (Rochester, Vt.: Inner Traditions, 2003), as well as my book *Brocéliande et l'énigme du Graal* (Paris: Pygmalion, 1989).

used by alchemists, is "the open door of the closed palace of the king." To find the key, patience is required, along with the ability to note the smallest signs that can put the seeker on the right path. Because these signs are by nature ambiguous, they must be interpreted, which sets up a bizarre game of Snakes and Ladders that Roger Caillois described so well in his work *Cases d'un échiquier* [Squares of a Chessboard]:

> Paradox of the Treasure. There are many novels of the *Treasure Island* type in which it is a question of rediscovering, by correctly interpreting a coded document, the fabulous buried treasures of the pirates, the Templars, or the pharaohs. The same paradox can be observed: The owners of the treasure, scattered freebooters, *persecuted sects, or dethroned monarchs,* appear to have been singularly preoccupied with *providing the clues necessary for someone else to take possession of it.* Hence the establishment of a complicated cryptogram intended to guide the possible seeker. Everything transpires as if the keeper of the treasure wished to reward ingenuity. He organizes a game of "Hide and Go Seek" in which the first comer has a chance, provided he is clairvoyant and shrewd. He who demonstrates the greatest perspicacity, not he who would have the most legitimate claim to an inheritance, takes the booty.[9]

We now see what the point is for all this: It is from these elaborate preparations involving codes and so forth that the "test" takes all its meaning. It is not always the legitimate heir—with respect to the current laws—who acquires the right to the succession. All the stories from oral folk tradition emphasize this point. Most often they involve a young hero, one who is poor, of course, but very intelligent, who finds the solution and weds the princess, though he has not the right, which in short permits him to *usurp* power. It is the prize of intelligence and cunning. The process is the *test* in all its fullness—and whoever passes the test is capable of succeeding at others. Such is the price of humanity's progress, in which human conciousness can exceed itself and attain the stage at which, as the Serpent in Genesis (himself a symbol of this

---

9. *Cases d'un échiquier* (Paris: Gallimard, 1970), 42–43.

torturous but effective intelligence) states, the human being, a poor creature that cannot even use a tenth of its mental capacity, could be "as a god." This embodies the sin of pride, perhaps, but without pride, what would the future hold?

What these stories about hidden treasures give us is a lesson of metaphysics and theology, for these treasures are *hidden,* with all the shadowy zones this word holds. Of course, shadow can be both good and bad. This is why Roger Caillois stresses

> . . . the double nature of treasures: they are secret, hence the hiding place; they are talismans, thus necessarily consisting of materials that are intrinsically valuable, charged with legends, and history, and almost superstition.[10] They consist of gems, jewels, and, if need be, antiquated coins. A treasure is not imagined as consisting of bank notes, I.O.U.'s, and checks payable to the bearer. All fiduciary currency is excluded.

This imagined nature of treasure stems from the idea that paper currency is not *reliable* and that it cannot be cloaked in that magical *aura* that is indispensable to the effectiveness of the treasure-talisman. In addition, this treasure can come only from the Past. It is a symbolic remnant of what could have been a beginning, during that *illud tempus* that is the base for any itinerary belonging to the Sacred. And the Sacred, like the shadow that protects it, is both good and bad, beneficial and maleficent. Hence the double attitude of the seeker—both attraction and repulsion—and the dual nature of the treasure, which can provoke either the best or the worst.

Taking all of this even further, treasure has a life that is almost independent from that of its owner. Roger Caillois writes:

> He who has amassed or discovered it, does not profit from it, nor do his descendants, nor even those who aided him to accumulate it. The treasure is, so to speak, always at stake and will pass again

---

10. This obviously brings to mind the jewels that carry bad luck. But the very notion of cursed gold, cursed treasure, belongs to this category.

into the hands of the most skillful. For this individual it is a token of fortune rather than the fortune itself: We have never seen a hero spend the treasure he discovered. It is the guarantee of his exceptional destiny, not a kind of open account. I suppose that at the moment of his death, he will compose a rebus in turn and begin a new contest.

This is the case with Béranger Saunière and should cast doubt on the accusations lodged against him concerning the flashy luxury of his construction. It was not for his personal gain but rather for his work that he spent the fortune (whatever its origin) he had amassed, and the allegations about his sumptuous parties and Pantagruel-like feasts are only idle gossip. In fact, under examination we may see that Abbé Saunière never personally profited from what he had discovered. To the contrary, it substantiates the theory that he would have left an obviously coded, symbolic message to indicate to others this "door on the inside" that can be opened only by those who hold the *key*.

The detractors of the Saunière affair have vainly denounced the inconsistencies and obvious errors noticeable in what is considered his "work," as well as those in the work of those who have approached it. These inconsistencies are countless and the errors are incontestable. In contrast, the partisans of the affair (who, after all, is the affair for?) emphasize all these inconsistencies and mistakes by saying they are too obvious not to be intentional. *They are hiding something.*

So let us try to open the door.

8

The Door Is on the Inside

Legends are tenacious, especially when they are only a mere twenty years or thirty years old. Some people wish us to place complete faith in the one concerning the Rennes-le-Château affair. According to the legend, Béranger Saunière was a poor pawn shamelessly used by Abbé Henri Boudet, in a chess match in which someone (who?) had a considerable vested interest. To listen to those who stand by this interpretation, it was Boudet who, in the name of the ever-mysterious "brotherhood," guided his younger colleague Saunière in his excavation, research, and achievements. Now we know from a sure source and supporting testimony that Abbé Boudet was not at all a diabolical hierophant who remained in the shadows while allowing Saunière to move about on the stage, or rather before the altar. Abbé Mazières, who wrote several books on the Razès, said of Boudet: "Those who knew him are surprised when they hear it said that he wished to leave a message. His mind was not at all disposed to that." Boudet was certainly an honest priest with integrity, and even a puritanical streak.[1] But he

---

1. A characteristic anecdote about him was recounted in the *Bulletin de la Société d'études scientifiques de l'Aude* (1973), 221. Henri Boudet had a passion for archaeology and gladly took part in excavations. One day toward the beginning of the twentieth century, while excavating a Roman site, he and his coworkers found a very beautiful statue of Venus. She was depicted nude, however, and Abbé Boudet, horrified by this nudity, refused to pick it up or touch it. Is this the attitude of a man ready to do anything to carry out the commands of a fairly unorthodox brotherhood—especially when they require committing the worst kinds of misappropriations?

made a mistake in writing and publishing *La Vraie Langue celtique et le cromlech de Rennes-les-Bains*. This work, which enjoys great success today, would have fallen into total oblivion if by happy—or unhappy—chance Boudet had not been the priest of Rennes-les-Bains while Saunière was priest of Rennes-le-Château.

To be fair, it should be stated that Abbé Boudet certainly could have done without publishing a work that earned him nothing but ridicule while he was alive and the label of insanity after his death. Nor would it have been any great loss to science if he had abstained. But in the end, what's done is done. The opinion that is most widely shared by those researching the Saunière affair is that *La Vraie Langue celtique* holds the key that allowed Saunière's secret drawer to be unlocked.

La Vraie Langue celtique et le cromlech de Rennes-les-Bains is an astounding work that starts from a series of linguistic equivalencies (completely aberrant ones) based on observations from Rennes-les Bains and the surrounding area, and from these claims demonstrates that the Celtic language is the oldest language in the world. Further, Abbé Boudet goes on to declare that the patois spoken in the Razès (he never uttered the name Occitania) is a very pure remnant of this archaic "true Celtic language." "One thinks one is dreaming when hearing these Celtic expressions, treated scornfully today as wretched and vulgar, as clearly the original language Adam taught to his children."[2]

This declaration is disconcerting. It is not new, however, for in the latter years of the eighteenth century, the famous "Celtomaniacs" La Tour d'Auvergne and Le Brigant made low Breton the mother language of humanity, the tongue that was spoken in Eden. Le Brigant thereby recognized in all modern languages an obvious Breton root and found arguments to persuade his readers to share his view. Henri Boudet proceeds in a similar fashion, but his originality lies in his observation that in addition to the Languedocian patois, the purest representative of this ancient Celtic language is quite simply modern English. It is true that Boudet had a degree in English, but this assertion nonetheless led to some astonishing conclusions, including, for example, the explanation he gives for the name of the Rialsès River

---

2. Boudet, *La Vraie Langue celtique et le cromlech de Rennes-les-Bains*, 213.

north of Rennes: "The *Rialsès—real (rial)*, "real, effective"; *cess*, "tax"—flows from sunrise to sunset in a valley whose fertile soil allowed the inhabitants to pay the tax that the Celts imposed on lands that grew crops easily."[3] All that was required was for someone to think of it.

Obviously, the cromlech that Boudet speaks of does not exist. It is purely a product of his imagination. But this imagination is supported by a landscape that forms a kind of amphitheater—with Rennes-les-Bains at its center—from which emerge natural rocks, though Boudet considered them to be megaliths, or rather "druid stones," as they were called during the time of the Celtomaniacs. Boudet, however, extended his study far beyond the Razès. Here, for instance, is how he explains the name of Locmariaquer in Morbihan: "Locmariaquer is a place near Vannes Lake.[4] Here is the composition of this word: a lake that prevents hunters—*loch (lok)*, "lake"; *to mar*, "prevent"; *yager (iagueur)*, "hunter."[5]

And while he is at it, he explains the origin of the name Sarzeau on the peninsula of Rhuys: "All the authors concerned with Celtic industries have taught us that horsehair cloth was a Gallic invention, but they cannot tell us the site of its invention and fabrication. Sarzeau, on the peninsula of Rhuys, teaches us much on this topic—*sarce (sarse)*, "tammy, horsehair cloth"; *to sew (sô)*, "attach, sew."[6]

And on it goes. The whole book continues in this vein. Boudet pores over all the ancient and modern tongues and rewrites the history of humanity in his fashion. We thereby learn that the name Cain comes from "to coin," to mint money, to invent. Isn't Cain regarded as the ancestor of smiths and metalworkers? We also learn that Sodom comes from "sod," the ground, and "to doom," to judge or condemn, which justifies the destruction of this city. Whenever he can, Boudet brings his explanations back to a regional expression of his native land, a place-name, a part of his "cromlech."

His foggy, murky considerations fit the tone of nineteenth-century

---

3. Boudet, *La Vraie Langue celtique et le cromlech de Rennes-les-Bains*, 227.

4. In other words, the Gulf of Morbihan.

5. Boudet, *La Vraie Langue celtique et le cromlech de Rennes-les-Bains*, 156.

6. Ibid.

Celtomaniacs. He drew his conceptions of Celts and Celtic civilizations from Henri Martin, Amédée Thierry, members of the Celtic Academy, and romantic historians. For him as for them, the megalithic monuments were obviously druidic and were used for sacrifices.

Henri Boudet took his work quite seriously, it seems, and sent his book to numerous people as well as to scholarly societies of his day. In this way he attracted rather ironic reviews, such as this one from the Toulouse Academy of Sciences, Inscriptions, and Belles-Lettres:

> We cannot enter into a detailed criticism of this book in order to discuss its eccentric theories and declarations that are as gratuitous as they are audacious and would seem to betray the presence of a very fertile mind. Taking a stand from an exclusively religious point of view, the author ceaselessly introduces authorities who have nothing to do with linguistics such as it is understood today . . . We were greatly surprised to learn that the unique language spoken before Babel was modern English, preserved by the Tectosages. But this is what Mr. Boudet has demonstrated with his prodigious etymological tours de force.

The reaction of The Société d'étude scientifiques de l'Aude was no gentler.

> It is regrettable that this author bases his only suppositions on vague and arbitrary etymologies from which he has drawn highly unorthodox proofs, and cites only ancient authors . . .

But as Philippe Schrauben noted in his preface to the reissue of *La Vraie Langue celtique,* this book:

> . . . is a large mosaic of extracts from carefully selected nineteenth-century works chosen to create a more or less coherent unity. It is made up of not merely short citations, but entire pages transcribed verbatim and placed end to end. Was the intended purpose a rebirth of the true Celtic language as desired in the Celtifying mode of the end of the nineteenth century? Or was it an attempt to set up boundaries for a hypothetical "Celtic cromlech" in Rennes-les-

Bains? After finishing the book, one has the impression that Boudet believed in neither one, but wandered from subject to subject, topics as different as water cures and Greek mythology . . .[7]

By all evidence, *La Vraie Langue celtique* forms part of the body of work written during the nineteenth century by county seat scholars, as they are called, who thereby seek to show the love they bear for their region despite the fact that they have had no scientific training and rely on no serious reference works related to the topic they have studied. Henri Boudet's passionate investigation of his own region did not prevent him from taking an interest in others.

Much to the detriment of fans of secret treasures, Abbé Boudet's personal papers, which still exist, testify to a lifetime of intellectual labor and research. Their consultation successively shows that this learned priest had thrown himself into the etymological study of a great number of villages and locales in the Aude region . . . So Rennes-les-Bains was not an isolated case. . . .[8]

A yet-unpublished introduction reveals again that Abbé Boudet did not regard his theories as nonsense and that his writings were not cryptograms for mystics to use in their search for loot waiting to found.[9]

But the fact is this: Since the launching of the Abbé Saunière story, Abbé Boudet has been made into the inspirer and accomplice of the priest from Rennes-le-Château, and *La Vrai Langue celtique,* with its unlikely assumptions, aberrations, and stupidities, has become merely a gigantic rebus that provides the key Saunière used to enter the cave where the treasure was stored. The book is no longer The True Language of the Celts, but instead "the true language of the birds," a name used to designate traditional hermetic language. All that is required to find

---

7. *La Vraie Langue celtique* (Nice: Éditions Bélisane, 1984). This is the only authentic and complete republication of the original 1886 text.

8. P. Jarnac, *Histoire du trésor de Rennes-le-Château,* 28.

9. Ibid., 289.

the solution to the mystery of the cursed treasure and the famous "door that is on the inside" is to decipher Abbé Boudet's work.[10]

This is how Abbé Boudet has been presented to posterity, which is certainly not how he imagined it would be. Now why should we throw ourselves into the dangerous adventure of decoding a text that is only a jumble of clichés drawn from all kinds of nineteenth-century works and embellished by an adulterated sauce? Why add more absurdities to the ones that already exist in the text? Abbé Boudet was an honest man even if his linguistic theories are highly eccentric. Nothing useful is gained in adding to these eccentricities. If we wish to find our way back to the treasure, *La Vraie Langue celtique* is absolutely the last place to start looking. The insistent emphasis on Boudet's book is simply one more intoxicated manipulation to divert the attention of seekers. The more the curious are sent astray, the safer is the secret—if there is, in fact, a secret.

This is the appropriate perspective from which to examine the Church of Mary Magdalene in Rennes-le-Château, both its surroundings and its interior, for here too there has been no shortage of interpretation and speculation. Its odd ornamentation and the real anomalies it contains all lead us to believe that something is hidden within it. Therefore, if Abbé Saunière had wished to leave a message, he would not have been better served to have it viewed otherwise. The problem is that we do not know whether or not Abbé Saunière left a message. There would necessarily be one from a man who had discovered certain things, but not all that others have attributed to his finding. This is what is so irritating about the Saunière affair; only some pieces of the puzzle have been put into place, but the whole picture still remains hidden.

Abbé Saunière wished to restore and refurbish his church from the moment he first arrived in Rennes-le-Château. He did so and for a highly laudable purpose: to give a new dimension to his parish while at the same time making his own mark and leaving a memorial, both perfectly human desires. But in the course of his activity he found himself embroiled, willy-nilly, in events he had not foreseen. He made discov-

---

10. In *L'Or de Rennes*, Gérard de Sède devoted some time to this little decoding game, or rather some other people did it for him or whispered in his ear what he needed to do. Since then many others have followed him down this trail. Because I believe everyone is free to his own opinions, I prefer not to mention any names or cause anyone any problems.

eries that certainly allowed him to move his project forward, but which nonetheless were not intentional.

As we've seen, the decoration of Saunière's church is unusual and bizarre due to the fact, it seems, that he did not have a very developed sense of aesthetics. Yet there are certain constants that can be found in the church's ornamentation.

The first is an exultant style of baroque poor taste. Everything is completely disordered and overloaded, including the inscriptions, the decorations, and the statuary. It seems that the mind that conceived all this sought to include the maximum amount of information in the minimum amount of space, leaving no empty places. There could be a very simple reason for this: The church structure itself is small and Abbé Saunière suffered somewhat from delusions of grandeur. His attempt to rebuild a triumphal porch leading to the cemetery is revealing. He wanted something grandiose but lacked the means, hence this pale, miniature copy of the famous porches on the parish grounds of Nord-Finistère. But we can wonder if this excess might not be justified: Perhaps the worthless rubbish—worthless artistically speaking—serves to conceal important information.

The second constant is a kind of bias toward the reverse or the opposite of what is usual. The so-called Visigoth pillar that holds up the statue of Our Lady of Lourdes is quite characteristic of this. A priest like Abbé Saunière, accustomed to the shape of the cross, would know full well that the one depicted on this pillar was displayed upside down. This can mean one of two things: Either one of his workers made a mistake, and Saunière did not dare or was unable to make him rectify his error, or else it was on his explicit command that the pillar be placed in this position. Which of these two solutions is the right one? There is no way to say. This preference for the reverse is again found in the arrangement of the Stations of the Cross. The first station is placed to the left of the altar, even though it is usually placed to the right. There is the opposition on either side of the altar of the Virgin Mary and Saint Joseph, each accompanied by a child (is it really Jesus?). And what reason is behind the unusual presence of the devil at the entrance to the church? The devil, as we know, is the very symbol of reversal, the opposite of good. This apparent justification for the devil's presence here is the punishment of bending his knee and holding up the holy water stoup with an expression of great suffering on his face, thereby testifying to his servitude. What could be more orthodox in this portrayal, even if it may be somewhat surprising to the faithful, who are accustomed to a more peaceful atmosphere in church?

It is true that we are warned ahead of time: *Terribilis est locus iste,* "This place is terrible." But this phrase, borrowed from the story of Jacob in Genesis and displayed prominently, is nevertheless tempered by the inscription that frames it: *Domus mea domus oratorionis vocabitur,* "My house will be known as a house of prayer."[11]

On the vaulting of the porch another phrase appears: *Hic domus Dei est et porta coeli,* "Here is the house of God and the Door of Heaven." This more reassuring inscription is arranged around a keystone of the vault on which are carved the coats of arms of Monsignor Billard, bishop of Carcassonne, and Pope Leo XIII, bearing the words *lumen in coelo,* "light in heaven." The triangular tympanum above it is fairly odd. There is a cross at the top surrounded by an inscription laid out in the shape of a horseshoe, *in hic signo vinces,* which literally means "in this sign you will triumph." In the center of the tympanum there is a statue of Mary Magdalene holding a cross in her arms. The one strange element in the statue is the snake uncoiling upon her dress. It is an odd detail in a depiction of Mary Magdalene and seems more appropriate to a statue of the Virgin Mary. Above the statue is the inscription *Regnum mundi et omnem ornatum soeculi contempsi propter amorem domini mei Jesu Christi quem vidi quem amavi in quem credidi quem dilexi,* which means, "I have scorned the kingdom of this world and all adornment of this century because of my lord Jesus Christ, whom I saw, I loved, in whom I believed and loved." The word *dilexi* is quite ambiguous, for it means generally "I have loved," but with a significant subtlety: *quem dilexi,* which is the usage that appears here, means "in whom I have taken pleasure." And these are words that Mary Magdalene is supposed to have spoken. The least that can be said about this tympanum is that it is somewhat enigmatic. We should recall that in the Middle Ages it was by carefully examining the facades of churches and cathedrals, especially the stylobates and

---

11. But this phrase spoken by Jesus is incomplete. Why didn't Abbé Saunière include the line that follows it: "But you have changed it into a den of thieves"?

tympanums, that the master builders, the members of the brotherhoods, the alchemists, and other "initiates" discovered what they were seeking.

What is most striking inside the church is the double representation of the infant Jesus; he appears both with Joseph and with Mary. It could be that what was intended in this dual portrayal was a depiction of the exoteric path (Joseph) and the esoteric path (Mary), or even, as the Cathars would interpret it, a real Jesus and a mystical Jesus. Another doubling occurs with Saint Anthony. The depiction of Saint Anthony the Hermit refers to he who was tempted in the desert, but the other saint, Saint Anthony of Padua, is the one to whom we pray *when searching for something that has been lost.*

Other oddities in the church are the scene over the confessional, one of the shepherd looking for his lamb in an underground landscape; and the large fresco on the back wall portraying Christ on the Mount of Blessings. If Béranger Saunière commissioned this painting, he did so obviously to display the goal of his ecclesiastical vocation. The inscription beneath it is quite revealing: "Come to me those who are suffering and overwhelmed, and I will ease your pain." It is the most ineffable kind of bounty that inspired Saunière to install this evangelical depiction, which justifies the expenses incurred in building the tower and the villa. Apparently, when he was still only envisioning the construction, Abbé Saunière already knew what its final purpose would be: to provide a shelter for the poor and underprivileged, all those without resources. We know in fact that he wanted to make the Rennes estate into a retirement home for aged and infirm priests.[12] There can be no question that this was his intention.

Saunière named his villa Bethania and his tower Magdala, two names associated with Mary Magdalene. Interestingly, in different areas of the fresco we can see symbolic representations of the town of Bethany and the town of Magdala. It would be hard to get any more explicit. We know, however, that religious images often have double meanings. What, then, is the significance of the ruined Corinthian capital to the right at the foot of the hill? Couldn't this painstakingly depicted landscape bring to mind the area surrounding Rennes-le-Château? And couldn't the mountain of

---

12. P. Jarnac, *Histoire du trésor de Rennes-le-Château,* 162.

flowers over which Christ is triumphing be a discreet allusion to the Rosicrucian knight de Fleury, son-in-law of Marie de Négri d'Hautpol? How are we to know? There are definitely some curious coincidences.

On the other hand, the path of the Stations of the Cross, over which the most audacious and wildly varying analyses have been made, is of absolutely no significance. There is nothing original about it. This was an achievement of the Giscard House of Toulose and there are similar examples throughout the region, notably in Mouthoumet. An absolutely identical one has been found in Rocamadour in the Lot region, which is the second most popular pilgrimage site in France after Lourdes, and it was inaugurated in 1887—in other words, just before Saunière had one set up in Rennes-le-Château. It is perfectly useless, then, to consider the Stations of the Cross a catalog of clues, as has been repeatedly said in all quarters. As to whether the Stations here are of Masonic inspiration (because of certain distinctive scenes), that is another matter entirely. But before we interpret as we please a traditional work of frightful banality, it would be better for us to question Mr. Giscard Jr.'s membership in the Freemasons. Giscard the younger was a prizewinner and member of the jury of the School of Fine Arts, "owner-producer" of the Manufaturing House of MM. Giscard and Son, whose "establishment and large studios" had their "main entrance" on 25 rue de la Colonne in Toulouse, according to the bill for 2,310 francs that was sent to the priest of Rennes-le-Château in 1887. The Giscard House was the regular provider to Abbé Saunière of allegedly artistic religious objects. If there are Masonic symbols in the path of the Stations of the Cross in the Church of Saint Magdalene, it is surely not due to Béranger Saunière.

The same is true of the Masonic checkerboard—the black-and-white flooring—which is apparently more common in a lodge than a church. Whoever can discern anything in it beyond banal decoration must be exceedingly clever. If it was really a checkerboard, with all the attendant symbolism, it would have only sixty-eight squares, but simple examination will show that there are quite a few more than this in the church and that the installation of this flooring has nothing whatsoever to do with some kind of esoteric concern. As for the presence of Blanche de Castille's coat of arms above the tabernacle, this can be explained by the fact that the Church of Saint Magdalene was expanded during the time of Saint Louis and that the renovation benefited from a personal donation made by the queen mother, who, as we have seen, took a close personal interest in the Razès.

We could still discuss the light effects that occur at certain times in the church, mainly on January 13 and at the beginning of April—but these are phenomena that can be noted almost everywhere, because the architects and master stained-glass makers knew how to use sunlight to magnify their work and at the same time remind people that the sun is the symbol of divinity. Isn't it *Lumen Christi* mentioned in the Christian liturgy of Easter Eve? This kind of play with light, quite frequent in numerous sanctuaries, has always intrigued the fans of the mysterious, who are always ready to ask, "What could this mean?" In Rennes-le-Château it means nothing. Sunlight was simply made to take part in the liturgy, and in the most orthodox fashion possible.

In short, then, the interior of this church would prove to be extremely disappointing, and we would be apt to accept that Abbé Saunière had left no message, if one other constant did not exist: the permanent presence of the theme of Mary Magdalene. We can in fact count the references to her: the tympanum on the church's porch, the extremely Saint-Sulpician statue on the right when facing the altar, a stained-glass window above the altar, a painting beneath the altar table, and finally the allusion to it in the large fresco on the back wall. These add up to quite a few. But after all, aren't we in a church dedicated by name to Saint Mary Magdalene?

Yet these multiple occurrences within the church, in conjunction with the abbé Saunière's exterior—if not profane—structures, Villa Bethania and the Magdala Tower, do prompt a justified curiosity. We should also note that when Saunière built his grotto in the church garden with stones brought from the Stream of Colors, he had, according to local testimony, placed in it a small statue of Mary Magdalene in prayer, which has since disappeared. We might rather have expected to find a statue of Our Lady of Lourdes in this grotto. Here, then, is another anomaly and we should recognize it as such.

There are certain details in this "invasion" of Mary Magdalene that will catch the eye of an observer. On the tympanum, where she appears with the uncustomary serpent, we can see that Mary Magdalene is on a vessel. This depiction conforms with the tradition that maintains that

Mary Magdalene traveled to and disembarked on the shores of southern France, either at Marseilles, Saintes-Maries-de-la-Mer, or somewhere else much closer to the Corbières. The statue portrays her holding a cup in one hand and a cross in the other, with a human skull at her feet. The cup could be the jar of perfume with which she anointed the feet of Christ, but it looks more like a chalice than a perfume jar. The round stained-glass window behind and above the altar depicts Jesus and his disciples sitting around a table and talking. Mary Magdalene can also be seen in the picture; she is bent over the feet of Christ as she washes them. In the large fresco, Mary Magdalene is weeping to the right of Jesus.

But the saint's strangest presence by far is in the fresco beneath the altar table. In it Mary Magdalene, dressed in extremely beautiful clothes, kneels and prays before a cross made of tree branches stuck into the ground. She is in a grotto and there is a human skull nearby. Outside the grotto there is a fairly melancholy natural landscape with some ruins that can be distinguished in the background. This painting is the work of an unknown artist from Carcassonne, but we do know that in his youth Abbé Courtauly helped Abbé Saunière touch up the painting with some "improvements" to the original outline, which leads me to believe that Abbé Saunière had a particular fondness for this work and wished it to have some importance.[13]

---

13. While in the presence of a former bishop of the diocese, it appears that Jacques Rivière, author of *Le Fabuleux Trésor de Rennes-le-Château,* had a curious experience in Carcassonne in 1981 with regard to this painting. On a topographical map of the department that indicated the area's highest altitudes with black lines, Rivière projected a slide of the image of Mary Magdalene in the grotto. The result was that the black lines exactly reproduced the contours of the saint in meditation, with the city of Carcassonne sitting atop her like a crown. This information is provided by Pierre Jarnac in *Histoire du trésor de Rennes-le-Château.* In a footnote he adds: "But this is not the most disturbing thing! In fact, at the exact point where the branches of the cross intersect, the point at which Mary Magdalene is staring, reads the name Puicheric, a small village of Capendu. In the church in this commune there is a stained-glass window that displays the exact replica, though reversed, of the Rennes-le-Château bas-relief portraying Mary Magdalene!" Pierre Jarnac, recopying the layout proposed by Jacques Rivière, further claims that Mary Magdalene's eye is not on Rennes-le-Château itself but right next to it, at a point called "les Justices," near Leuc. While it is sometimes permissible to laugh openly at the attempts at sacred geography that currently flood the public, it must be acknowledged that Rivière's experience with Mary Magdalene's image is rather strange.

Mary Magdalene is certainly the patron saint of the parish in Rennes-le-Château. Her role is further and explicitly stated in the Latin inscription at the bottom of the grotto painting beneath the altar table: JESU. MEDELA. VULNERUM + SPES. UNA. PENITENTIUM. PER MAGDALENAE. LACRYMAS + PECCATA. NOSTRA. DILUAS—in other words, "Jesus, remedy of wounds, sole hope for those who regret,[14] by the tears of Magdalene dissolve[15] our sins." While she is the symbol of the repentant sinner in a certain Christian tradition, she is not necessarily playing that role in this painting. So what was Béranger Saunière's opinion of this very special saint? It would be interesting to know, because the famous *key* bestowing access to the cursed treasure of Rennes-le-Château is there in the grotto where Magdalene is kneeling—not the legendary grotto of the Holy Balm,[16] but a symbolic portrayal that responded to the priest of Rennes-le-Château's intention in every detail. Who, then, is this Mary Magdalene who apparently haunted the waking and sleeping hours of Father Béranger Saunière?

---

14. *Penitentes* is the present participle of the impersonal verb *paenitet*, which literally means "to regret. The modern word *penitent* has a much more precise meaning than did its Latin predecessor.

15. The word *dissolve* here means literally "lave" [the French word for "wash"—*Translator*], which forms a double allusion: Initially it refers to Mary Magdalene's tears but one also calls to mind the fact that she washed Christ's feet.

16. The word *baume* or *balm* is a pre-Indo-European word meaning "grotto."

9

That Odd Mary Magdalene

I adorn myself as if for a ball; I perfume myself as if for bed. My entrance into the banquet room caused all talk to cease; the Apostles rose up in great alarm at the fear of being infected from a touch of my dress; in the eyes of these men of good, I was as impure as if I were continuously bleeding. God alone remained lying on the leather bench. I instinctively recognized those feet worn down to the bone by all his walking over every path of our hell; that hair inhabited by a vermin of stars; those vast, pure eyes like the sole morsels of his heaven remaining to him! He was as ugly as suffering, he was as dirty as sin. I fell to my knees, swallowing my spit, incapable of adding any sarcastic rejoinder to the horrible weight of this Godly distress. I saw immediately that I could seduce him, for he would not flee from me. I undid my hair to better cover the nakedness of my transgression; I emptied before him the phial of my memories. I realized that this outlaw God had slipped through the gates of dawn one morning, leaving behind him the other members of the Trinity, astonished at finding themselves only two. He found food and shelter in the inn of days; had given unsparingly of himself to passersby who refused him their soul but demanded of him all tangible pleasures. He had tolerated the company of bandits, contact with lepers, the insolence of policemen. Like me, he consented to the atrocious fate of being available to everyone. He placed on my head his large cadaverous hand that seemed already empty of blood. We only change our enslavement; at that very moment the demons left me and I became possessed by God.

This is how Marguerite Yourcenar, in her book *Marie-Madeleine ou le Salut* (Mary Magdalene or Salvation), speaks of Magdalene's first meeting with Jesus. But who really was the person who spoke these magnificent words of love? Mary Magdalene remains an enigma because she, an enchanting and far from ordinary individual, has been removed, seemingly deliberately, from the official texts of Christianity, though we can guess that she played a starring role in the life of Christ and his preaching.

We are familiar, of course, with the scene of the repentant sinner. Mary Magdalene appears in Luke 7, the chapter in which Jesus is a dinner guest at the home of a Pharisee named Simon. All at once a woman, who appears to be of ill repute, enters the house seemingly to seduce the "prophet." But touched by grace, she instead washes Jesus' feet with her tears, dries them with her hair, and pours perfume over them, and Christ forgives her all her sins. It is a touching story, although it appears to have been fabricated to show that Jesus forgave prostitutes. The other three Evangelists are mute on this episode, but they recount a somewhat similar incident, which, they say, took place in Bethany before the Passion, in the villa of Simon the Leper (according to Matthew and Mark) or in the home of Lazarus shortly after Jesus brought him back to life (according to John). In both Matthew and Mark's versions, there was a *woman* who came and anointed the feet of Jesus, but in John 12, plausibly based on eyewitness testimony, there are precise and exact details that provide us with additional valuable information:

Six days before Easter Jesus arrived in Bethany, where he found Lazarus, whom he had resurrected from the dead. A meal was made that Martha served, and Lazarus was among the guests. Mary took a pound of nard perfume that was pure and quite expensive and anointed the feet of Jesus with it. She then dried them with her hair and the entire house was filled with an aromatic fragrance.

This clearly resembles the scene in Luke involving a prostitute, but here there is no prostitute, only Mary, Martha's sister, and therefore the sister of Lazarus. This is not Mary's first appearance in the Gospels; she is mentioned earlier in connection with the resurrection of Lazarus, in what may be the most mysterious passage in the entire Gospel of John. Indeed, Lazarus appears to have been a friend of Jesus, but at the announcement of his illness, then of his death, Jesus presents a facade of complete indifference. Yet "Jesus loved Martha and her sister and Lazarus" (John 11: 5). It was four days following the burial of Lazarus when Jesus arrived in Bethany. A disturbing scene then takes place: Martha is brought to meet Jesus and vehemently reproaches him for not coming sooner. "If you had been here, my brother would not lie dead" (John 11:21). Jesus reassures her and tells her that her brother will live again, but he seems in no hurry to put action behind his words. Martha then goes off to find Mary and tells her, "The Master is here and he calls for you"—which is manifestly false. But Mary races before Jesus, who is still far from their house and is in no apparent hurry to arrive. In fact there must be a large lapse of time here, for Martha is able to return to the house to speak to Mary, who then has time to make the same journey in the opposite direction. What happened next everyone knows. On reaching Jesus, she throws herself at his feet and scolds him in terms identical to those of her sister. It is then that Jesus decides to act. He asks to be led to the tomb of Lazarus, where he brings Mary's brother back to life. "The dead man emerges, with his feet and hands still wrapped in binding cloth and the shroud still covering his face" (John 11:44).

Exactly who is this Mary, sister of Lazarus? We see her again on Golgatha, during the crucifixion of Jesus: "Near the cross of Jesus stood his mother, and the sister of his mother, Mary, wife of Cleophas, and Mary Magdalene" (John 19:25). The other Evangelists remain mute on this female presence at the Crucifixion. It is at Jesus' resurrection that the story of Mary takes on its true significance. In the Gospel of Luke, three women, who have "come from Galilee with Jesus," show up at his tomb to embalm the corpse. According to Luke 24:10 their names are "Mary Magdalene, Joanna, and Mary, the mother of James." In the Gospel of Mark it is only two women (Mary, mother of Jesus, being oddly absent) who, Mark 16:1 tells us, witness the placement of Jesus in the tomb by

Joseph of Arimathea. The two—Mary Magdalene and Mary, the mother of James—return the day after the following day to tend to the body (they could not return the following day because it was the Sabbath), accompanied this time by a third woman, Salome. In Matthew 18:1 there are only two women who come to embalm Jesus: Mary Magdalene and the *other* Mary. We can admire in passing the alleged concordances of the so-called synoptic Gospels. Even more admirable is the sugary dialectic of the orthodox exegetes who achieve stunning feats of language to explain the monumental contradictions and notable absurdities that can be found in the canonical texts—those recognized by the Roman Catholic Church as being the unshakable foundation of Christian dogma. No, this is not another issue altogether; *it is the issue,* because the message of Abbé Saunière—and he did have a message—specifically concerns Mary Magdalene, whoever is concealed behind that name.

In the Gospel of John (20:1), which is apparently the most reliable because it is based on eyewitness testimony (that of John himself or of people close to him), we find the figure of Mary Magdalene at Christ's tomb, but in this version she is alone, and John does not say whether she has come with the purpose of embalming the corpse. "Mary Magdalene came to the tomb early in the morning, although it was still dark, and she saw that the stone had been rolled away from the tomb." She refuses to enter the tomb and instead goes straightaway to find Simon Peter and "the other disciple beloved by Jesus," meaning John (19:2). Both disciples rush to the tomb, but John, who is the faster runner, is the first to see that Jesus' body has vanished. The disciples return home then, firmly convinced of Jesus' resurrection.

Mary Magdalene, however, does not follow them. In John 20: 11–13 her attitude is at first mysterious. It would seem that she should be rejoicing. Instead:

Mary remained next to the tomb, standing and her eyes full of tears. Still crying, she leaned over the tomb and saw two angels dressed in white seated at the top and bottom of the bench upon which Jesus' body had been placed. "Woman," they asked her, "why do you cry?" She answered, "Because someone has carried off my Lord and I do not know where they put him."

Apparently she does not believe at all in Jesus' resurrection, only that his enemies have carried off his body to prevent people from worshipping it, as was then customary. It is at this point that she turns around and sees a man standing close by. She does not recognize Jesus and thinks instead that it is a gardener. We must recall that the scene takes place on the property of Joseph of Arimathea, in the garden where he had a tomb constructed for his own personal use but which he offered as a sepulcher for the person whose teachings he had been following in secret (for Joseph of Arimathea was a high-ranking figure among both the Jews and the Romans).[1] The man asks her why she is crying, and at this Mary Magdalene grows angry, but in a way that speaks volumes about her own intimate feelings for Jesus: "Lord, if you are the one who carried him off, tell me where you put him, and I will take him away" (John 20:15). There could be no more direct expression of amorous passion.

This is the beginning of a scene with a marvelous wealth of possible interpretations (John 20:16–18):

> Jesus called out to her, "Mary!" She turned around and said in Hebrew, "Rabbouni," which means Teacher. Jesus added, "Do not touch me,[2] for I have not gone back up to my father.[3] Rather, go tell my brothers that I am ascending to my father, to my God and your God."[4] Mary Magdalene thus went to tell the disciples that she had seen the Lord and he had told her of this and that.[5]

---

1. He must have been of very high rank to obtain Pilate's consent to take possession of Jesus' body, because this did not comply at all with Roman law, which stipulated that the crucified rot on the cross.

2. This is the famous *noli me tangere*. This exclamation must mean that Mary is rushing toward him.

3. All of this is quite obscure. The most plausible explanation is that the "metamorphosis" of Jesus, meaning his "fulfillment" in the form of a "glorious" body, had not been fully completed.

4. This is not the Ascension, for Jesus will later appear to the disciples before his final ascension and tell Doubting Thomas to touch his wounds. In reality, Thomas is the "twin," for this is the meaning of Thomas's other name, Didyme.

5. The use of this expression indicates that Jesus said much more to Mary Magdalene than the few phrases recorded in the Gospel of John.

That is all. There is nothing else in the canonical texts on Mary Magdalene, though what is there is both a lot and a little. One question arises immediately: What do the three Mary Magdalenes depicted in the Gospels have in common? (They are the sinner who is won and forgiven by Jesus; Mary of Bethany, the sister of Martha and Lazarus; and finally Mary of Magdala (thus Mary Magdalene), who, according to Luke, has come from Galilee with Jesus.) It is known that divine figures were often depicted in the form of triads in ancient times. A remnant of this can be seen in the Christian doctrine of the Trinity. It was the Celts who placed a special emphasis on the *three faces* of a god or hero. This is why we often finds groups of "three mothers" in Gallo-Roman statuary, or even three-headed gods such as the Cernunnos of Reims. In the mythic epics of Ireland, the Triple Brigit is often cited or the same figure can be recognized under three different names and three different aspects. It cannot be said that this makes for simplified understanding; nevertheless, it is part of a logical system that simply does not have much affinity with the Latin. Could the same be true for the three Marys of the Gospels, who can also be seen beneath a varnish of folklore in the legend of the Holy Marys of the sea?

In the Gospels, then, we have three female figures who can be commingled and identified as one and the same woman: the sinner whom Jesus forgives; Mary of Bethany, the sister of Martha and Lazarus; and Mary Magdalene, whom Luke says has come from Galilee with Jesus. Can the chaste Mary of Bethany be identical to the prostitute who made her way into the house of Simon the Pharisee with the intention of seducing Jesus, about whom she had heard so much? If we are to go by the words of John (11:2) at the beginning of the story of Lazarus's resurrection—"This Mary was she who anointed the Lord with perfume and dried his feet with her hair"—there would seem to be no doubt about this. But because John does not mention the episode of the prostitute at the house of Simon the Pharisee, which is included only in Luke's account, some hesitation is permissible. Luke, however, specifies that the incident takes place in Bethany, where Lazarus lived. This creates a strong case that the prostitute (a high-class one, of course, who could very well be a rich woman leading a so-called life of pleasure without consideration of financial remuneration) is the sister of

Lazarus, Mary of Bethany. But Bethany is in Judea, and we learn from Luke that Mary Magdalene came from Galilee (Magdala is in fact in Galilee). Luke also adds that she is one of a group of women "who had followed Jesus." Thus there is nothing specific to suggest that we cannot identify the three Marys as one and the same woman.

But there is more: Mary of Bethany, the sinner, and Mary Magdalene are rich members of high society. Could this mysterious Mary have been one of the first disciples of Jesus when he was still in Galilee? This is not absurd or impossible. Indeed, this is the opinion of Jacques de Voragine, the author of the famous *Légende dorée* (Golden Legend), a hagiographic text in which it is difficult to distinguish the fantastic from the real, but which provides useful pieces of information for anyone who takes the time to strip them out of the superfluous text. In fact, Jacques de Voragine's Mary is born to a noble family of royal lineage from whom she would have inherited a vast fortune in goods and properties, including the house in Bethany that she shared with her sister, Martha, and brother, Lazarus. She might even have inherited the stronghold of Magdala (hence her name), a place with a wide reputation for immorality. She was therefore wealthy, but devoted to hedonism, which the scene recounted in Luke clearly shows. Christ then forgives her and chases out the seven demons that have been possessing her. From this point on Jesus refuses no grace to Mary Magdalene. This is the story told by Jacques de Voragine and we must admit that it holds up well. It is even corroborated by Luke 8:1, which refers to the entourage of Jesus: "The twelve accompanied him, as well as several women . . . cured of evil spirits, of whom Mary, nicknamed the Magdalenian, was purged of seven demons."

The triple face of Mary Magdalene, disciple of Jesus, can therefore be accepted without great reservation, along with the fact that she, with the help of her sister and brother, in some way *sponsored* the activities of Jesus. She had the means, after all. We should keep in mind that during the three years of his preaching, Jesus did not work. Yet he certainly required food and lodging, as did his disciples. Even the Son of God cannot live off the spirit of the age. Jesus was a man; he ate, drank, and slept, as did his disciples.

It even seems that among Jesus' disciples, Mary played a privileged role. Why, then, did the Roman Catholic Church feel obliged to almost totally erase her role and almost entirely remove her presence? Is it because of the misogyny, now conclusively proved, that existed at the heart of the Church from the early Middle Ages? The Christian conception of femininity, which has certainly greatly evolved in the modern world, especially since Vatican II, is due to both the Greco-Roman legacy and the Hebraic alternatives. Excepting the female characters in Genesis, who are gripping figures, to say the least, the scribes of the Bible have lowered Woman by making her impure and ineligible to play a sacerdotal role. The idea that Mary Magdalene enjoyed total equality with the apostles was a claim that has never crossed any theologian's mind. Because priests are the legitimate heirs of the apostles, this would make Mary Magdalene a priestess—how horrible!—and one of the foundations for the apostolic sacerdotal filiation.

And yet the scene in which Mary of Bethany washes Jesus' feet and anoints him with expensive perfume, which Judas, the group's treasurer, feels could be put to a more profitable use, is a kind of sacerdotal and royal ordination. What is more, in this instance it is Mary who performs the ritual; it is she who is the *priestess.*

> Is it forbidden to think that Mary of Bethany, over the course of those long moments spent at the feet of the Lord, heard what he said and grasped it in its entirety, or at least sensed the full scope of Christ's mystery? Jesus persistently tried to get his disciples to realize this—if only in the brilliance of the Transfiguration! But their hearts remained curiously closed all the way to the end. Mary, however, did perceive and accept it. On that day she knew the moment had come to manifest this mystery in chiaroscuro. Through a kind of prophetic intuition, Mary anointed the head of Jesus, recognizing and displaying him as king and priest, and anointed his feet as Messiah and as one sent from God.[6]

This obviously involves a rite of enthronement that can be performed only by a person symbolically vested with sacerdotal powers. Jesus is fully aware of this when he answers Martha's reproaches by saying that Mary "had the best part."

---

6. Georgette Blaquière, *La Grâce d'être Femme* (Paris: Éditions Saint-Paul, 1981), 163.

In Israel there are two sites named Bethany: a town two miles east of Jerusalem, where Mary, Martha, and Lazarus lived; and a place on the left bank of the Jordan, just before the Dead Sea, a ford where John the Baptist baptized. This place by the gates to the desert was also called Bethabara, "the house of passage." Each in his or her own way, John and later Mary granted baptism, initiation—that is to say, the right of passage, the crossing of the threshold. The two Bethanys seem to mirror each other. Magdalene extends the echo of the precursor of Jesus, John the Baptist. One is the man clad in hides and the other is the woman with her long mane of hair. The chief difference between them is that John stays within a harsh and terrible place, screaming the call to repent and launching curses (an example of Essenian rigor), whereas in the Bethany on the opposing shore, where all is blooming and gay, Magdalene speaks of love and forgiveness and the transition from one world to the next. Jesus received the baptism of water from John, but unlike the ancient kings, he did not receive an anointing or consecration by oil. Just before the Passion, however, and his "baptism by spirit and fire" (the Crucifixion), he received the perfumed oil from the female Mary Magdalene.[7] The old and ancient notion of the priest-king applies to Jesus. But this royal unction, let me repeat, can be performed only by a priest—or priestess.

The unction in Bethany is surely one of the most important events in the life of Jesus. Furthermore, in his words to his disciples, who are always more or less hostile toward the whims of Woman, he declares that in fact this woman truly did "what she had to do," and even adds, according to Mark 14:9: "In truth, I declare to you, everywhere the Gospel is to be spread, throughout the whole world, one will also recount, in memory of her, the deed she has done." This is acknowledgment of an uncommon power possessed by Mary that may seem out of proportion—and this is what the first disciples clearly thought—with a gesture that could pass for female vanity. This statement underscores the importance Jesus gave Mary Magdalene in his very words.

Why, then, is this Mary Magdalene relegated to such a minor role in the evangelical tradition as revised and corrected by the Church Fathers? Is the Christian sacerdotal class ashamed to owe so much to a woman?

---

7. Jacquéline Kelen, *Un Amour infini* (Paris: Albin Michel, 1983), 52–53.

And I cannot forbear from asking myself: What has the memory of the Church done to these words of Jesus? Isn't there something yet to be explored there? And wouldn't this something be the consecration of a specifically female ministry of a prophetic and charismatic nature that Jesus would himself have recognized and proclaimed as existing in tandem with the apostolic and sacerdotal ministry? What a unique place woman would hold in the very heart of the Church, if this was the case![8]

The question has been clearly raised. And it seems that Abbé Saunière may have answered it in his own way in the church of Rennes-le-Chateau.

The fathers of the Church, followed by the "philosophers" of the Middle Ages, all beholden to the Church, only justified and codified "this hatred of women, a hatred that in fact came from a fear of women taken to delirious proportions, that was hung from the most minor physiological details, which were exploited in such a way as to make them impassable prohibitive barriers."[9] It is true that in everything they undertook, Christian theoreticians were slaves of the famous verse in Genesis after the transgression, when the Lord tells Eve: "Your desire will draw you to man, and *he will rule you.*" This premise is responsible for many misunderstandings. "Christian dogma has no fear of going to absurd lengths, as is shown by its declaration that the mother of Christ conceived without any sexual intervention, thereby condemning the Savior to being simply a half man, like Bacchus."[10] And yet, as the just revenge of things would have it, in Christian worship the place of the Virgin Mary, mother of God and consequently a woman, is absolutely beyond all common measure.

It would just require a little impetus, though. The text of Pope John Paul II, published on the occasion of the Marian year 1988, contains a proposition that goes much further than we might think at first glance. In fact, John Paul II pays a sustained homage to Mary Magdalene, and after reminding us that according to the Gospel of John she was the first

8. Georgette Blaquière, *La Grâce d'être Femme* (Paris: Éditions Saint-Paul, 1981), 165.

9. André de Smedt, *La Grande Déesse n'est pas morte* (Paris: 1983), 165.

10. Ibid., 225. The author of these lines is a Catholic priest.

person to have seen Christ after he emerged from the tomb, he adds, "It is for this very reason that she is called the Apostle of Apostles. Mary Magdalene was, before the Apostles, eyewitness to Christ's resurrection, and for that reason, she was also the first to testify to it in the presence of the Apostles." This observation has the merit of considering the importance of the very circumstances that surrounded the event. When you think about it, in fact, it seems "enormous." Jesus, who belonged to a preeminently patriarchal society, who is depicted as leading a troop of exclusively male apostles, chose the first witness of his resurrection to be a woman—and not his mother, but a woman with whom he seems, if we read between the lines, to have shared a privileged relationship.

What is the meaning of this scene at the tomb? A historically based reading, such as the kind practiced by the official commentators of the Church for twenty centuries, does not cast any doubt as to the reality of the facts. Yet through an event that can be accepted as authentic, the presence of Mary Magdalene—especially alone, according to John, the most reliable witness—is quite odd.

In his address concerning the Marian year 1988, John Paul II, incidentally a highly talented and dramatic author who is perfectly cognizant of the problems faced by women, made this observation that definitely warrants our interest:

> A woman is strong because of her awareness of this entrusting, strong because of the fact that God "entrusts the human being to her," always and in every way, even in the situations of social discrimination in which she may find herself. . . . If the human being is entrusted by God to women in a particular way, does not this mean that Christ looks to them for the accomplishment of the "royal priesthood?"[11]

A "royal priesthood" is truly what is involved here. Without trying to come to any conclusion about the question of faith, if we consider the symbolic meaning of the scene in which Jesus comes back to life and addresses Mary Magdalene, it can be seen that this scene is of mytho-

11. John Paul II, *Mulieris Dignitatem,* Rome, 1988.

logical, alchemical, metaphysical, and of course religious significance, all wonderfully combined in an image that can be engraved into collective memory. The tomb is the earth's womb (that of Mother Earth, the primordial deity). The dead Jesus is placed therein ("if the seed does not die . . .") so that he can ripen and be re-created and regenerated like the *prima materia* of alchemists. His is an inert body subject to the rigidity of death, then decomposition—but by virtue of that, to purification. He will, at the end of a symbolic gestation period of three days (in fact, forty-eight hours), emerge from the athanor—that is, the alchemical crucible (or the womb of Mother Earth). This is a veritable *birth,* but who is presiding over it? It is certainly not the Roman Juno. It is a woman, but it is not his mother. It is an *Other.*

In short, in this "symbolist" version of the story of Jesus' resurrection Jesus is the equivalent of the moon god (originally this was the Hebrew Jehovah's role)—in other words, the moon man in his tomb, who (like the void moon, for several days) is still in thrall to the night of the unconscious, who lies in the shadows of the nonrealization of his royal priesthood. If this identification is accepted, then what would Mary Magdalene be if not the sun woman, the dispenser of warmth and life, the embodiment of full and complete awareness who causes this consciousness to surge into the unconscious awareness of the moon Jesus as he leaves the tomb of an undifferentiated night? Mary Magdalene, who here holds the role of the New Mother, carries a number of characteristic solar aspects. We should remember too that this takes place at the dawn of the third day.

All of this brings to mind a certain parallel between this evangelical scene and the legendary tale of Tristan and Yseult. I know this might scandalize some people, but I cannot put it otherwise. Yseult and the majority of doomed heroines in tales of Celtic origin represent aspects sometimes adopted by the Goddess of Beginnings, the sun woman without whom the moon man cannot gain awareness of his existence and his royal priesthood. Mary of Magdala, the mysterious Magdalene, like the Virgin Mary for whom she is only the new image, rejuvenated and rejuvenating, is the sun woman in all her intensity, splendor, and burning power. In this role she permits Christ to fulfill the Scriptures, to establish on the earth an era where mind will prevail over matter—

which is only an emanation of mind, as we often fail to remember. Mary Magdalene, like all the traditional Celtic heroines, is she whom André Breton, under the pretext of defining beauty, described as "convulsive, veiled erotic, magic circumstantial," under penalty of not existing at all otherwise. Indeed, no one can deny the eroticism and magic of Mary Magdalene washing the feet of Christ with her tears and drying them with her long hair. It is perfectly understandable that the resurrected Jesus appears first to her.

But the New Testament ultimately grows mute on the fate of Mary from Magdala, the woman who "dared love Jesus." This was the starting point for the legend, the cult, and the controversy. In the early days of the Church, Gnostic writings and even certain Church Fathers acknowledged Mary Magdalene as a power of sacred seduction. She was even extolled by Saint Augustine. Her worship intensified toward the tenth century, when Odon of Cluny composed a hymn to her. The legend expanded further in the thirteenth century. It did not matter that a new generation of theologians was casting doubt on the identification of the three Marys. To popular piety she became the image of the repentant sinner. Those in Provence believed she had made a journey, landed in Marseilles, and, as legend had it, from there retired to a grotto in Sainte-Baume. A Burgundian legend recounts her departure from Palestine in the company of Martha, Lazarus, and Maximin on a boat that sank off the shores of Provence. This same legend tells us how Maximin preached the Gospel in the Côte d'Azure; how Martha settled in Arles, where she tamed the Tarrasque; how Mary Magdalene retired into a grotto; and primarily how the very precious relics of this saint ended up in Vézelay, thanks to Girard de Roussillon, a semilegendary, semi-historical figure, who was a hero in several chansons de geste in the Charlemagne cycle. At this same time, however, the basilica of Exeter in southern England— or more exactly in the ancient realm Dumnonia of the British Isles, the ancient metropolis of the Dumnonii—boasted of possessing the same relics. The worship of Mary Magdalene spread throughout Europe, but took hold particularly in Occitania, where not only churches are consecrated to her, but also hills, grottos, and mountains. Under these conditions, why would it be surprising that the church of Rennes-le-Château should bear the name of Saint Mary Magdalene?

Of course, the tradition of Mary Magdalene has undergone many transformations. It could not be otherwise, for we have absolutely no concrete information about her life after the essential moment of the Resurrection. The course is thus clear for speculation to develop at will. In addition, the mystery that already surrounds Mary Magdalene in the Gospels lays the groundwork for all kinds of hypotheses.

It is incontestable that she was in love with Jesus. Saying so cannot shock anyone, because the canonical events offer sufficient proof of it. While not one of the Gospel writers says one word concerning a "liaison" between Mary Magdalene and Jesus of Nazareth (or rather, Jesus the Nazarene), novelists and filmmakers are free to imagine what they want: The seeds of their plot lines already existed in the Gospel of Saint John, and here is a case where one guarantee is as worthy as another.

One theory is that Mary Magdalene was the wife of Jesus. A meticulous analysis of the story of the Wedding in Cana reveals some perplexities in this regard. According to the text, Jesus, who was allegedly invited to this famous wedding in the company of his mother (it is the first action of his public life), behaves like the master of the house and gives orders to the servants, telling them to fill the jars with water so that he can turn it into wine. The servants obey him.[12] There are other oddities throughout the Gospels: A *rabbi* would not have had the right to bear that title unless he was married. Jesus maintains close relations with Martha and Lazarus. The house in Bethany seems to serve Jesus as a residence in between his travels and preaching. According to John, Mary Magdalene is present at Jesus' crucifixion and immediately following his resurrection. Then there is the *noli me tangere* that Jesus fires at Mary, who seemingly wants to rush to him. There is no lack of grounds for presumption of a wedded relationship. But there is no proof. Of course, nor is there any strictly historical proof that Jesus actually existed.

---

12. See M. Baigent, R. Leigh, H. Lincoln, *Holy Blood, Holy Grail* (New York: Delacorte Press, 1982). It goes without saying that while I consider these authors' arguments concerning the Wife of Jesus to be extremely interesting, I do not share their conclusions, just as I hold many reservations based on the mentality that animates this book. Although completely impassioned, it is quite suspect from a variety of perspectives, particularly because of its problematic ideology.

The so-called apocryphal gospels certainly do not fail to testify to the bonds uniting Jesus to Mary Magdalene. For example, we can read in the gospel attributed to Philip a passage that could not be any more explicit:

> The Savior's companion was Mary from Magdala. The Christ loved her above all the other disciples and often kissed her on the mouth. The other disciples took offence at this and made no attempt to hide their disapproval and asked Jesus: "Why do you love her more than any of us?" And the Savior answered them: "Why wouldn't I love her more than you?"

What we must keep in mind, however, is that the Gospel of Philip is a Gnostic text in which everything is symbolic. It also includes a long dissertation on the nuptial chamber that has nothing to do with the reality of a Jesus, God incarnate. But this text does contain one constant: Jesus is always accompanied by three women—his mother, his sister, and Mary Magdalene.[13]

All of this is hypothetical, of course, but no more than hypothesis is required to prompt the hatching of speculation that is thrust upon us as historical fact, which is occasionally embellished by miraculously rediscovered documents that actual analysis reveals to be forgeries. This is the case with the story of Mary Magdalene disembarking on the shores of Occitania with her family and the children she had with Jesus. These descendants of Jesus are said to have settled in the south of Gaul and taken root there, so that today it is possible to rub shoulders with authentic descendants of Jesus Christ.

The story grew more absurd when a fusion was created with the legend about Magdalene and another legend circulated by the Merovingian chronicler Fredegar. (In fact, it is an apocryphal text, which another chronicler of the time, Gregory of Tours, did not even mention because he considered it stupid). This story involves the mythic—hence divine—origin of the Merovingian dynasty, those "long haired" kings who practiced both magic and war. But then, in so-called primitive societies, all

13. See Pierre Crépon, *Les Évangiles apocryphes* (Paris: Retz, 1983).

war is magical, and when men learn to handle weapons, they necessarily learn feats of magic to be used to best adversaries.

The myth is as follows: Merovech, founder of the dynasty (it is not certain he actually existed), had two fathers, for after his mother had been impregnated by the Frankish king Clodion the Long-Haired, she was carried off while bathing by a mysterious creature that Fredegar describes as a *bestia Neptuni Quinotori similis*. This "beast similar to a Quinotaur of Neptune" recalls another fabled animal from Greek mythology. Now this "beast" sexually assaults the queen, making her pregnant again, so that when she gives birth to a son, the famous Merovech, he possesses two different bloodlines, one of a Frankish king and one of a fantastic—and divine, of course—creature who has come from over the sea. This theme is far from original and births resulting from two conceptions are not at all rare in Celtic mythology.[14] It is likely that Fredegar found this legend in an old mythological source common to both Celts and Germans. Whatever the actual source, great men have always been the product of a birth or conception that is out of the ordinary: Romulus was the son of a vestal virgin and the god Mars; the Irish hero Cuchulainn was given two fathers and experienced two births in succession; the great Welsh bard Taliesin was first Gwyon Bach before being eaten by the goddess Ceridwen and being reborn from her womb. We can guess at the significance of Pharaoh's daughter finding Moses floating on the Nile. Every ruling family has needed mythic ancestors, and Julius Caesar went to great pains to spread the legend that he was a descendant of Iulius Ascanius, son of Aeneas, who was himself son of Venus. This prompted Julius's successor Augustus to encourage the poet Virgil to compose his *Aeneid* for the glory of Rome—and the imperial family, the *gens iulia*. And the Plantagenets claimed descent from a fairy or the Lusignans, who were of the line of Melusine.

In the recent past—and it concerns the Rennes-le-Château affair—certain authors have thought it made sense to combine the Merovingian legend with that of Mary Magdalene, wife of Jesus and mother of many children. In doing so they explain that the sea monster is only a symbol of a man who came from across the sea, but with a divine connotation.

---

14. See J. Markale, *Epic Myths of Celtic Ireland* (Rochester, Vt.: Inner Traditions, 2000), and J. Markale, *l'Épopée celtique en Bretagne,* 3rd Édition (Paris: Payot, 1985).

As you may guess, this sea monster is actually symbolically designating a son of Jesus and Mary Magdalene, meaning, consequently, that the Merovingian kings are the descendants of Jesus. They are not merely kings by divine right; they are *divine kings*. This leads to propping up the theory of those who claim that legitimate and pure-race descendants of the Merovingians still exist, meaning that there are today descendants of Dagobert II, a genuinely historical king who was assassinated circa 678 under ill-explained circumstances, but probably through the impetus of Pippin of Heristal, true founder of the Carolingian dynasty. Any of Dagobert's power restored to a cadet branch of the Merovingians would be an illusory power, however, for at the time of his death the real levers of command were already in the hands of the Pippins. This era of the Slothful Kings remains obscure enough to permit any kind of speculation, and unfortunately any invention.

As an example, it is claimed that Dagobert II wed Gisela of Reddae, daughter of a Visigoth princess. At the time of Dagobert II's murder, his son, Sigibert IV, was allegedly rescued and led by his sister Irmine to a hiding place in the Razès at the home of his grandfather Bera, count of Reddae. Sigibert would have succeeded Dagobert and given birth to a kind of clandestine dynasty, authentically Merovingian, whose obviously enthusiastic offspring (the *plant-ard*) are still recognized today—at least in certain self-styled esoteric milieus.

The sad truth of the matter is that nowhere is there record of a marriage between Dagobert II and Gisela of Reddae. In addition, at the time of Dagobert's death his son, Sigibert (whose existence has not been proved), would have been only three years old, while his sister Irmine, who allegedly took him to the Razès, could not have been more than four. Obviously a very precocious family! It must be true that the blood of Christ is mixed with that of the Franks! The same obscurity hovers over the so-called Bera, count of Reddae. There is no record of him, and the first count of the Razès was William of Gellone—Saint Guilhem—a historical figure who entered into legend under the more familiar name of William of Orange, named to this position in 781 by Charlemagne. We are thus pretty far from the Merovingians. Yet we are told that documentation exists that could prove the contention of Merovingian descent: "These documents that could reestablish the truth are those discovered by Abbé Saunière in Rennes-le-Château. Among these parchments was one bearing the seal of Blanche de Castille, we are told, and that it proves the Merovingian descent through Sigibert IV."[15] But yet another unfortunate fact emerges: "[T]he documents of Abbé Saunière have never been seen by anyone. Why not make them public, for their content has been revealed for decades?"[16] This is a pertinent question, and one for which we are still waiting to receive an answer.

We can always expect a miracle, of course. After all, aren't the Merovingians who are living today the descendants of Jesus and Mary Magdalene? It is true that the present time is not a propitious one for miracles, however. Though Jesus was an authentic thaumaturge, his descendants may not be. Finally, today we know that the farther back we trace our ancestry—as far back as is possible—a well-known law of arithmetical progression is established so that we find our ancestors to be those of millions of people. In other words, human beings are all more or less from the same family.

In all this phantasmagoria—which is very well orchestrated, by the way, and echoed by talented authors—and without having to resort to a "fabulous race" that came from *elsewhere,* there do exist some certitudes and undeniable realities. Among these is the existence of a church, Saint Magdalene in Rennes-le-Château, a strange church whose entire ornamentation seems to have crystallized around Mary Magdalene. That is the most important reality.

---

15. Richard Bordes, *Les Mérovingiens à Rennes-le-Château,* 15.
16. Ibid., 27.

10

The Shepherds of Arcadia

It is certainly not by chance that we find on the Arques road through the area of Peyrolles an isolated tomb that is an exact replica of the one depicted in Poussin's painting *The Shepherds of Arcadia*. What is of note is that Poussin did not model his tomb on the one found on the Arques road because this tomb did not exist in the seventeenth century. We must clearly acknowledge that the tomb was built *after Poussin painted his scene*. But then another question arises: Why is the countryside depicted in Poussin's painting identical to the very real landscape behind this tomb? Here is yet another anomaly in a region that has more than its share of inspiration for incessant speculation and keen polemic.

The tomb is not ancient. It dates from the time of Father Saunière, and the precise circumstances surrounding its construction are known. In 1902, the grandson of an industrialist who twenty years earlier had purchased the property on which the tomb sits had decided to make a sepulcher on a small rise located some sixty yards away from the road. In order to achieve this he turned to a master mason, a Mr. Bourrel of Rennes-les-Bains. The tomb was used to house the mortal remains of several members of the owner's family. In 1921, however, the deceased were exhumed from their graves and transported to a vault in the Limoux cemetery. Shortly afterward, the property was put up for sale and purchased by another industrialist—an American named Mr. Lawrence. The tomb remained as it was then and still is today—that is to say, empty. It can be seen, half hidden by the trees, on a mound at the edge of a sheer drop, near a small bridge that spans a small, now dry streambed. If Nicolas Poussin's landscape is committed to memory, it can be seen that the landscape behind the tomb is identical to the one in the painting.

This is well worth considering. It is certain that the person who commissioned the tomb knew this painter's work. He would not have chosen this site or made a tomb in imitation of the one imagined by Poussin if this was not the case. But why did he do so? No one ever knew what his motives may have been, and when the similarity was noted, it was too late to ask the man responsible, for he had long since vanished. The mystery therefore remains intact.

It is plausible that Poussin had taken his inspiration for his painting from this landscape. But something in this notion is not quite right. Nicolas Poussin was born in Andelys, but left France at an early age to take up residence in Rome. "It would be an extraordinary occurrence if Poussin, who stayed in France for only two years—from December 17, 1640, to September 25, 1642—could have left Paris for the three months or more that would have been necessary to paint a landscape in the Corbières region. If Poussin had visited this area, some unambiguous clues and testimonies would certainly have remained. To the contrary, it can be proved that he did not leave Paris, where he had been entrusted with an official mission and where work was heaped upon him."[1] Another point is that Poussin's painting, currently on display at the Louvre, is not the only one he composed on this theme. There is a second painting with a different composition that has been housed for the last two centuries in the Gallery of the Dukes of Devonshire in England. Further, Poussin was not the first painter to use this subject matter; a Guercino painting dating from around 1618 may have served Poussin as a model.

What distinguishes these three paintings is both the depiction of shepherds reading the inscription on a tomb and the inscription itself: *Et in Arcadia ego,* meaning "Even in Arcadia [am] I." This enigmatic phrase (which can also be translated as "I, too, *have been* in Arcadia") has attracted a great deal of attention from analysts, as has the posture of the figures, which clearly reflects notions of symbolism. In the Guercino painting, two shepherds leaning on their crooks are looking at a tomb set

---

1. R. Descadeillas, *Mythologie du trésor de Rennes,* 141–42.

in a fairly tormented landscape. On the tomb is an impressive death's head, which has a hole in its skull that is reminiscent of ancient Germanic rituals intended to prevent the deceased from reincarnating. Poussin's English painting depicts three shepherds, one of whom is seated in a kind of despondent posture while the other two are viewing the tomb with a kind of trepidation. A shepherdess with her right breast almost entirely exposed is standing on the left and bears an air close to indifference.

The painting in the Louvre, however, is the one that is the most polished and worthy of interest. It is also considered to be an exceptional example of perfect artistic harmony, the Golden Mean. This famous ratio, 1.618,[2] is honored in the composition to the extent that everything is arranged to make the inscription the fictitious but absolute center of the entire composition. The painting consists of three shepherds and a shepherdess grouped around a tomb. The shepherd on the left is leaning on both his staff and the tomb with an expression of curiosity on his face. Another shepherd on the left is kneeling with his left knee on the ground; he seems to be drawing the inscription with his right finger. The third shepherd is on the right. Slightly stooped and supported by his staff, he is pointing at the inscription with his left hand while his head is turned back toward the shepherdess with a questioniong air. She is standing with her hands on her hips, her face leaning slightly forward, with an expression that suggests she knows the meaning of the inscription while the shepherds do not. The landscape is mysterious and somewhat tormented. Mountain peaks appear in the background against a sky that is blue on the right, cloudy in the center, and red on the left as if sunset is approaching.

This painting has been the subject of a wide variety of interpretations. The art experts of course see nothing mysterious about it. When he painted *The Shepherds of Arcadia*, Poussin was gravely ill and knew

---

2. Poussin's painting is considered to be a "golden rectangle" because it is entirely constructed according to what Pythagoras called the "divine proportion"—the ratio of the length to its width equals the marvelous number 1.618003399. In ancient times it had been observed that this number was the ratio between the first and second finger and the second and third finger on the hand, and that the navel divided the body according to this same proportion. The golden number, which results from extremely precise mathematical calculations, has always been cloaked with a sacred, even magical virtue.

his days were numbered. He had availed himself of this preexisting theme as a way to translate the idea of death and the flight of time in the midst of life. His personal drama was therefore made one with a universal human reality. It is also known that this painting was executed on behalf of Cardinal Rospligosi, the future pope Clement IX, who had asked Poussin to paint him a work that could express a "philosophical truth." Hence the subject of the well-known myth of Arcadia.

Geographically, Arcadia is a mountainous and fairly wild area of the Peloponnesus. It is in fact a kind of amphitheater surrounded by a crown of mountains, a somewhat remote region that was heavily forested for a long time. This region became a mythological place in ancient times. The name Arcadia was explained as a derivation of Arkas, the name of the hero who was the son of the nymph Callisto. According to the myth:

Zeus seduces the nymph Callisto who is a hunting companion of Artemis. She is changed into a bear by Zeus himself, according to some, in order to hide her from the eyes of his wife, Hera, and by Artemis, according to others, as punishment for breaking her vow of chastity. Callisto is then hounded by Artemis's pack, while Artemis herself shoots arrows at her at the instigation of a jealous Hera. To save her life, Zeus picks her up and raises her into the sky, where she becomes the constellation known as the Big Dipper.[3] The Little Dipper supposedly represents either a dog or the son of Callisto, the ancestor of the Arcadians.[4] This myth is revealing. The name Arkas comes from the Indo-European root *orks*, which means "bear." It has engendered the Greek *arktos*, the Irish *art*, and the Breton *arz*, as well as the Latin *ursus*. This implies that Arcadia was a place rife with bears, but when the bear's symbolic value is taken into account, it can easily be seen that Arcadia has become a kind of Other World, a parallel and sometimes underground world in which death is unknown. Winter is in fact the time when the bear hibernates, only to emerge when the sun is shining again. This brings to mind the

3. [The Big Dipper is known as the Big Bear in French. —*Translator*]
4. Michel Praneuf, *L'Ours et les hommes* (Paris: Imago, 1989), 37–38.

myth of Arthur, who is hibernating on the isle of Avalon. Arcadia can be considered as the Greek mythological equivalent to the Isle of Avalon and even the Celtic Other World of underground mounds, where dwell the gods and heroes of ancient times.

We know that Nicolas Poussin was greatly attracted to hermetic doctrines and that he spent time with people known for belonging to more or less secret "brotherhoods." No doubt the painter was himself a member of one of these "initiatory" societies that were proliferating in Italy and even in France during the seventeenth century. We also know that he was a protegée of Nicolas Foucquet and that the latter interacted with the painter. As minister of finances in 1655, Foucquet sent his brother Father Louis Foucquet to Rome "with the secret mission of acquiring art works intended for the adornment of Belle-Île, Saint-Mandé, and the castle of Vaux-le-Vicomte." Louis Foucquet obviously turned to Nicolas Poussin for assistance. But was this "secret mission" intended to traffic only in works of art? A letter sent from Rome by Louis to his brother the minister casts significant doubt on this. It includes this very curious passage:

> He [Poussin] and I have projected certain things that I shall with ease be able to explain to you in detail—things that will give you, through Monsieur Poussin, *advantages which even kings would have great pains to draw from him, and which, according to him, it is possible that nobody else will ever discover in the centuries to come.* What is more, it would not occasion much expense and could even be turned to a profit, and these are things that are so keenly sought after that all that exists on the earth could not have greater fortune and perhaps not even equal it.

Obviously this letter could concern bribes and graft and other shady methods of procuring art at a cheap price. There are references to these in other letters from Louis to his brother, but the terms used here seem disproportionate to a simple deal involving paintings. They clearly appear more significant. Of course, we can imagine all sorts of possibilities regarding what this passage may be referring to, but one thing is sure: Shortly after the time of this letter, Nicolas Foucquet was sentenced to life imprisonment because of a secret he held and never divulged. Following Foucquet's imprisonment, why did Colbert undertake so many searches of the archives of the Razès? What was he looking for? The imbroglio is complete and the mystery continues to thicken.

As it happens, Nicolas Poussin chose a rather curious personal seal, one depicting a man holding a boat or an ark, with the inscription: *tenet confidentiam,* translated as "he holds the secret." Given this, what should we make of Maurice Barrès's posthumous work, *Le Mystère en pleine lumière* (The Mystery in Full Light), a collection of several studies of painters in which the author gives vent to some rather strange observations? Barrès informs us that numerous painters belonged to initiatory brotherhoods, the chief one being the mysterious Angelic Society, which he associates with Delacroix, taking a particular interest in the "angelic aspect of his work." He makes a more explicit reference with regard to Claude Gellée, better known as Claude Lorrain, saying of him that we "clearly feel that he was not born all at once, but *was prepared.*" This means that Claude Gellée was a member of a spiritualist group that dictated some of his inspirations. Barrès adds, "If one truly wishes to know Gellée, it is necessary to have the drawing by Sandrart in which he reveals himself to be a most worthy companion of his friend Poussin." Should we conclude from this that Nicolas Poussin was a member of the same "brotherhood?" Still speaking about Claude Lorrain, whom he likens to Poussin, Barrès goes on to say, "He would be nothing if the Angels were not holding his hand, if he was not a member of celestial society, if he drew away from what enchants him, supports him, and uplifts him. *He knows his poem, outside of that he knows nothing.*" There could be no clearer reference to the existence of an Angelic Society to which the majority of painters (and authors) of any era belong. Even better, Barrès goes on to openly reveal the password: "It is necessary that we manage to contrive in some corner of our work a tombstone with the famous inscription: *Et in Arcadia ego.*"

If anyone still doubts the existence of this Angelic Society whose rallying or recognition sign appears to be the phrase inscribed on the tomb painted by Poussin, then he or she should read a letter George Sand wrote to Gustave Flaubert, dated November 17, 1866. Here is what the "good lady of Nohant" has to say: "In any event, all I am good for today is setting down my epitaph! *Et in Arcadia ego,* you know." The "you know" speaks volumes more than any discourse would. Before she became the "good lady of Nohant," George Sand took part in all the movements of utopian inspiration and was fully aware of where things stood in those "brotherhoods" that were the heirs of the Bavarian Illuminati and certain clandestine orders of the Middle Ages. Before writing *La Mare au diable* (The Devil's Pool), she wrote a book entitled *Consuelo* in which she makes several revelations about a mysterious brotherhood she calls the Sect of the Invisibles: "They are the instigators of every revolution; they are at work in the courts, guide all business, decide war or peace, redeem the unfortunate, punish the scoundrels, and cause kings to tremble on their thrones."

We cannot help but recall Nicolas Foucquet, who gave Louis XIV cause to tremble on his throne before giving way himself, probably because Nicolas *betrayed* the "brotherhood" to which he belonged. Acts of betrayal are not forgiven by these kinds of associations, and the Invisibles are where they need to be: "It is not known if there is a place where they stay, but they are everywhere . . . It is they who murder many travelers yet also lend a hand to others against brigands, depending on whether they have deemed these travelers worthy of their protection or deserving of punishment."

This cannot help but bring to mind Father Gélis, who was murdered in the Coustaussa presbytery for no apparent motive. In fact, we will recall that the inscription written on the cigarette paper found near his body said: *Viva Angélina.* Who could still harbor any doubts about the presence of this Angelic Society that had as a member Nicolas Poussin and as a mythic country Arcadia?

The Illuminati are a reality, even if masked by spiritual appearances. Louis Blanc praises them discreetly in his *Histoire de la Révolution:*

Solely through the attraction of mystery and the force of association, they compel thousands of people in nations around the world to move with a single will and breathe with one breath . . . Gradually and slowly they educate these people to become entirely new beings; make them irrationally obedient to the death to leaders who are invisible and unknown; with such a legion, weigh secretly upon the courts, envelop the sovereigns, direct governments and even Europe at their will to the point that all superstition is abolished, all monarchy torn down, all privilege by birth is declared unjust, the very right of property abolished. All this was the grandiose plan of the Illuminati.

Louis Blanc had cause to rejoice because at bottom this was his desire as well. We now know that the French Revolution and the Russian Bolshevik Revolution, just like the establishment of Nazism in Germany, were long incubated in advance within secret societies that dared not speak their names but clearly displayed philanthropic and spiritualist objectives. We must remake the world! This phrase of Karl Marx, which is also that of Arthur Rimbaud, is fraught with ambiguity. What ideology should be used in remaking the world?

The early Christians constituted a more or less secret sect. It was from the time that Christianity became the official and unique religion of the Roman Empire that the scales were tipped and other sects, born and maintained in obscurity, sought to destabilize Christianity and contrive its fall. That is the way of the world.

What is truly unnerving in Louis Blanc's exposé is his expression *"solely through the attraction of mystery."* Here we find ourselves plunged straight back into the Razès and the Father Saunière affair. Could the priest from Rennes-le-Château have been a member of the Angelic Society, or was he merely its pawn and finally its victim? There is no possible answer, though we can feel invisible presences around Father Saunière because the mystery is effective. In a posthumous work published in 1910, Saint-Yves d'Alveydre described an underground kingdom he called Agartha. He could just have easily called it Arcadia. In this shadowy land are an unknown people who live in cavities in the earth and are ruled by the King of the World, whose envoys are sent to the overworld, where they pass unseen and run governments. This simply recycles a conception developed earlier in a novel by Edward George Earle Bulwer-Lytton that appeared in English under the title *The Coming Race*. Bulwer-Lytton is best known for his book *The Last*

Days of Pompei, but here the theme is openly borrowed from the Illuminati tradition: Beneath the ground dwells a race of strange beings—the Anas—who are clearly spiritually and technologically superior to the poor humans on the surface of the earth. They have long moved beyond social problems, have formed a classless society, and have an incredible energy source called Vril. Their world can be entered only by means of a mine that connects to "a gulf whose walls are jagged and scorched, as if this abyss had been uncovered in some remote age by a volcanic eruption." The power of the Anas is irresistible because their civilization is superior to our own. Further, they possess an ultimate weapon that will one day allow them to rule the world. This is all quite mysterious and even a little alarming.

But the Anas merit further study. In the novel it is the Anas themselves who claim to have descended from a Celtic race. True, Bulwer-Lytton (1803–1873) was a minister under Queen Victoria, an Englishman, a Rosicrucian, and a member of that astounding brotherhood known as the Golden Dawn, which has been implicated in the development of some sects that gave birth to Nazism. Bulwer-Lytton was himself the descendant of a famous seventeenth-century alchemist and was well versed in Celtic mythology, at least the traditional Welsh and Irish texts that were just then beginning to be translated and published in Great Britain. It is not hard to identify the Anas. They are the Anaon of Armorican Brittany, the departed souls who can be seen wandering the moors and riverbanks at night. In Wales they are the sons of Don— in other words, the ancient, magical gods of the druidic religion. In Ireland they are the Tuatha de Danann, the ancient gods who live in mounds *(sidhs),* the huge megalithic cairns scattered throughout Great Britain and Ireland that are really the Other World, the marvelous underground world of Faery. The Tuatha de Danann, the "people of the goddess Dana," have extraordinary powers: Most tellingly, they can leave their mounds, mingle with humans, and manipulate them as they will. They are a real part of Celtic daily life in folk tradition. Not an Irishman alive would deny the sneaking presence of the *banshee* (literally, "woman of the mound"), a mysterious fairy or deity who influences human destiny. The Irish word *sidh* means "peace." Thus the underground world described by the Celts is the "peaceful world," where time no longer exists and space is infinite. There are no logical limitations there and anything is possible. Magic, fantasy, and the marvelous are given free rein in this evocation of the underground kingdom. We can easily see Bulwer-Lytton's considerable debt to ancient Celtic tradition—but he has integrated it into a new context, that of the Illuminati of Bavaria, the Rosicrucians, and the Golden Dawn, which makes this work of fiction more revealing of what was actually transpiring in the intellectual milieus of Great Britain at the end of the Victorian era.

All of this is connected to the Grail myth, which is phenomenally fertile in all its various incarnations. The energy Vril in Bulwer-Lytton's novel is nothing other than the green ray Jules Verne describes in a book called *The Green Ray*. Given that everything Jules Verne writes is very logical, his green ray's scientific explanation is that it is a natural phenomenon. In other science-fiction novels of that time, the green ray is nothing other than the ultimate energy, and whether it is good or evil depends upon the person using it. In this and other ways it is similar to the Grail as Chrétien de Troyes describes it: a mysterious vessel emitting a light that causes the sun to pale by comparison, or even the chalice carved from the emerald that tumbled from the forehead of Lucifer (the Light Bearer) when he fell into the abyss of eternal darkness and suffering following the revolt of the rebel angels. I am not so bold as to claim this force is atomic energy, but it is quite close. Vril is absolute energy. It is what the Grail holds, for the Grail is only a receptacle. It is the green ray emanating from the sacred vessel that Perceval the Welshman sees by chance and must then strive ceaselessly strive to track down.

Given this information, why wouldn't a sect that calls itself Norman, or Viking rather, or even the Church of Odin seek to spread the news that hidden somewhere in Rennes-le-Château are *emerald tablets* of a very specific kind? These tablets are what Fanny Cornuault describes in her book *La France des sectes*: "Each of these old Visigothic tablets contains a large emerald capable of harnessing the cosmic rays from the planet Vega. Norman initiates knew how to then direct with destructive force these green or violet radiations (the violet are the most carcinogenic) against an enemy."[5]

---

5. F. Cornuault *La France des sectes* (Paris: Tchou, 1978).

Don't worry, we are not digressing too far from Nicolas Poussin. In fact, he:

> . . . entered the secret crypt where the Visigoth kings had once amassed an immense war treasure. They had inventoried their booty then gradually transported it to another crypt located between the Black Mountain and the Corbières range. But Poussin feared that in the coming centuries the guards of this treasure who succeeded him in this duty would lose its esoteric filiation. So in Rome at a much later date he painted his famous work *The Shepherds of Arcadia,* in which a woman, a Halowyn,[6] is seeing to the deciphering of an inscription on an ancient tomb.[7]

All of this is in reference to a very common tradition maintaining that somewhere in the world there exists an emerald tablet capable of concentrating cosmic energy, a kind of dreadful condenser that under certain conditions could become the ultimate weapon. In Maurice Leblanc's *L'Île aux trente cercueils* (The Island of the Thirty Coffins), Arsène Lupin uncovers the secret of an amazing emerald that can burn flesh and kill, but can also provide power and life—a kind of cursed treasure with a dual nature, similar to radioactivity. Nothing is either good or evil; all depends on the way a power is put to use.

This is also reminiscent of the *Tabula Smaragdina,* that famous Emerald Tablet attributed to Hermes Trismegistus that serves hermeticists as a kind of bible or book of initiation that contains all and permits all. The origin of this tradition, beyond all shadow of a doubt, is to be found in so-called apocryphal gospels that mention the famous emerald that shines from Lucifer's forehead and serves as a kind of prima materia in the "holy" Grail, at least in certain versions of the legend. The green color is quite mysterious and has been the subject of

---

6. A priestess of the god Odin-Wotan.

7. "Hin Heilaga Normanniska Kirkja." *Tribune des Nationalistes normands catholique et odinistes et Jésuites panscandinaves restés fidèles à la doctrine raciste de saint Ignace* (title vouched for), March 1, 1965. Rather than citing the name of the author of this article, it is better to simply denounce again the diversion of European myths for the benefit of the most dubious ideologies.

countless studies demonstrating its essential role in plant growth. The function of chlorophyll is not the invention of some poet with heavenly inspiration—it is real. Too bad if legends almost everywhere mention precious stones that have strange properties either to engender illnesses or to bring about healing. There are even stones that can be bearers of good or evil. In short, the Grail, in Wolfram von Eschenbach's German version of the story, is nothing other than a stone with marvelous powers that can be as dangerous as they are beneficial.

But where can we find such stones? Assuredly we cannot on the surface of the earth, but we can find them within, in some secret cavern that is of course guarded by extremely vigilant, invisible powers. Here we find ourselves back again in Arcadia, that "land that lies elsewhere," that Other World, which appeared particularly smiling and luminous in the Razès. As early as the seventeenth century, certain authors had pointed to the Razès as the equivalent of the Greek Arcadia. But we should avoid be taken in by appearances. There is always a hidden face behind the visible one, and not everyone can discern it. This may bring to mind another novel by Jules Verne, *The Black Indies,* which is set in Scotland. In it the author recounts, with many Masonic allusions, the adventures of a young engineer who descends to the bottom of an abandoned mine in which he hopes to find a seam that has not yet been exploited. This is the opening of a series of extraordinary adventures, for the hero and his companions become lost and cut off from the outside world. They are saved thanks only to the intervention of a young girl who lives in this underground world with her father, a mysterious and misanthropic man. After numerous ups and downs, everything works out, except that the father loses his life—but this fits the template of the myth—and the hero weds the young woman when they return to the earth's surface. In short, the hero makes his descent into hell and returns with Eurydice. More cunning than Orpheus, however, he does not look back before returning to the light of day.

We are, then, fully within the domain of myth—as is Rennes-le-Château. The stories told about caches hidden throughout the region are variations on this same theme. It is the myth of Orpheus and of Gilgamesh; of Lancelot of the Lake, who strives to free Guinivere from the infernal kingdom of Meleagant; and of all those young peasants in folktales who free a young girl held prisoner by a monster in a cave or a well or beneath a somewhat diabolical fortress. The region of Rennes-le-Château lends itself marvelously as the site for this kind of myth, as we can see in the unlikely crystallization of traditions from all over that can be found in this area. Yes, Arcadia is here beneath our feet, but we must not forget that it is necessary to have the key that opens the door leading underground, where the shepherd tried to find the lost lamb. Béranger Saunière knew this well, for he secured for his church a depiction of this scene.

We ask whether something is history or myth. The question is moot, for myth is history and history is myth. Most important is to know what we are seeking when we enter the underground corridors of the Other World.

11

The Queen's Gold

When comparison is made of all the tales or analyses of Rennes-le-Château and its cursed treasure, it is clear that *something* is hidden underground there, whether in a cave or a man-made chamber or even one of those fairy realms endlessly extolled in folktales as lands of peace and prosperity. Rennes-le-Château could be Arcadia, for example, where the bear waits for the arrival of spring before emerging from its deep sleep. The interior of the earth easily charges the imagination and serves as a support for numerous versions of the primal myth, that of Mother Earth whose generous womb gives birth to all living things and nourishes them with her own blood. The maternal womb is both comforting and terrifying. It has all the ambiguity of the Sacred, the chill of the tomb, and the warmth of the sun. In the fifth book of Pantagruel, which may not be due entirely to Rabelais but does in any case show the mark of an esoteric filiation, the priestess Bacbuc, after having led her illustrious visitors Pantagruel, Panurge, and Father John to the Holy Bottle, makes a speech to them. In it she tells them that contrary to appearances, all life, all creation, and all movement arises from below. "Once you have returned to your world," she tells them, "bear witness to the great treasures and admirable things that lie under the earth." Then after an allusion to the myth of Proserpine she adds, "What has become of the art of calling the thunder and fire of heaven out of the skies? You have certainly lost it; it has left your hemisphere but is still in use here beneath the earth."

For Rabelais and the tradition that enwrapped him, it was incontestable that the world below was the holder of the secrets of the universe just like the prima materia of the alchemists that held within itself exclusively all the components of the philosopher's stone. It is incontestable that the priestess Bacbuc is quite disposed to welcoming those who approach her and to revealing these secrets by having her visitors drink the water from a divine spring. In fact, we may recall that a little to the south of Rennes-les-Bains flows the stream Trinque-Bouteille, which merges with the Blanque before becoming part of the Sals River. Isn't *Trinck!* [drink] the word spoken by the Holy Bottle—the only word, according to the pompous interrogation initiated by Panurge? Most assuredly, the water of this spring is capable of causing true intoxication, when we are possessed by the Spirit.

Again, this Spirit should not be thought of as evil. The obscurity that is the chief characteristic of the world below can easily lead to confusion. Gérard de Nerval was not fooled, however. At one point in his story *Aurélia* he shares a strange vision that possessed him concerning the symbolic history of the Creation from the time of the Seven Elohim of the beginning. Eventually the Elohim fell into a relentless war among themselves.

I have no idea for how many thousands of years these wars stained the world with blood. Three of the Elohim, along with the Spirits of their races, were finally relegated to the middle of the earth, where they founded vast kingdoms. With them they took the secrets of the Holy Kabbalah that connects the various worlds and they gained their power from the worship of certain stars, to which they continue to correspond. These necromancers, banished to imprisonment within the earth, had agreed among themselves to transmit their power to each other. Surrounded by women and slaves, each of their sovereigns had taken steps to assure themselves rebirth within the form of their children. Their life span was one thousand years. When death approached, powerful kabbalists would shut them into heavily guarded tombs, where they existed on elixirs and strong preservatives. For a long period of time they would maintain an outer semblance of life; then, like the chrysalis that spins its own cocoon, they would fall into a forty-day sleep from which they would be reborn in the form of a young child who would later be called to take up the reins of empire.

Now here is something truly worthy of the name cursed treasure. Here it is nothing other than necromancy, even if it is capable of prolonging life or of transmitting one body into that of another.

Meanwhile the vivifying resources of the earth were being exhausted in order to nurture these families whose blood, never renewed, coursed through generation upon generation. In vast underground chambers hollowed out beneath catacombs and pyramids, they had amassed all the treasures of vanished races as well as certain talismans that protected them from the wrath of the gods.

This clearly describes a parallel humanity that escapes the common law. These "necromancers" survived all cataclysms, every upheaval of the earth, all wars, and all floods: "The necromancers huddled in their underground lairs, gloating over their treasures in silence and in darkness. Sometimes they emerged stealthily from their retreats in order to strike terror among the living or spread the deadly teachings of their sciences among the wicked."

It is known that Nerval ceaselessly skirted this world below as much in his frequenting of certain "brotherhoods" as in his madness. This descent into underground chambers where magicians performed their deeds was one he personally experienced and whose dangers he measured. The characteristic feature of the cursed treasure is to convince those who lay hold of it that they have the power to rule the world. The poet added in a kind of sob: "I shuddered as I depicted the hideous features of these cursed races. Everywhere the suffering image of the Eternal Mother continued to languish, weep, or die."

There is no need to stress Nerval's idea of the Eternal Mother; she is *simultaneously* mother, virgin, and prostitute; Isis and Aphrodite; Cybele and Mary; as well as his own mother, whom he never knew and whom he looked for in all the women he met. She is also Aurélia, that radiant figure who shed light on his nightmares and stirred up the burning need in his life. In the text of *Aurélia,* however, he showed this Eternal Mother as a victim of the struggle among the Elohim.

Three of the Elohim had found refuge on the highest peak of the mountains of Africa. They began to fight among themselves. Here my memory grows hazy and I do not know the outcome of this supreme combat. The only thing I can still see is a woman they abandoned on a peak lapped by the waves; shrieking and with hair disheveled she was struggling for her life. Her forlorn cries rang out above the roar of the waves. Was she saved? I do not know. The gods, her brothers, had condemned her; but the Evening Star shone over her head, raining its fiery rays upon her face.

This magnificent evocation is reminiscent of the unusual image that we can see on the tympanum of the church of Rennes-le-Château: that of Mary Magdalene on a sort of boat, with a snake against her robe and a cross crowning her head. For here Mary Magdalene is truly taking the place and posture normally taken by the Virgin Mary. She could even be the Virgin's double. This is surely the case, but there is more: From the light cast by Nerval's vision, we may glean a completely different understanding of the distinctive décor of the Rennes church and the omnipresence of Mary Magdalene in it. We should certainly admit that despite appearances, all that is in the church hardly conforms with orthodoxy. To the contrary, the décor plunges us into an entirely Gnostic context in which Mary Magdalene, while still being who she is, also represents what the Gnostics called the Soul of the World. Nerval's Eternal Mother is also this Soul of the World, driven away by her brothers, the Elohim, and lamenting while she awaits the moment when she can recover fullness. The Soul of the World separated from the world is only a prostitute desperately seeking a sign of light. But the Evening Star shines above her head; it is hope and still contains a little of the divine light that once flooded her.

The circular journey of the Anima Mundi would be as follows: the celestial Virgin (the Pleroma of the Gnostics) falls into the world and is cleaved in two. Widowed and in mourning, she awaits her missing portion. Then she is scattered, hidden, and murdered beneath the various faces of the Prostitute. Through the meeting with the One she again becomes Bride of Yahweh, the Virgin of the Original Garden, Light undivided. Mary Magdalene experienced all these trials—solitude, the death of those dear to her, humiliation, mockery. Like all mystics, in love and silence she fulfills the circle (crown of thorns and wheel of fire), which allows her return to the limitless land of Immortality.[1]

Now we return to the depiction of Mary Magdalene on the tympanum of the church. The ship or ark could also represent the boat on which she crossed the Mediterranean, if we believe the legend as well as the *archou,* meaning the chest in which a treasure is stored. But for Mary Magdalene, this treasure could be a vessel of perfumes and other objects containing what we today call cosmetics. In any event, Magdalene is the guardian of something, ship or chest, and the snake is there to confirm this role. We note that the snake is not trampled here or held underfoot by Mary as is usual in depictions of the Virgin Mary, or of other saints such as Marguerite de Cortone. On the contrary, this serpent seems friendly to Mary Magdalene and there is no sign of any visible struggle in the image. The serpent, or the dragon, is always the guardian of treasure hidden in the earth, generally in a cave. In addition, from the alchemical point of view, its role as guardian stems from the fact that the snake is the symbol of mercury that has not yet been purified and therefore contains the seed of the philosopher's stone. In addition, we should recall that the serpent has always been a symbol of knowledge (this is what it symbolizes in Genesis) because it winds its way everywhere and knows every secret, even those that are the best guarded in the entrails of the earth. This is accompanied by a certain amount of ambiguity, which Nerval emphasizes by the necromancers who could prolong their lives at will, but who used their powers, their knowledge, for malefic purposes.

In the entrails of the earth: This is, in fact, the location of the sanctuary in which, tradition maintains, the treasure lies. Among the Greeks,

---

1. Jacquéline Kelen, *Un amour infini* (Paris: Albin Michel, 1983), 116.

the master of the hells (that is to say, a world below, the dark underground realm) is the god Hades, "he who sees all," whose other name is Pluto, a name connected to the same root as *ploutos,* "rich." The master of the world below is therefore the seer and the wealthy one. This is reminiscent of the rich Fisher King from the romances of the Holy Grail, the lame king who pretends to rule over the kingdom of the Grail, which has become a sterile desert since the time the Fairies of the Mounds were raped by men and especially by the king, who thus performed a major sacrilege. This Fisher King, who, according to certain tales in the Arthurian cycle, is named Pelles, which is merely a "courtly" form of an ancient Welsh god named Pwyll Penn Annwfn, is a remarkable man and uncle of Perceval-Parzival. But this king is nothing without the intervention of a divine woman, who is the Grail Bearer in the medieval story; Mélisande in Maurice Maeterlinck's play (in which Pelleas is no other than Pelles); and the enigmatic horsewoman Rhiannon in the Welsh story from the First Branch of the *Mabinogion.* It so happens that Rhiannon is a figure of the utmost importance. This horse-riding goddess, often incorporated into the Gallo-Roman Epona, is in fact the Great Queen, whereas Pwyll Penn Annwfn is literally Pwyll, "chief of the abyss." The word *annwfn* (or *annwyn*) is a designation of the dark, underground world where the secrets of life and death are held.[2] We know that King Pelles, who, according to one version of the Grail legend, was an expert in "nigromancie" and could take on any form, *is the guardian of the Grail,* which he protects in a castle that everyone passes by without seeing. The only ones capable of entering this castle are those whose *eyes are opened,* the eye symbolizing knowledge, inspiration, and initiation.

It is around this figure of the Great Queen, then, that the entire story of Rennes-le-Château is organized. But who is this Great Queen? Popular tradition maintains she is Blanche de Castille, but the local legend of a white queen who came to take the waters does not really involve the mother of Saint Louis. Instead it concerns an alleged Spanish queen who came "to take the waters" at Rennes-les-Bains, in particular at the spring known as the Bains de la Reine (Baths of the Queen), with all the wordplay that the name suggests. We should also

2. See Jean Markale, *L'Épopée celtique en Bretagne* (Paris: Payot, 3rd édition, 1985), 27–42.

not overlook that Rennes-les-Bains was called the Bains de Règnes (Baths of the Kingdoms) for a long time. If we summarize the legend as it was transcribed by Louis Fédié, there are certain details that cannot help but surprise us. We in fact see the Spanish queen depicted there "seated beneath an old weeping willow whose branches lean over the crystalline waters," where "she spent many long hours giving vent to her laments of exile and weeping over her fate as a woman without a husband and a queen without a crown." Strange. It should first be pointed out that this queen, through a series of unfortunate circumstances that took place in the fourteenth century, according to historical tradition, was the wife of Pierre II the Cruel, king of Castille, who abandoned her three days after their wedding in order to live with his mistress. Incarcerated in a fortress, the queen was freed by Pierre the Cruel's natural brother, Count Henri de Trastamare, and was taken by him to the castle of Peyrepertuse. Through this historically constructed fable we can see the broad outlines of the Celtic (specifically Welsh) myth of Rhiannon: As the result of a series of circumstances, Rhiannon was rejected by her husband, Pwyll Penn Annwfn (he accused her of murdering their child) and condemned by him to remain at a mound where she would serve as a mount for all those traveling to the royal fortress (hence Rhiannon's incorporation into Epona, the mare goddess). This is certainly no coincidence, and the famous White Queen, more mythological than real, is the very soul of a new myth, that of the treasure of Rennes-le-Château.

In fact, based on the local legend, this white queen was stricken with an illness while staying in Peyrepertuse. She had herself taken by litter to the Locus de Montferrando et Balneis—which is nothing other than Rennes-les-Bains—a thermal spa whose merits had been praised to her. She remained there for a period of time and was cured of her illness. It is in memory of her and her cure that the spring in which she bathed bears the name Bains de la Reine. But there is another detail in this traditional tale that should command our attention: This queen who wept while taking the waters one day dropped a silver goblet that rolled away into an abyss. Some versions of the story say a shepherd retrieved the goblet. Others declare that it still lies somewhere *in the entrails of the earth.*

Legends are always a blend of fantasy and reality. While there is a spring in Rennes-les-Bains known as Bains de la Reine, there is another much farther south of the village, between the Sals and the Blanque, that is called Source de la Madeliene (Magdalene Spring). Those of an empirical mind-set will say that this spring takes its name from a woman who came to bathe there in 1871, a time when it is possible to find objective verification for a piece of information. But nobody will be fooled, for the older name of this spring is Fontaine de la Gode. It so happens that the word *gode* or *gote* means "cup" in Occitan, which is quite revealing. It is made even more so by the fact that this word reappears in the name of the famous Goudils, who are figures in makeup that take part in the carnival-like parades of Limoux and the surrounding area accompanied by masked Fécos, as well as on Ash Wednesday accompanied by the hermits of Bugarach. Further, the promontory that hangs over this spring bears the name Goundill, in which the term *gode* is clearly recognizable. We should not overlook that the territory of Rennes-les-Bains has given up a certain number of archaeological objects from the Gallo-Roman era, most of which are representations of a female deity. It is quite clear that in the remotest past Rennes-les-Bains must have served as a regional sanctuary. In short, the Celtic *nemeton* was located there near the springs and in the middle of the forest, within a sacred clearing. But what is this legend concealing? What are its connections to Mary Magdalene?

Not far from this spring, in a place called Cap de l'Homme, meaning "man head," on the prominence named Plas de la Coste that overlooks the valleys that converge toward Rennes-les-Bains, another archaeological discovery was made: a head, no doubt that of a deity, which, as we know, is now displayed in the garden of the presbytery of Rennes-les-Bains. It is clearly the head of a female deity, with a deep perforation in the top of the skull.

There is no need to look far afield for the explanation for this. The answer can be found in the skull discovered in the cellar of the Magdalene church in Rennes-le-Chateau—a skull that is presumably Merovingian and was *ritually pierced*. This rite was observed not only to prevent the soul of the deceased from reincarnating (a Germanic belief), but also to protect a treasure or *a valuable hoard* from any kind of defilement. Now we recall that at the feet of Mary Magdalene inside the Rennes-le-

Château church, both on the statue and in the painting that adorns the lower part of the altar, there is a skull with this same ritual hole.

Abbé Saunière's message is to be found at the church in Rennes-le-Château and nowhere else: It is Mary Magdalene herself. The parish church of Rennes-le-Château had certainly borne her name since the ninth century, but Béranger Saunière made every effort to multiply her image: the statue, the fresco beneath the altar, the fresco on the back wall, the stained-glass window in the choir, the tympanum on the out-side, *not to mention Villa Bethania and the Magdala Tower.* There are many, many depictions and clues. As Gérard de Nerval said in his mag-nificent and inimitable way:

> *My forehead is still red from the kiss of the Queen.*
> *I have dreamed in the grotto where swims the Siren.*

The gold of the Queen, with all its play on words, is not far away:

> Certain treasures lead us on a veritable "Queste" that is undertaken one day for no conscious reason and never ends, a queste through nature, people, history, art, a queste that is total and absolute. This is the reason such an approach is eternal, and it could well prove that the gold one hunts for is much *more a spiritual as opposed to material gold* that may be everywhere and nowhere, in each place spirit may breathe, each step that human knowledge takes forward.[3]

There is no question that in addition to a treasure of old coins and pieces of jewelry, Abbé Saunière found some documents. The witnesses wholly support this conclusion. What, then, became of these famous parchments? Those that have reappeared are authentic *fakes*. What became of the parchments he discovered in the pillar of the altar of the Saint Magdalene Church of Rennes-le-Château? *No one has ever been able to answer this question.* Béranger Saunière never supplied an answer. Marie Denarnaud never spoke of them. The law of silence has been respected.

---

3. Gérard Lupin, *Le Trésor d'Alaric,* unpublished.

But pay heed, whispers the author of *Aurélia,* Gérard de Nerval, who knew too much on matters like these and was found hanging from a street lamp on the rue de la Vieille Lanterne in Paris (suicide? surely not); pay heed. "[T]he magical alphabet and the mysterious hieroglyphs have come down to us in truncated form, either distorted by time or *by those who benefit from our ignorance;* let us but rediscover the lost letter or the *effaced sign,* let us recompose the dissonant scale, and we shall gain in strength in the spirit world."

But especially in our time, when confusion is spread intentionally, it is not always easy to reconstruct an entire puzzle when three quarters of the pieces are missing. The documents discovered by Saunière must have been priceless; this is a certainty, for someone made sure of their disappearance. This brings up another question: For whom would they have value beyond price? Here again we can come up with no answer, or at least the answer cannot be expressed. For as Nerval again says:

> *And twice I have victoriously crossed the Archeron:*
> *Modulating in turn on the lyre of Orpheus*
> *The sighs of the Saint and the cries of the Fairy.*[4]

Nerval says he crossed twice victoriously. Yes, but the third crossing took place on the rue de la Vieille Lanterne. Don't be fooled.

And what if Saunière was only what secret agents call a "goat," meaning someone intended to attract attention while other events of great interest were transpiring elsewhere? And what if Rennes-le-Château was a single tree concealing an immense forest? Or at least the smallest outcropping of a colossal iceberg? Or even a kind of noise intended to psychologically prepare us for something that would put into question centuries of certitude?[5]

The question has been raised, and this is enough for the answer to emerge from the unconscious, where it has been dazed by centuries of

---

4. G. Nerval, *El Desdichado.*

5. Gérard Lupin, *Le Trésor d'Alaric.*

hibernation, like the bear of Arcadia or like Arthur of Celtic legend, or even like Mary Magdalene, whom the Evangelists mentioned only because she scared them. Mary, in fact, solely through her enigmatic presence, causes us to question some twenty centuries of Christianity. Her challenge is not to its foundations, which remain the same, but to how its message has been transformed—in other words, to its betrayal of the message of love, beauty, knowledge, and serenity.

If we truly seek Béranger Saunière's message, we must go in this direction to find it. It is Mary Magdalene who is the key to the priest's entire life. For contrary to all that has been said about him, contrary to all those malicious souls who seek to cast him as a priest who had illegally returned from banishment, as a heretic, and even as an adept of some rather disquieting and definitely negative brotherhoods, it can be stated that the priest of Rennes-le-Château was *an inspired man.* Certainly he was muzzled following his discoveries; by whom, no one knows. But the parchments discovered in the altar pillar still exist somewhere . . . And if Béranger Saunière never said a word on this subject, if he refused to give his bishop an explanation for the funds he had at his disposal in order to realize his construction, then he must have had his reasons.

Saunière had the good—or bad—fortune to discover the *Queen's gold.* Whether this is real gold or only the treasure of knowledge changes nothing about the matter. In either event it could be only a cursed treasure. We cannot disturb with impunity a society that has its customs, rules, and interests. We cannot preach with impunity against the prevailing ideology unless we can be satisfied with following the example set by John the Baptist and preach in the desert.

This is a little bit like what Saunière did. But he never forgot that he was a priest and that as a priest he had a duty to fulfill toward others. He folded before adversity, defended himself poorly, and every day wondered what new setback was waiting to greet him. He never set foot in Paris to have his documents analyzed by an expert. He never knew the Satanist Jules Bois. He was never Emma Calvé's lover, no more than he was the lover of Marie Denarnaud. He never trafficked in Masses. He was a monarchist and a fundamentalist, certainly, but was hardly the only one in his time. Saunière died a pauper, as did Marie Denarnaud. Her heirs never discovered the royal treasure, whether it was that of the Visigoths, the Templars, or the Cathars. The legend constructed around Béranger Saunière is a vast, intoxicated undertaking to better hide whatever might be visible.

What is visible is primarily the dignity of a man others sought to sully *post mortem.*[6] Certainly Saunière knew a secret, and an important one to boot. He was never able to divulge it, but arranged matters so that he could transmit it by the simplest means possible. But why leave things simple when they can be complicated? The work of Béranger Saunière exists. It is visible. It is even *legible.* Are there just as many illiterates today as there were in the decadent era around 1900? Why is there a need to distort history for the benefit of a kind of ideology of dubious taste?

The *cursed* gold of Rennes-le-Château, which can also be that of Rennes-les-Bains, is stained with malediction only to the extent that the Sacred is terrifying. We tremble before the Lord; if we take the Bible at its word, Yahweh never showed his face to the prophets without placing a screen between himself and humans. Ever since the time man was chased out of the earthly Paradise, an angel holding a fiery sword has been keeping watch over the entrance to a world now buried in the shadows of the Unconscious. For the Garden of Eden, whatever it really is, holds a lost treasure, and all the energy of the Creature of God is crystallized toward the rediscovery of this treasure, even if this absolute quest skirts the dangerous precipices from which the odors of fire and brimstone emanate.

But what treasure do we seek? Just what is this gold that legend claims is cursed, perhaps because those who manage to reach it do so at the risk of losing their souls? Is it a material treasure, the sacred objects from the Temple of Jerusalem or the Sanctuary of Delphi that Alaric's Visigoths carried from Rome and buried somewhere in the Razès, in the middle of the woods or on some arid plateau riddled with undiscovered caves? Could this material treasure lie in the grotto of

---

6. I am in a perfect position to assert this because of my own spiritual father, Abbé Henri Gillard. Since the time of his death, inane stories about him have circulated, despite the fact that this man was always a model of human dignity and priestly devotion. Yet he also had the audacity to take an interest in things that were better not stirred up and to carry out with his own funds the—odd—restoration of the church of which he was the rector.

Mary Magdalene, or that of the Gode, with its strange name that recalls the primordial chalice in which Christ's blood was collected? We know that according to one of the Gospels, Mary Magdalene was there at Jesus' descent from the cross and shrouding, and thus witnessed Joseph of Arimathea's collection of Christ's blood in the Grail.

But is the treasure truly a material one? Wouldn't it instead be a great secret that could not sensibly be divulged yet because it poses a serious challenge to centuries of history and a certain conception of Christian spirituality? No one ever learned what the manuscripts discovered by Saunière actually contained. They have disappeared. But that does not mean that they might not reappear one day and be acknowledged. It cannot be denied that Saunière did know what became of them. But only he knew, though a man who has devoted his life to a work, even one so debatable and odd as the church of Rennes-le-Château, could not carry his secret to the grave without leaving behind some signs.

Now, signs are always symbolic and are generally drowned in a flood of details intended to mislead those who do not have in mind a clear idea of what they seek. This is where the virtue of the test appears; all the great myths of humanity stress this essential aspect of the quest. Close inspection of Saunière's work leads to a very simple conclusion: If he left a message—and it appears undeniable that he did—it could be only in the image he gave Mary Magdalene, one that was too strong and blinding to be taken into consideration until the present.

Her ubiquitous presence is itself an indication, even if there is a logical reason for this presence in a parish dedicated to her. As we have noted, Mary Magdalene's depiction takes the place ordinarily reserved for the Virgin Mary, and she is not in this church depicted as she is elsewhere. This is especially true of the scene in which Mary Magdalene is kneeling in a cave, facing a rustic cross with a perforated skull at her feet, a revealing detail. The presence of this pierced skull forms an admission: The death's-head is in some way a symbolic and *magical* element traditionally placed near a treasure. It is quite dark inside this cave, but light from the outside floods the face of the meditating woman. "I despised the kingdom of the world and all the adornment of the century"—these are the words recorded as spoken to Magdalene. Does this imply that the treasure she appears to be guarding does not belong to this world and will thereby acquire exceptional importance in the overall message of Christianity? The serpent of knowledge that crawls up Mary Magdalene's robe on the tympanum of the church only reinforces this idea, and the ark, or chest, at her feet can just as easily signify her sea voyage to Gaul as it could the preservation of a precious object hidden from the eyes of others.

Mary Magdalene is the image of the Feminine in its highest expression. She is the "revealer" of the resurrected Jesus. She performs the royal anointing of Christ. She is the one who loves Jesus and whom Jesus loves above all other women, she who gave him the Second Life, that of the Spirit and the body of glory. Hers is a message of a love that can transform the world. The Occitan troubadours knew this, repeating ceaselessly that it was through woman that one attained God. But Magdalene also symbolizes "convulsive" beauty, which can also be "explosive-fixed," meaning the generator of an eternal becoming toward Perfection. For the moment, however, in a world that is not yet capable of understanding this supreme message, Beauty conceals itself within a cave. Gérard de Nerval phrases it thus:

> *Do you recognize the temple with the immense peristyle*
> *And the bitter lemons holding the imprint of your teeth*
> *And the cave, fatal to imprudent guests*
> *Where from the vanquished dragon sleeps the ancient seed?*[7]

In the final analysis, perhaps the cursed gold of Rennes is the sleeping seed of that vanquished dragon. Perhaps Saunière's message is not to awaken the Dragon. This is where the quest can reveal itself to be dangerous, fatal even for one not prepared for this kind of confrontation. We must dare to enter this cave, for as Nerval (himself an initiate) admits: "the Saint of the Abyss is more holy to my eyes" ("Artemis," from *Les Chimères*). This is without question an invitation to go hunting not for the gold of Rennes but for the gold of the Queen [Reine] buried in the same cave where the ancient dragon sleeps, in a coffer that Mary Magdalene holds precisely between her fairylike hands.

---

7. "Delfica," from *Odelettes*.

Index

Books of Related Interest

Cathedral of the Black Madonna
The Druids and the Mysteries of Chartres
by Jean Markale

Montségur and the Mystery of the Cathars
by Jean Markale

The Templar Treasure at Gisors
by Jean Markale

The Grail
The Celtic Origins of the Sacred Icon
by Jean Markale

The Gospel of Mary Magdalene
by Jean-Yves Leloup
Preface by Jacob Needleman

The Woman with the Alabaster Jar
Mary Magdalen and the Holy Grail
by Margaret Starbird

The Goddess in the Gospels
Reclaiming the Sacred Feminine
by Margaret Starbird

Magdalene's Lost Legacy
Symbolic Numbers and the Sacred Union in Christianity
by Margaret Starbird

Inner Traditions • Bear & Company
P.O. Box 388
Rochester, VT 05767
1-800-246-8648
www.InnerTraditions.com

Or contact your local bookseller